THE EDUCATION OF A NATION

Gareth Elwyn Jones is Research Professor of Education, University of Wales.

THE EDUCATION OF A NATION

GARETH ELWYN JONES

UNIVERSITY OF WALES PRESS • CARDIFF • 1997

British Library Cataloguing-in-Publication Data.
A catalogue record for this book is available from the British Library.

ISBN 0-7083-1403-1

Published with the financial support of the Arts Council of Wales

Typeset at the Midlands Book Typesetting Company, Loughborough
Printed in Great Britain by Dinefwr Press, Llandybïe

TO THE MEMORY OF A TRUE FRIEND

PROFESSOR DAVID J. V. JONES

Contents

Preface

I am as convinced now as when I wrote the first of the essays in this book that the history of education in Wales remains a Cinderella subject, a concern of far too few scholars.

I believe this to be particularly unfortunate since the history of state education in Wales has been so central to social change. I remain as convinced that a historical perspective is essential to intelligent debate about the implications of the revolutionary changes which have taken place in the education system in Wales and England since 1988 and are still proceeding apace. I hope, therefore, that these essays, concerned with education in Wales over the last two hundred years, will make some contribution to focusing attention on the Welsh dimension of present radical change.

Within the overall theme there is a sub-plot. In none of these essays did I set out to impose a pattern, still less to indulge any theory of history. However, as they accumulated, I became increasingly convinced that there is a recurring characteristic of the evolution of education in Wales within the context of the 'England–Wales' state. This conviction was cemented as I prepared a chapter on the 1847 report of the commissioners into the state of education in Wales (chapter 2). I argue in this essay, which appears for the first time in print in English, that there is substantial circumstantial evidence to indicate that the essential motive of Sir James Kay-Shuttleworth, and perhaps the commissioners, was to use the example of Wales to shame central government into improving its provision for elementary education and teacher-training across England and Wales. If this is the case, it reflects attitudes towards educational development in Wales over two centuries.

From time to time, notably in 1889 with the Welsh Intermediate Education Act, there has been separate provision for Wales, designed to meet different circumstances prevailing there. Throughout the twentieth century there have been devolutionary measures which, at least superficially, have invested Welsh institutions with increasing control of education. Underlying realities reflect a very different situation. The pattern which I believe was established in the 'Blue Books' of 1847 – that of using Wales to serve the needs of England – has continued. The Welsh have been seen as marginal, forced to fit whatever Procrustean educational bed has been designed for the wider state. This was certainly true in the wake of the 1902 Education Act (chapter 5), in the inter-war years (chapter 8) and in the wake of the 1944 Education Act (chapters 3, 4 and 7). At these times, even after 1944, government policy for education in England and Wales was, in the main, reactive. What makes an essentially condescending attitude so significant in contemporary Wales is that educational change in recent decades has been dramatically pro-active. There has been an educational revolution since 1988, brought about by an unprecedented spate of education acts. For a time I was convinced that, on balance, education in the schools of Wales was profiting, and this optimism is reflected, guardedly, in chapters 9 and 10. The potential of the National Curriculum in Wales, coupled with a period of enlightened activity in the Curriculum Council for Wales under creative chairmanship seemed to indicate that the limited educational autonomy allowed to Wales might prove adequate to safeguard the nation's interests. I am now convinced that this optimism was misplaced. The events of 1993 and after are dealt with in chapter 11 and in previously unpublished work in chapter 12 and the conclusion. Central government action, in the form of the 1994 Dearing Report and subsequent legislation, indicates that attitudes towards Wales have, at their core, hardly changed since the nineteenth century. The approach is more civilized, epitomized in the visits of Sir Ron Dearing to Wales, when he was at his emollient best, but the essential message is the same: modification of the curriculum takes place according to priorities perceived to be relevant in England. The government intends to impose structural changes – such as voucher schemes for pre-school children, or the undermining of the comprehensive principle by selection – on Welsh parents whether they like them or not. The question at the heart of this book, therefore, is whether such a situation is still acceptable.

The majority of these essays have been published previously and I am much indebted to the editors of the relevant books and journals for their kind permission to include this material. The staff of the University of Wales Press have seen a number of my books through the press. They have done so with efficiency and patience. They now put up with idiosyncratic editing with great tolerance and I am most grateful to them.

The academic debts which I have incurred over the years during which these essays have been written are too numerous to list. I have been particularly inspired by discussions with my colleagues in the University departments of education in Swansea and Aberystwyth, and in the Swansea history department, not least the librarians.

In special circumstances prevailing since July 1992, academic and personal debts have fused and accumulated in perhaps unprecedented fashion, and defeat cataloguing. It is impossible to do more than express a heartfelt gratitude for the support which has motivated my determination to continue with research and writing. In dedicating this book to the memory of David Jones who, in the company of David Howell, was a very present help, I acknowledge a far wider, and so often unspoken, debt to my friends and colleagues. I must make special mention of my mentor for four decades, Sir Glanmor Williams.

The process of research and writing is now a team effort. My son and daughter are highly efficient members, when available. My wife, Kath, makes my writing, and everything else, possible.

GARETH ELWYN JONES
Swansea, September 1996

Acknowledgements

Most of these essays have appeared in print previously and their location is indicated below. I am particularly grateful to the editors and publishers of the books and journals concerned for their ready permission to reproduce the material.

Chapter 1. *Education for Development*, 10 (1) (Spring 1985). Special number: *Perspectives on the History of Education in Wales*, 2–12.

Chapter 2. Published in Welsh as 'Llyfrau Gleision, 1847' in Prys Morgan (ed.), *Brad y Llyfrau Gleision* (Llandysul, 1991), 22–48.

Chapter 3. Prys Morgan (ed.), *The Glamorgan County History (VI), Glamorgan Society, 1780–1980* (General editor, Glanmor Williams), (Cardiff, 1988), 315–32.

Chapter 4. D. W. Howell (ed.), *Pembrokeshire County History, IV, Modern Pembrokeshire 1815–1974* (Haverfordwest, 1993), 389–417.

Chapter 5. Kenneth O. Morgan (ed.), *Welsh History Review*, 14 (3) (1989), 417–38.

Chapter 6. Ned Thomas (ed.), *Planet*, 76 (1989), 82–7.

Chapter 7. W. Gareth Evans (ed.), *Perspectives on a Century of Secondary Education in Wales 1889–1989* (Canolfan Astudiaethau Addysg, Aberystwyth, 1990), 60–76.

Chapter 8. This lecture, subsequently published, was delivered on the occasion of the fiftieth anniversary of the Higher Education Committee in Wales of the National Union of Teachers, June 1984. I am most grateful to Mrs Peggy George for the kind invitation to deliver it.

Chapter 9. This paper was given as one of the series of Callaghan lectures organized by the University College of Swansea Education

Department and subsequently published. M. Williams, R. A. Daugherty and F. Banks, *Continuing the Education Debate* (Cassell, 1992), 97–106.

Chapter 10. This lecture was delivered at a conference organized by the Welsh Office Education Department and subsequently published in Owen E. Jones (ed.), *The Welsh Intermediate Education Act, 1889: A Centenary Appraisal* (1990), 149–67. It is reproduced by permission of Her Majesty's Stationery Office.

Chapter 11. Sally Brown (ed.), *The Curriculum Journal,* 5(1) (1994), 5–16.

Chapter 12. This previously unpublished lecture was delivered at a conference of primary-school headteachers in Mid Glamorgan in 1995. I am most grateful to Robert Jones for his invitation to deliver the lecture.

1
Education in Wales:
a historical perspective

Paradox pervades Welsh education, past and present. There is even an historical paradox. One of the distinctive features of Welsh education is supposed to be its centrality to our history. It has certainly not been central to our historiography. In the renaissance in historical writing in Wales over the last thirty years attention to the history of education has been marginal. There have been a few excellent theses, articles and monographs, but generally, distinguished Welsh historians have construed educational history as a rivulet feeding the political, religious or economic mainstream.

Is it that the history of education in Wales is seen as 'tunnel' history, a line of development best hived off from the generality of social history? If such is the case it compounds the felony since the only worthwhile history of education assumes its centrality in the wider society. Such an assumption underlies the excellent introductory text of Lawson and Silver[1] for English education. More likely, the history of education is seen as of lesser significance than that of the politics and economics of Wales. This, in turn, may be partly due to the fact that the Whig interpretation of history is especially seductive when it comes to education; whatever the indices, educational provision is better today than it was fifty years ago. School-leaving age, grant aid, provision of materials, proportion of gross national product, training of teachers, teacher-pupil ratios have all improved since the war. When, as now, we regress, the shock is the greater precisely because of entrenched expectations of constant improvement.

The tale of that improvement has been related often in histories of English education or, more tellingly, for Great Britain, in such standard works of not very long ago as those of Curtis[2] and Barnard.[3] Curtis (7th edn., no less) still remains an ideal source to quarry for the facts of acts. It may be that Curtis's title *History of Education in Great Britain* (separate chapters for Scotland) tells a story –

perhaps for Welsh historians it has told the whole story. Do we have another paradox, that one of the distinguishing features of Welsh education is that we constantly hear of its superiority to that of England, yet the histories of both countries in the twentieth century have so converged, that the Welsh educational dimension has syncromeshed its way out of existence?

Here, then, may be the difference of perspective in Wales and Scotland. The Scottish education system, as with its law, has always retained a distinctive administrative structure. It has similar proud claims on national sentiment as the Welsh, but fundamental similarities with English developments have been packaged under different labels. The result is that there are at least three orthodox histories of Scottish education. A standard history, by James Scotland,[4] has emerged relatively recently. In Wales we have no standard history, no one who has imposed on events a historically respectable Whig interpretation. England has produced Marxist re-evaluations, particularly in the work of Brian Simon.[5] In Scotland, historians are beginning to counter James Scotland's orthodoxies.[6] In Wales we have no orthodoxies to undermine. We have not reached first base.

This is serious, not only because education is part of the warp and weft of our social fabric in Britain but also, as Welsh nationals, it is fundamental to our understanding of the nature of Wales and Welshness, myth and reality, past and present. The Welsh are, we all know, at least as educated as they are musical. Despite the occasional dent in the image these days, accumulation of fact and myth since the eighteenth century results in a concept of a nation concerned for education, formal and informal. Inextricably intertwined with the notion of the *gwerin* – rural, peasant backbone of Wales, the true Wales, farmer-poets, philosophers and theologians – the appetite and respect for education is second to none. There is a residual compelling image of a poor society, desperately manufacturing its own culture, leadership and democratic identity in the face of hostility from an anglicized, exploiting gentry through the self-help of response to Griffith Jones, Hugh Owen and, in a changed context, O. M. Edwards. Circulating schools, the university founded and run on the pennies of the poor, and the county schools, provide a potent image of concern for the finer things in life in the face of material deprivation.

More recently, national pride and self-congratulation engendered by this idealized picture would appear to have been dented in the Loosmore report and its aftermath. Doubts have been cast on the performance of Welsh comprehensive schools, especially in their ability to deliver examination results for the middle-ability ranges.[7] Here again, paradox. The researchers concerned suggested that one of the reasons for this worrying disparity in the performance of Welsh and English schools was the inheritance of a grammar-school ethos in the new comprehensive schools, an ambience conducive to concentration on 'academic' subjects, a continuation of the hierarchical structures of the old grammar schools. Certainly there are still speech days which celebrate academic success as they did in the 1900s, if less ostentatiously. There are still photographs in evening papers of pupils destined for punts and glittering prizes, not for Salford and Aston. But the perpetuation of such 'grammar-school' practices has not led to popular questioning of the county/grammar-school ethos and practice – far from it. The alleged shortcomings of Welsh comprehensive schools (and even here the picture muddies with each succeeding study) have led, instead, to a nostalgia for the old schools and the old standards and the old days of a secure meritocracy.

There is more than hearsay evidence that, in the absence of professional history, the old stereotypes suffice in the best circles. An English reviewer in *The Times Educational Supplement* adjudged some years ago that 'being Welsh like being Jewish traditionally means respecting education'.[8] The old story of the future Sir Henry Jones walking miles to see a Bachelor of Arts is well known. What is striking is that there are modern equivalents among greater heroes. Barry John, asked in a television interview how he felt on learning that he had been awarded his first Welsh cap, could hardly find words to describe that transcendental moment: 'It was like learning you'd got your Ph.D.' Some might swap.

Such reactions are rooted in a different social history from that of England. Myth-making stems from the historic role of Welsh education in providing economic and social mobility in a society in which both have been restricted compared with England. So, consciousness of the importance of educational opportunity has seared itself into the Welsh psyche, and that opportunity has been most dramatically associated with the county/grammar schools of the first half of the twentieth century. Carwyn James, teacher, littérateur, greatest of all rugby coaches, Welsh to the core, wrote:

Came, alas, the destruction of one of the best educational systems in the world. Came the levelling down process. A disbelief in Plato's gold, silver and brass. All children are equal and none is more equal than another. Comprehensive. The new in-word. Big and beautiful. Hours of business strictly nine-to-four. Special responsibility allowances a must. Preferably no Saturday morning games.[9]

Perhaps Gwyn Thomas was too close to the chalk face for too long for such an endorsement of the county/grammar system to be so disingenuous. But in a more modified, more realistic form he sees a more distant, thus perhaps more potent, sunlit age:

From the University College . . . came a legion of eager harvesters, the shining centurions on a march that was to endow the common folk with a new power and dignity. Seen in our present gloomy penumbra, our cultural mange, the last statement might sound odd, a jape from a dog-eared and disavowed comedy script. But there was a day, not too long ago, when the truth of these words rang out like the stroke of a golden bell. Learning was to be mankind's new and magic robe. It would put a new face on the absurdity of endless labour in places from which grace and beauty had been removed as if by surgical excision.

The early native graduates who staffed the county school during the end of the last century and the beginning of this were a remarkable band of pioneers. They were the first across the Missouri, not yet plagued by a clear view of the Rockies of recalcitrance, failure and breakdown that for many of them lay ahead. They were lucky men. They were in their day anointed princes. They were Tibetan Lamas of infinite wisdom and authority set in the context of shorter mountains and taller pretensions. The teachers in the early days of mass education, if they were a people blessed with a deep vanity, lived in a school climate as balmy as Barbados . . . Given the often demented pride that parents felt for them, the deep respect instinctively shown them by their pupils, and the wide-spread awe felt for them by neighbours still stuck in their ancient traps, it is wonderful that so many of the native graduates in the post-1870 era remained loyal to the serene egalitarianism of their radical tradition.[10]

Indeed, but their *raison d'être*, their social function in the schools which so many served so faithfully for so long, was to promote inegalitarianism. We even need to be wary about those Welsh Tibetan Lamas. They did tend to remain in a single school for much of their careers, though this might have had something to do with the restricted career opportunities of the day. That same restricted career structure ensured that some of our most eminent scholars served their apprenticeships and more in the secondary schools; they were the best academic posts available. W. J. Gruffydd, most distinguished of scholars, professor of Celtic, playwright, poet of outstanding talent, began his career as a teacher at Beaumaris Grammar School. Historian David Williams wrote: 'his old pupils there still speak with emotion of the undisguised disgust with which he regarded them and his duties'.[11]

It is uncomfortable to question myths. They are especially important to a nation as precariously poised in history as Wales, emanating, as they often do, from that precariousness. Nights of Long Knives help compensate for an oft-felt ubiquitous aimlessness, particularly apparent in contemporary Wales since 1979. And we are allowed our legends since they seem to carry no political or social danger. But myths are dangerous. They develop a life of their own which serves a nationalistic and political purpose as real as the fact which underlies them.

Such a process is not confined to Wales. With all its historiography that same process can be observed at work in Scotland and in that inelegantly labelled entity, England and Wales. Here, too, a strait-jacket of historical interpretation can all too easily be imposed which it becomes almost disloyal to question. There are, for example, some striking parallels between the 1889 Welsh Intermediate Education Act in the Welsh context and the 1944 Education Act in the context of a wider nation. One similarity is that historians interpret both Acts as the enlightened provision of enhanced opportunity and greater egalitarianism by progressive politicians fighting entrenched back-woods attitudes in Treasury and educational establishments. It is almost heresy to question the 'breakthrough' of the 1944 Act in inaugurating free secondary education for all pupils, raising of the school-leaving age and the rest. The steady erosion of the educational consensus, particularly since 1979, has had something of a similar effect on our perspective of the 1944 Act as has the Loosmore Report in Wales on our conception of Welsh county/grammar schools. Where Conservative educational policies since 1979 might have led to questioning of the impact of the 1944 Act and its inadequacies it has instead led to the consensus politicians falling back on the Act as a kind of beacon of educational enlightenment. In the 1980s this was manifest in the debate over the charging of fees for university tuition – its Tory opponents centred their opposition on the breach of the principle of free tuition enshrined in the Butler Act. An idealized interpretation of the 1944 Act serves a political, hence social, purpose now. It can be construed very differently. Its blueprint had been etched before the war, in the Spens Report of 1938. This was rejected, in the time-honoured way of governments, as too expensive, in a refrain which had disguised class ideology of secondary education since the birth of state secondary schools in England in 1902. For Wales, continuity with a pre-war pattern was yet more marked. The main provisions of the 1944 Act echoed trends already long apparent in the Welsh system – particularly that of free entry by ability to a selective system. No debunking of the 1944 Act need obscure the achievement of R. A. Butler in reconciling powerful religious pressure groups which had helped scupper Labour attempts at reform in 1929 and 1930. Even though Butler had to buy off these interests, he required all his considerable political finesse even to create the atmosphere in which money talked. But he was responsible for legislation within which central direction of the education system, often disguised, produced a rigorously enforced bipartitism. The major element in the Act – free secondary education for all up to the age of 15 – was remarkable not for its originality of concept but because it actually happened. The Act provided the framework within which civil servants and educational administrators, with the aid of a succession of Labour and Tory conservatives, could perpetuate the divisions of a society, especially in Wales where they had to work far harder to do so. But succeed they did, in the face of educational and organizational logic. That divide in the system of schooling has been centrally significant since the state began to intervene massively as the forces of change in industrial society became too much for voluntary organizations to handle. Through the nineteenth century and early in the twentieth century the divisions were openly discussed in class terms. From the 1920s it became less acceptable for officialdom openly to comment on the necessity for the superiority of a paid-up middle-class education over that of the working class. Fee-paying had to secure something better, and be seen to be leading to something better – jobs, pay – else economic logic, indeed the fabric of society, would be undermined. Another weapon of discrimination was conveniently at hand, the intelligence test, and its accompanying tests of attainment: the scholarship. In effect these tests performed the same social function as payment of fees – and they operated in tandem until 1944. IQ became a shibboleth; absolute assessment at the magic age of eleven (just when administratively convenient). We now know that the 1944 Act's provision of second-ary education for 'age, aptitude and ability' disguised a decision taken in 1941 by the Board of Education's senior civil servants to perpetuate the bipartite discriminatory post-eleven provision. Multilateral schools were accorded merely the most grudging experimental status. The first pamphlet of the new Ministry of Educa-tion, *The Nation's Schools*, indicated that 'future employment will not demand any measure of technical skill or knowledge'. The major-ity would be 'the hewers of wood and the drawers of water'.[12] Labour ministers, though not the rank and file, faithfully followed the mandarins, mystified. Later Conservative governments, naturally, endorsed the system fabricated for them by those civil servants who were the product of the most highly selective educational system in the world. They perpetuated that system in their own image. Yet it was skilfully done in a framework of consensus.

Disillusionment with the system produced by the 1944 Act mounted in the 1960s and the progression to a comprehensive system produced its own backlash. But with the erosion in recent years the 1944 Act has become a kind of touchstone of progressivism and enlighten-ment. This is dangerous. The historian, as well as the educational-ist, has the duty to point out that the author of the 1944 Education Act, when Chancellor in 1953, produced a list of savings for his cabinet colleagues which included levying fees in state schools, rais-ing age of entry to six and lowering the leaving age to fourteen.[13]

In Wales we are, of course, part of this wider scene but we need to be even more conscious that education is part of the fabric of society. The education system is the product of that society and it reflects and helps perpetuate it. But it also helps to modify it. In short, if we are Welsh we must have a Welsh education. An 'English' education (in whatever language) will not do.

In the Musée du Louvre there is a striking statue of a scribe of the old Kingdom of Egypt. It is about 4,500 years old. He is carved in limestone and painted – hair black, flesh brown, eyes of alabaster, rock crystal and copper – an alert crossed-legged figure, ready with his papyrus scroll. To be so memorialised in stone the scribe must have played an important role in the eyes of his contemporaries. This was because he had mastered the major technique in civilized communication – he could write ... Because he could write and cypher he could receive written instructions and eventually but inevitably became the man who could most easily execute them. Thus he became, whether high or low in the scale of royal servants, a member of an educated secretariat that directly or indirectly wielded the power behind the throne.[14]

The interaction of education, social mobility, class, politics, power, if true for ancient Egypt, has never been so easily analysed since. But the fact of that relationship has been fully appreciated by monarchs and governments. The study of the history of education in Wales must take cognizance of this at all points. For example in the eighteenth century in Wales the Society for Promoting Christian Knowledge and Griffith Jones, whose circulating schools made much of the nation literate, expended considerable energy on reassuring their wealthy supporters that they were not educating the poor out of their station.

The social dimension of the history of education tends to disappear from the Welsh historian's view when he has dispensed with Griffith Jones. The graph of state activity, and of state expenditure on education in Wales, seems to proceed ever upwards – grants to British and National Society schools (1847 a watershed), board schools, training colleges, a university, a state system of county schools from the 1890s, Hadow-type reorganization (not such a success story this), the 1944 Act, the excitements of the expansion and reorganization of the 1960s. The detail of that story, based on careful research into the mass of printed and documentary primary sources, would be invaluable both as a work of reference and as a framework within which alternative interpretations might be placed. Our knowledge of those schools which have educated the mass of the Welsh population since the industrial revolution, the elementary schools, voluntary and board, and the primary schools is indeed sparse. Larger issues are rarely treated. There has been little fundamental questioning of processes by which groups or classes in Welsh society have sought to preserve the education system in their own image and to best serve their immediate interests. We have only hints here and there. But the history of modern Wales requires these questions to be asked at every point. While it would be absurd to deny the contribution of the *gwerin* and their pennies to the development of secondary and university education in a Wales transformed by the industrial revolution, and churlish to minimize the efforts expended by Hugh Owen and O. M. Edwards, it is unhistorical to rest content with some residual glow of a golden age, when the sun shone at every sports day. *The*

Corn is Green syndrome, so seductive for the playwright, is the hallmark of a relatively poor, inegalitarian, educationally and socially blighted society. It is the stuff of self-sacrifice; it is the stuff of ruthless competition. It evokes community appreciation and help – a transferred *cymorth*; it produces alienation and division. In pre-industrial Wales, indeed for much of the nineteenth century, community flourished in poverty. Wales paid for its centrality to the Industrial Revolution by becoming part of a society in which such community was inevitably transmuted. One of the major agencies of the metamorphosis has been education. And here the situation in Wales gets more complex than that in England, more exciting. The county schools of Wales were no accident. The Industrial Revolution fed on itself. It created the need for vastly increased numbers of literate and numerate people as primary industry, then commerce and service industries, grew apace. Blackcoat jobs were created on some scale. For Wales, a world centre of primary industry in the second half of the nineteenth century, the result was a burgeoning middle class which did not have the appropriate grammar-school education to perpetuate itself as it was doing successfully and exclusively in England, though there, too, there was a thrust towards increasing secondary provision as demand outstripped supply. For reasons of Welsh national prestige and respectability, as well as for wider social and political reasons, the vacuum had to be filled. That it took the form of the Welsh Intermediate Education Act and its schools was due to individuals acting in a particular political and administrative context. That the schools came into existence was due to economic, social and class forces. Welsh historians have yet to explore the interaction in detail.

Such profound social and educational changes forced fundamental questions to be asked about Wales and Welshness. National respectability for the leaders of opinion in Wales, at least since the 1847 Blue Books, had been bound up with the question of education, whether for enlightenment, or social control or industrial and commercial efficiency. National respectability for Welsh leaders of the nineteenth and early twentieth century involved loyalty to Britain and to the Empire along with loyalty to Wales. After all, it was the economic imperatives of the British Empire which were moulding the new Wales. That respectability in Victorian times could only be conferred and cemented by an educated middle class, providing leaders and opinion-formers for the nation. To this process a system of secondary schools was essential. Hugh Owen was acutely aware of the dynamic relationship between education, Welsh society and Welsh nationalism.

The Welsh county secondary schools took in a far wider social mix than the English. On a greater scale than was the case in England the county schools and the municipal secondary schools after 1902, educated the sons and daughters of a working class as well as those of a middle class. But they educated an élite, and that élite was inexorably anglicized, not only in language but also, far more fundamentally, in attitude. Indeed, in one sense, this was part of the purpose. There was then, and remains, no such entity as a distinctively Welsh middle class, as opposed to a middle class in Wales. That term itself is one signifying accommodation into a wider society. The Welshness of the people so designated must lie outside that which makes them 'middle class'. What distinguished them as a middle class tended to extinguish them as Welsh – at least in traditional terms. That élite was concerned not only with creating a Wales after its own image but also perpetuating its distinguishing advantages. The education system was central to this, though in less stark terms than in England. Such a social function of the secondary schools, in a context of a view of Welsh history which highlighted the community and national role of an educated, enlightened, respectable, rural, classless, peasant *gwerin*, led to the Welsh national disease of schizophrenia among educators and social analysts. Owen M. Edwards struggled desperately and, of course, unavailingly, to reconcile the irreconcilable. He, too, saw clearly the interrelationship between education, society and nationalism in the Wales of the early twentieth century.

It is not evident that present-day analysts of education in Wales are aware of the centrality of the relationship, and historians must be held partly responsible. Of course the Welsh language figures centrally in education debate, rightly. Examination results, as in O. M. Edwards's day, can spark off acrimonious exchanges. The point, now as then, seems to have been missed. O. M. Edwards and Major Edgar Jones, the classic protagonists of the 1909/10 controversy over yardsticks of success by which the county schools might be measured, were arguing from irreconcilably different premises.[15]

One of the sadder features of the controversy surrounding the Loos-more Report was that no one seemed to take the O. M. Edwards line – that education was about more than examination results. The meritocratic ethos seems finally to have overwhelmed all else in Wales.

None of this can be adequately and fairly discussed without recourse to the history of a long-standing debate, combined with an appreciation of the centrality of education to the economic, political and social structure of this – or any – nation. It is not the historian's task *qua* historian, to analyse the present predicament in Welsh education. The historian may legitimately indicate that the history of Welsh education, in so far as it *has* been written, leads inexorably to the conclusion that questions about the state of Welsh education are questions about the state of Welsh society. When we ask what sort of education we want in Wales we ask what sort of Wales we want. Myths are no basis on which to start addressing that question.

2
Matter, myth and motive in the 'Blue Books' of 1847

Introduction

> Now, what I want is, Facts. Teach these boys and girls nothing but Facts. Facts alone are wanted in life. Plant nothing else, and root out everything else.
>
> Charles Dickens, *Hard Times*, 1854.

'Facts' were what Mr Gradgrind wanted, and he reflected a Victorian passion for them. While the kind of information which Gradgrind valued has become a byword for barrenness we should not lose sight of the reasons why the Victorians wanted their facts and the invaluable service they did to posterity by collecting them. If Royal Commissions and Commissions of Inquiry seemed as much a growth industry as those supplying their context it was for very good reason. As social change proceeded at a pace which decreed an unparalleled degree of social dislocation, the Victorians had to find out what was going on. Wales, particularly, with its frightening tendency to riot with Rebecca and march for the Charter, had to be investigated, and that social context is made clear in the first few pages of the Reports.[1] Ralph Robert Wheeler Lingen's report on the three counties of Carmarthen, Glamorgan and Pembroke, takes forty-two pages. Already, by page 6, he feels confident enough to diagnose the Welsh character, conditioned solely by a 'theological bent of mind isolated from nearly all sources . . . of secular information'. The result was that 'poetical and enthusiastic warmth of religious feeling', chapel-going and relative absence of crime were associated with 'the most unreasoning prejudices or impulses; an utter want of method in thinking or acting'. What are the two examples of this cast of mind provided by Lingen? They are participation in the Rebecca riots and the Chartist movement.

It is in the context of a total incapacity of commissioners of the social, educational, religious, national and class background of such as Lingen to comprehend that anyone would contemplate support for such aberrant movements that we must see the Report. There was a total lack of empathy on the part of the commissioners. Yet that lack of empathy should not be reflected in our own assessment. This Report on education was an attempt to understand a situation which seemed to pose fundamental threats to social structures. So the Report had to be about the Welsh character. Its political context was that of a government apprehensive of the uncontrolled Welsh. David Griffiths has argued that the investigation resulted not merely from a request by the Welsh MP for Coventry, William Williams, but from a government initiative for which Williams was merely the agent.[2] Griffiths has argued that while specific documentary evidence is lacking, the circumstantial evidence is powerful, and indeed the speed with which government accepted the initiative is significant. His case is convincing. However, I would argue that if what the government envisaged was an answer to Wales's social problems what they ended up with was something very different and wholly inimical to their thinking. And the essential message was not confined to the Welsh situation. What emerges from the Blue Books is a statement about education in England and Wales. The Report of 1847 embodies a philosophy of elementary education and a remedy to educational ills in England as well as in Wales.

David Griffiths argues that it has become fashionable to see the commissioners as able, talented and conscientious, but misled.[3] He is right to question their supposed naïvety. He goes on to ask whether the answer to the riddle is that the *government* had Wales in mind for an experimental system of national education. This would certainly be commensurate with the educational arguments advanced by the commissioners, especially by the most outspoken of them, J. C. Symons. The case is less convincing in relation to government philosophy and practice in the 1840s. Frank Smith, Kay-Shuttleworth's biographer, has argued that the requirement to examine the 'moral' dimension in Wales resulted from an alteration by an unidentifiable source to Kay-Shuttleworth's own draft terms of reference.[4] I believe that the probable explanation of the thrust of the various arguments in the Blue Books is that, simplistically, the government was concerned to find out how it might better control the behaviour of the Welsh and Kay-Shuttleworth, and at least Symons and Johnson, were concerned with providing irrefutable evidence for the necessity of a state system of education – and not only in Wales.

Some facts

The *Reports of the Commissioners of Enquiry into the State of Education in Wales* were published in 1847. The statistics of the Reports, as well as those contained in them, are a formidable tribute to Victorian labours and thoroughness in a world in which not even science fiction had yet imagined the word processor. William Williams's motion in the Commons had been put forward on 10 March 1846. Instructions, or terms of reference, to the commissioners went out from Kay-Shuttleworth on 1 October 1846. Lingen's response on the three counties of Carmarthen, Glamorgan and Pembroke was submitted on 1 July 1847. It comprised forty-two pages of report, nineteen pages of statistics and 207 pages of statistical appendices. The detailed reports, hundred by hundred, parish by parish, took up a further 266 pages, twelve pages of 'Evidence respecting the Mining and Manufacturing Districts' ensued. The Report concluded with three pages of data relating to night schools in the three counties.

Part Two of the Report concerned the counties of Brecknock, Cardigan, Radnor and Monmouth. Jelinger C. Symons had an easier task than Lingen, and completed his section on 6 March 1847. His analysis was longer than Lingen's – sixty-eight pages. Appendix A comprised the evidence of seventy-seven witnesses in fifty-five pages, with Appendix B, notes on parishes and schools in the area, taking a further eighty pages. This is followed by a further fifty-nine pages of appendices. The report on Monmouthshire occupied another sixty-four pages.

Part 3 of the Report relates to the north Wales counties of Anglesey, Caernarfon, Denbigh, Flint, Merioneth and Montgomery. It was returned to Kay-Shuttleworth in October 1847. Henry Vaughan Johnson took sixty-eight pages to set out his conclusions, which he supported with over 300 pages of evidence. The 1847 Report, with its various title pages and appurtenances comes to 1256 pages of detailed information. Much of that detail is about the education which was on offer in Wales. Much of it is about contemporary opinions of that system and what its deficiencies were. It is an unparalleled Victorian educational census.

Kay-Shuttleworth, in his terms of reference, called for such detail. The object of the total exercise has been made famous by posterity: 'an inquiry . . . into the state of education in . . . Wales, especially into the means afforded to the labouring classes of acquiring a knowledge of the English language.'[5] This was no new theme – the Act which brought about the translation of the Welsh Bible, credited with preserving the language, provided the Bible in Welsh in order that 'such as do not understand the said Language, may by conferring both Tongues together, the sooner attain to the Knowledge of the English tongue'. The labourers still needed enlightenment. Before this could be done, and 'measures . . . taken for the improvement of the existing means of education in Wales' the present inchoate structure had to be analysed. All was grist to the mill of the commissioners: endowments, physical conditions, tenure, size of schools, state of furniture and apparatus, number of children on roll, attendance, 'whether the children are instructed in the Welsh language, or in the English, or in both', together with an analysis of the teachers and their background.

The commissioners were warned to take careful note of the Sunday schools in Wales, the denominational complexities of which were doubtless well known to the secretary to the Committee of Council on Education: 'the Sunday-school must be regarded as the most remarkable, because the most general, spontaneous effort of the zeal of Christian congregations for education.' They had to be investigated and, in the process, there had to be no infringement of the civil liberties of the congregations.

Two other instructions are of significance. Kay-Shuttleworth stressed that the commissioners must try to be as 'complete and accurate' as possible in their returns if the Report was to have any value. They fulfilled this brief. Again, they were specifically instructed to 'keep in mind the amount, character and condition of the population . . .' and 'to form some estimate of the general state of intelligence and information of the poorer classes in Wales, and of the influence which an improved education might be expected to produce, on the general condition of society, and its moral and religious progress'. The commissioners fulfilled this brief too.

There is no reason to doubt that the commissioners were assiduous in their accumulation of the relevant details. In the south and west, for example, Lingen appointed three assistant commissioners, William Morris, a former schoolmaster, and David Lewis and David Williams who were members of St David's College, Lampeter. They went round the day schools of the three counties, schedules at the ready, and collected answers personally from the teachers 'and scholars also, when present'. The Sunday schools presented more of a problem. Superintendents of Sunday schools in Carmarthenshire and part of Pembrokeshire were interviewed personally, though of course the statistical information which they gave was not necessarily accurate since it was often undocumented. The inadequacy of the oral information, together with the sheer logistics of getting round brought about a change in method. The schedule of questions relating to the Sunday schools was printed in the main periodicals and journals published in Wales in both languages, with a request that the details should be completed by the time they were called for. The plan was unsuccessful. According to Lingen it neither saved labour nor resulted in greater accuracy. The various reasons Lingen identified for lack of accuracy included the fact that this was a 'first attempt to apply the rigid forms of statistical investigation among a class of persons who in general had neither the records nor the habits of mind corresponding to such an inquiry'. The remark is interesting. The impression is of condescension, of class-based prejudice. Of course it is. It is couched in language entirely typical of that class in Victorian society whose education and background fitted them for superior intellectual, social and political activities. Lingen was perfectly prepared to concede the remarkable achievements of the Sunday school. The language in which he conveyed his criticisms was as typically open as that of all contemporaries of his class.

The Report is far more than a parade of prejudiced opinion. There is no doubt about the genuineness of the attempt to provide an educational census. The work was carried out substantially by interview, with notes made on the spot and written up each night. Lingen, for example, stressed that in the case of those reports written by his assistants, he personally went over each one in the writer's presence. Each report relating to each school and district is directly identifiable or attributable either to Lingen or a specific assistant.

The social context

The commissioners realized that the traditional ambition of Church schools serving individual parishes not only had not been achieved but also was now an impossibility because the parish system itself had broken down. Symons noted that in Monmouthshire the eighteen western parishes which he investigated were small in area but housed over half the population, a population which, over the county as a whole, had nearly doubled between 1821 and 1841. Lingen realized that the schools attached to some of the new industrial works were the equivalent of the old parish schools since, he noted in a striking analogy, the works had replaced the manor. The redistribution of the population in Lingen's district meant that 'it is impossible to deal with its educational necessities through any adaptation of the existing parochial machinery'.

It was, of course, the industrialization of Glamorgan and Monmouthshire in particular which was responsible. The dislocation this caused was not only educational. The nature of the employment opportunities distorted the traditional age profile of school attendance. Compared with Pembrokeshire and Cardiganshire, in Glamorgan there were far more pupils under the age of five, and far fewer over the age of ten because of the job opportunities, which led Lingen to advocate not legislation on child labour but the concentration of educational effort on the infants' schools in the industrial districts.

The physical environment was linked with the moral climate and, in turn, with the remedial demands made of education, in a way which provides one of the major themes in the Report. Symons was the most outspoken in his condemnation of the ironmasters. He provided graphic descriptions of the degrading physical conditions of overcrowding and the lack of basic amenities for employees:

> I regard their degraded condition as entirely the fault of their employers, who give them far less tendance and care than they bestow on their cattle, and who, with few exceptions, use and regard them as so much brute force instrumental to wealth . . .

Symons went further. He associated the physical degradation which he encountered in Monmouthshire directly with social unrest. The followers of John Frost were associated, by inference, with 'evil in every shape', but that evil was not Chartism as such, it was the demoralization and brutalization to which the population had been subjected. In the rural areas Symons had to look for other explanations for such social unrest as the Rebecca riots. It was at this point that he made the direct link between lack of education interacting with the volatility of the Welsh character to produce such aberrations as Rebecca. But if Symons was less indignant about the poverty

of the countryside he certainly highlighted it. Of Breconshire, Radnorshire and Cardiganshire he recorded: 'The people in my district
are almost universally poor.' The implications of such poverty, the
resulting constraints on privacy and cleanliness, the consequences
for personal morality, were perfectly evident to Symons. To the
environmentalist, education could be a vital agent of change.

For a relatively sympathetic Symons, the social context of rural
and urban Wales were equally daunting in their effects. The difference he identified was that, in the rural areas, labourers could hardly
exist on what they earned but farmers could not afford to pay them
any more. In the areas of new industry, the employers were intent on
accumulating large fortunes, paid high wages, but took a totally
brutal view of their workforce in failing to provide any kind of
decent society for them to live in. He identified one aspect of this
cynicism as the employers' complete lack of interest in the education
of their workers.

The social structure of Wales militated against any spontaneous
development of education. Lingen noted that there was no middle
class in Wales, particularly in the works and, in one of his best
known strictures, attributed this not only to economic organization
but also to the influence of the Welsh language:

> My district exhibits the phenomenon of a peculiar language isolating the
> masses from the upper portion of society . . . Welsh element is never
> found at the top of the social scale, nor in its own body does it exhibit
> much variety of gradation . . . farmers are always smallholders; Welsh
> workmen never get into the office . . .

This refrain was also taken up by Symons, who highlighted the
inadequacy of the Welsh in coping with the demands of business,
the professions and, more surprisingly, agriculture, because the books
relating to agricultural improvements were written in English. The
commissioners were perceptive enough to realize that social
hierarchies and patronage structures tended to produce an educational
system in their own image. The inadequacies of the resulting system
in Wales were only too apparent.

The educational and religious inheritance[6]

In the absence of a substantial middle class the responsibilities of the
wealthy, whether gentry or industrialists, were all the more significant.

Of the three commissioners Symons was most ready to condemn them: 'Neither church nor school have been established by those who employ the people or own the land.' He reported that, in Monmouthshire, the only people who were indifferent to his inquiry were some of the ironmasters, who had done nothing to ameliorate the educational shortcomings or the physical degradation which the mass of the population had to endure.

The divided religious affiliations of the Welsh had had deleterious consequences on educational provision in an era in which that provision was a reflection of denominational strength. Organized provision of education was not the province of the state but of the British and National Societies. The first people whom the three commissioners 'deemed it expedient' to meet were the bishop of Hereford and the bishop of St David's. Here again, of course, Wales was a special case in its loyalties. In Cardiganshire, for example, 4,074 scholars attended Established Church Sunday schools (182 being aged over fifteen), while 23,057 (14,789 aged over fifteen) went to Dissenting Sunday schools.

The one spontaneous growth in Welsh education, the circulating schools, had been the only schools for the poor which, for complex reasons, had not been fatally flawed with denominational wrangling, though Griffith Jones had to work hard to persuade many of his backers of this. The circulating-school model of education had been inadequate in its day; by 1847 this inheritance was grossly so. It is sometimes forgotten that such schools, between twenty and thirty of them, were still in existence, though modified. They remained in one place for a maximum of three years, and the degree of charity was very limited compared with the amount which families contributed. All the commissioners condemned them. The temporary nature of the schools inevitably resulted in wholly inadequate buildings. There were, as always, limited aims, the teaching of the rudiments only of the three Rs, and pupils had to learn the catechism and attend the Established Church. Masters were paid a pittance – £25 a year. Above all, the schools' essential feature of transience was no model for the nineteenth century. To Lingen, they were a positive hindrance in that they inhibited the setting up of permanent schools. This degree of censure indicated the changed context of educational expectation in the mid-nineteenth century.

The Sunday school legacy was a different matter. By definition these schools were intended to be limited in time as in aim. The commissioners, even the acerbic Lingen, were highly complimentary.

The latter estimated that a fifth of the Welsh population attended Sunday school and 'half of this number is returned as being able to read the Scriptures'. There were thousands of voluntary teachers and the schools were 'real fields of mental activity'. In this context, the limited aims of learning to read the Bible in Welsh, and learning ever-extending chunks of it off by heart, were acceptable. Lingen was impressed by this Bible-owning, Sabbatically sartorial working class who knew so much about abstruse theology but with 'an utter want of method in thinking and acting'. Symons believed that three-quarters of the correct answers he got in day schools were the result of Sunday school instruction. As we shall see, he also found the Dissenting Sunday schools considerably more effective than those of the Church in that they were places of family spiritual improvement. He was outspoken in his praise: 'I must bear my cordial testimony to the services which these humble congregations have rendered to the community.'

It is clear, therefore, that the commissioners saw many of the complexities of the relationship between religion, class, economic structure and education which were the key to a school system which, in England and Wales, was increasingly perceived as being inadequate for a new society. Education was linked with social cohesion, right religion and economic competence. These were all considerations which the state had to bear in mind, but in the contemporary climate of political theory, the state could hardly yet countenance the practical implications of government funding. This was at the root of the widening gulf between provision and aspiration in England. It is hardly any wonder that commissioners like Symons, Lingen and Johnson could not come to terms with a situation in which the social structure, the religion and the language of Wales made even those promptings towards better provision more inconclusive. The only promptings with any hope of spontaneous success from within Welsh society were the Sunday schools. Yet, in the view of the commissioners, they could only, and should only, minister to the theological needs of the Welsh. The Welsh language allowed this, but 'its resources in every other branch remain obsolete and meagre'.

The educational ambitions of the Welsh

There was no doubting the total inadequacy of the educational inheritance in Wales as in so many regions of England. The charity model could not cope in the changed economic and social climate. Private enterprise would only be adequate if demand was universal and supply rose to meet it. The existence of large numbers of private adventure schools in the industrial areas indicated that there was demand, but the commissioners demonstrated its limitations. Symons noted of Monmouthshire, where he estimated that only just over half the pupils of an age to be in school actually attended, that children were taken away from school to earn a wage. We have already encountered Lingen's contention that the school population in Glamorgan was skewed towards the under-fives because of early leaving. A Baptist minister in Radnorshire contended that the poorest in Wales had little regard for the value of education.

Johnson, at least, was not prepared to blame any lack of appetite wholly on the Welsh. Indeed, his messages were distinctly equivocal. He came close to complimenting the Welsh on their rejection of the awful education which was on offer:

> It appears that considering the extremely small value of the instruction given compared with the expense, and considering the materials for instruction and the qualifications of the teachers, the scholars cannot reasonably be expected to be more numerous, more regular in their attendance, or to expend more time in an employment so unprofitable.

Elsewhere, the message from the commissioners, including Symons, was that the Welsh were hungry for a decent day-school education for which they were prepared to pay. What they wanted from this education was a mastery of the English language, although 'affection leans to Welsh'. Lingen was not sympathetic even to that affection. Although he rather tartly observed that it was not his position to comment, it is obvious that he did not even believe that the language of religion should continue to be restricted to Welsh or that mastery of two languages was more civilized than one. It is obvious that no one, at least of those reported in these pages, countenanced anything other than bilingualism.

The inference from Symons must be that the Welsh were as sensible of the limited social mobility conferred by the Welsh language as was Lingen. Indeed, Symons elsewhere made it explicit. He argued that the reason why only one day school in the three counties of Breconshire, Radnorshire and Cardiganshire taught Welsh was that the parents were desperate for their children to learn English because 'they find an ignorance of English a constant and almost an insurmountable obstacle to their advancement in life'. The problem was that a decent education in *English* was not on offer, either to native Welsh-speakers or, crucial to the argument, to native English-speakers. A similar message came from Vaughan Johnson in north Wales. Nearly half the schools in the northern counties were private adventure schools. Johnson reported that these schools were 'utterly worthless' in terms of teaching quality, attainment, apparatus, furniture and buildings. He argued that the proprietors were charging exorbitant fees and the only reason they were able to do so was because of the determination of Welsh parents to have their children educated. For religious reasons they would not send children to the Church schools, so they spent, in aggregate, a massive £7,000 per annum on private education, a sum which Johnson contrasted unfavourably with the £5,675 contributed to the provision of education of the poor by the rich. The message of the commissioners was that the Welsh wanted a day-school education for their children, they wanted it in the English language, and this demand was not being met to any worthwhile degree by the existing providing agencies.

Welsh achievements

The commissioners reinforced their view of the desire of the Welsh for education with words of high praise for the Sunday schools. Lingen's verdict was that 'these schools have been almost the sole, they are still the main and most congenial, centres of education. Through their agency the younger portion of the adult labouring classes in Wales can generally read, or are in course of learning to read, the Scriptures in their mother tongue.' In such schools, and at little expense, argued Lingen, 'the Welsh working man rouses himself', even though he proceeded to argue that this did not result in the cultivation of 'method in thinking and acting'. We have already seen that Symons was of the opinion that much of the information which he tested in day schools was the result of teaching in the Sunday schools. He was particularly unimpressed by most of the Established Church Sunday schools, in that they tended to cultivate mere rote learning. In so many of them he saw 'nothing to awaken the faculties, arouse the interest, soften the feelings, and reach the hearts of the children . . . the whole system is spiritless, and monotonous . . .'

He was much more complimentary about the Dissenting Sunday schools, where the presence of so many adults meant that the object was 'spiritual improvement for the congregation at large'. 'I must bear my cordial testimony', he said, 'to the services which these humble congregations have rendered to the community.' What appealed to him was the discussion and the creativity of thought; what he was against was the use of these schools to teach pupils to read, so ceasing to be 'seminaries of religious knowledge', instead 'sink[ing] into weekday schools of the lowest class'.

The message from north Wales was similar. The Welsh-language Sunday schools were 'the main instrument of civilisation' and 'have determined the character of the language, literature, and general intelligence of the inhabitants'. However, their concerns were theological. They left a population of the lower classes whose religious vocabulary, in the remarkable words of the commissioners, was 'rendered capable of expressing every shade of idea', but whose linguistic resources in branches of knowledge other than theology were meagre.

All the commissioners were therefore keen to attest the ability of the Welsh when educational conditions were right. It would be impossible to find a more outspoken tribute to the intelligence of the lower classes in any part of Britain than that they were able to manipulate abstruse theological ideas. Similar tributes to the mental powers of the Welsh came in the field of arithmetic. Lingen recorded that the pupils he saw seemed to have the potential to be very able in arithmetic, if only they had the right teaching. Symons, more prone to purple passages, waxed eloquent on Welsh children's arithmetical prowess: 'I have witnessed more proficiency after a small amount of instruction than I ever witnessed in any schools either in England or on the Continent.' In respect of Monmouthshire, Symons tempered his praise but broadened his scope. Considering their generally short stay in school Symons argued that Welsh pupils 'certainly attain as much facility in reading, writing, and ciphering as could reasonably be expected . . .' Elsewhere, Symons penned this striking tribute:

> I can speak in very strong terms of the natural ability and capacity for instruction of the Welsh people. Though they are ignorant, no people more richly deserve to be educated. In the first place, they desire it to the full extent of their power to appreciate it; in the next, their natural capacity is of a high order, especially in the Welsh districts. They learn what they are even badly taught with surprising facility. Their memories are very retentive, and they are remarkably shrewd in catching an idea.

For whatever purpose, the commissioners emphasized the Welsh capacity for education, so accentuating the deprivation of their actual educational experience.

Bench-marks

The curriculum of the day schools for the working class for most of the nineteenth century was, by our standards, an impoverished one. It consisted substantially of reading, writing and arithmetic, with religious instruction. History and geography were increasingly regarded in more enlightened circles as important. These subjects, sometimes vocal music, and, very exceptionally, such subjects as drawing or navigation, or some aspect of natural science, reflected current Welsh practice. The general conception was Gradgrind's – that education consisted of facts which should be learned. It was the only conception commensurate with the prevailing philosophy of education as, to the greatest possible extent, a private charitable enterprise.

There were more enlightened ideas abroad. A few individuals were influenced by Rousseau's child-centred notions, far more by those of Pestalozzi and Fellenberg. Fellenberg, for example, took for granted the supreme concern of the working class as manual labour, but advocated combining this with time for learning, and constant concern for intellectual discussion, even at work. Kay-Shuttleworth was aware of these ideas; it is likely that the commissioners were also.

Lingen, by far the least sympathetic, not only condemned the restriction of most elementary education in Wales to the three Rs, but also, and far more forcefully, the restricted outlook on the world which resulted. Here indeed was the credibility gap between the lawyer and the child labourer. The former found it impossible to understand a situation in which, he argued, pupils' ideas were as locally rooted as a millennium previously. In Lingen's view it is obvious that children who had no conception of what the capital of England was, or any understanding of the significance of William the Conqueror, were not only educationally deprived but beyond, even a danger to, the social system. 'What hold', he asks, 'has society upon the sense of interest, sympathies, or reason of such people?'

The wider brief which the commissioners took upon themselves, and which is, in my view, crucial to an understanding of the wider significance of their reports, is succinctly summed up by Symons:

> in the examination of the children I have striven to test the cultivation of their minds and the extent of their information, as well as to estimate the amount of their scholastic attainments; for I conceived my province to be less that of an inspector of schools than an inquirer into education. I have deemed the mental condition of the children the primary object of my attention . . .

To an extent these were laudable preconceptions. The short-term injustice of the assessment which they then undertook lay in concentrating on an end result which the pupils could not possibly have achieved, that is the general knowledge and 'mental condition' which the commissioners deemed appropriate. However, it must be the case that this unfairness was essentially devoted to an enlightened end. What the assessment itself revealed was pupils who, allegedly, did not know their own ages, did not know how many weeks there were in a year or days in a week. They knew nothing of what was manufactured in Manchester, of the landmarks of English history, that Ireland was a country. Symons made no secret of the fact that his examining of the pupils was 'nowise confined to the limited scope of the subjects taught in the schools visited, but [was] extended to most branches of ordinary information'. Of course such a procedure offends against all the tenets of fair examining, which insist that pupils should be tested on what they have been taught. In 1847 the purpose was not to be fair; it was to point out the wholly unacceptable consequences, as the commissioners saw them, of such a restricted system of education for the lower orders. The 1847 investigation was serving a wider purpose.

The inadequacies of the system

If the judgement made on the Welsh was not whether they were able to profit from the system as it existed but how deficient the system itself was, then there can be no gainsaying the unfairness of the 1847 Reports to individual Welsh children struggling to answer questions in English. With the *system* on trial there is another perspective. One thing is certain; gross deficiencies were not unique to Wales.

We are told of schools without benches in which pupils had to sit on the floor. We hear of 'eleven children . . . found in a small room, in which one of the children of the Mistress was lying ill in bed of the measles. Another child had died in the same room, of the same complaint, a few days before; and no less than thirty of the usual scholars were then confined at home with the same disease.' This is *not* information from the 1847 Report; it comes from reports of the Manchester Statistical Society in the 1830s. This society had been established partly as a result of the interest aroused by a pamphlet on *The Moral and Physical Condition of the Working Classes employed in the Cotton Manufacture in Manchester*. This pamphlet compares with Engels's writings in its description of the evils of the impact of uncontrolled industrialization. One of the essential elements of reform listed in the pamphlet was education for the poor. The pamphlet was written by Dr. James Kay, later Sir James Kay-Shuttleworth.[7]

The catalogue of inadequacies in Wales embraced all aspects of the schools and ascribed blame to many sources. At the heart of the problem was a dire shortage of funds. We have already seen that the social structure of Wales, its lack of any substantial middling class, was a structural problem. The commissioners were highly critical of the gentry and the clergy whose role in financing schools in England was central. In large tracts of rural south Wales, said Lingen, the gentry were neither resident nor did they subscribe to the education of the poor. In the whole of his district of Breconshire, Radnorshire and Cardiganshire Symons found only £1,196 in subscriptions and £1,167 in endowments, compared with £3,145 from 'school pence'.

The works schools in Wales have, on the whole, had a good press, perhaps because of the Guest educational edifice in Dowlais. This was not a view shared by the commissioners. In fact, the opposition of the commissioners to works schools is perhaps sufficiently stringent as to sow some seeds of suspicion as to their motives. Lingen pointed out that the workers paid for their works schools but had no control over them. Symons was not consistent, but he was scathing about the works schools system in Monmouthshire. He, again, points out that the workers provided the money and had no control either over the way the school was run or over any surplus money, which might find its way either to the employer or to an Established Church minister, despite the working majority being Dissenters. The schools were among the best in the county; the system of providing them was flawed.

Fundamental poverty, together with the failure of traditional agencies, produced an educational system which incurred the merited wrath of the commissioners. The resulting indictment is well known. It needs to be reiterated that such indictments were being made of educational provision for the poor in England as well. It was the immediate context, linguistic, religious, national, that gave the Blue Books their peculiar capacity to insult in Wales. The educational condemnation was justified, both in terms of the inadequacies of the system and in the expectation of preparing the ground for something better. In doing so the commissioners were providing an insight into what they believed to be the constituents of effective teaching in elementary schools. It is entirely commensurate with what we know of Kay-Shuttleworth's priorities.

The commissioners condemned the inadequacy of buildings, furniture and equipment. Schools were held in chapels, shops, kitchens and even bedrooms. The buildings were often private houses and many were little more than outhouses, without proper flooring, with no ceilings, with open chimneys and leaking thatch. Most had no toilets. In very few schools were there adequate books, maps or blackboards. Rarely were there textbooks which were favourably regarded by the commissioners. In most instances pupils had to buy their own books. The result was lack of uniformity, so that the teacher had to classify his pupils according to the books they possessed rather than their ability. The books which were in use were often ones which 'represent the subjects of which they treat in the most difficult and repulsive form, and to Welsh children remain at the close of their education as unintelligible as at the commencement'.

Another intractable problem was that, in the absence of both legislation and self-motivation, length of stay of those potential pupils was sufficiently short as to make their education particularly ineffective. Here again, the commissioners provided a contemporary measure which furnishes an insight into the thinking of the time. Twenty-nine years before education became, by and large, compulsory, the commissioners believed that children 'even of the working class' ought to spend a minimum of five years in day school between the ages of five and fifteen. Over one-third of pupils in Breconshire, Radnorshire and Cardiganshire did not meet this measure. But the more insidious evil was sporadic attendance in any one year. In Monmouthshire, according to Symons, scarcely 15 per cent of the pupils stayed in school long enough to profit. Symons reported that when he carried out a spot check in two Cardiganshire parishes he found that only 27 per cent of pupils between the ages of five and ten were in school. Lingen reported the custom in Pembrokeshire of pupils attending for odd quarters. In Cardiganshire the record was good: 21 per cent of those in school had more than two years of schooling. In Radnorshire, 63 per cent of pupils were in their first year. Johnson's verdict on the children in north Wales was similar: 'it appears that not more than 65.6 per cent of the number of alleged scholars are daily present in school throughout the year.' In analysing the reasons, the commissioners were sympathetic rather than condemnatory. They instanced the distance from the nearest school at which so many pupils lived, for example. We have seen that Johnson was outspoken in putting the case that the education on offer was so appalling that there was no profit in attending.

If the commissioners condemned what was on offer, did they isolate any peculiarly Welsh reasons for the shortcomings? Up to a point they did. We have seen that the ostensible leaders of society had come in for condemnation for their neglect of education. Johnson identified the catch-22 which partly, though only partly, lay behind this. The wealthy classes, he argued, belonged to the Established Church and would not fund education in non-denominational schools. The result was that Church of England schools were very badly attended, and then only by the poorest. Other parents had recourse to private adventure schools for their children, who were forced to pay exorbitant fees. Church schools were therefore deprived of the support of the lower classes, so they deteriorated. Where there were British schools, private adventure schools became extinct. He records that there were compromises. For example, Nonconformist pupils went to Church schools and learned the catechism – but were told by their parents not to believe it.

Then there was the bilingual difficulty. It is important to note that it was not a difficulty which Johnson, for example, saw as insurmountable educationally. His criticism was of the techniques involved:

> I have found no class of schools in which an attempt had been made to remove the . . . difficulty which occurs to a Welsh child at the very commencement of his course of instruction in consequence of his ignorance of the English language. Every book in the school is written in English;

every word which he speaks is to be spoken in English; every subject of instruction must be studied in English, and every addition to his stock of knowledge in grammar, geography, history, or arithmetic, must be communicated in English words; yet he is furnished with no single help for acquiring a knowledge of English. As yet no class of schools has been provided with dictionaries or grammars in Welsh and English . . . in the mean time it is difficult to conceive an employment more discouraging than that of the scholars, compelled as they are to employ six hours daily in reading and reciting chapters and formularies in a tongue which they cannot understand, and which neither their books nor their teachers can explain.

It would seem that the commissioners were, at the very least, inconsistent. Lingen argued that the Welsh were held back by their language; Johnson argued that even if the teachers were fluent in English and had the right kind of books, Welsh parents were averse to teachers using Welsh, even as a means of explanation. Johnson, at least, realized that the route to fluency in English lay through bilingual instruction. It was not a lesson which should have been so neglected in Wales. It was, after all, the basic instructional precept embodied in the Act for the translation of the Bible into Welsh in 1563.

Johnson's strictures, even in this regard, were substantially brought to bear on the teachers. The message which was hammered home time and again in the Reports is that the teaching and learning experience in schools in Wales was wholly inadequate, indeed usually counter-productive. The bilingual situation was a complicating one, and it accentuated the aridity and futility of much of what went on in schools of 'charity', but the essential message would have been true of the education of the lower orders in any part of England. Essentially, a combination of teachers of the lowest social status and teaching methods which consisted mainly of rote learning were wholly ineffective. The offending catalogue of teaching inefficiency is lengthy. Teachers were paid a pittance and therefore there was no incentive for them to make any effort. Symons recorded that a puddler could earn more in a week than a teacher could earn in a month. More of an indictment of teachers' pay, he recorded that in his district of Breconshire, Radnorshire and Cardiganshire, 401 of the 625 teachers were paid less than agricultural labourers. Teachers came from all kinds of backgrounds – mining, weaving, quarrying – usually occupations in which they had picked up a smattering of English. Often teachers from the more respectable backgrounds were ministers or clerks who were teaching as a second job. Training in a normal school or college was very rare.

Not surprisingly, the combination of poor premises, a real bilingual problem and a teaching force being paid a pittance resulted in teaching methods which the commissioners unanimously and constantly condemned. It is the reiteration of the ineffectuality of the methods of teaching going on in the schools which punctuates the reports like no other topic. Lingen argued that the near universal use of the Bible as a reading book was 'worthless . . . as a means of conveying religious or any other knowledge'. Pupils just chanted sentences, picking up successive verses as it came to their turn. Pupils had little sense of the meaning. Similarly meaningless activity often went on in the teaching of writing, whereby pupils just copied out line after line, so that they were never actually taught to put their writing to some use. Generally what they were given to copy was ungrammatical and inappropriate. The rules of arithmetic were not explained or understood. The learning which took place was rote learning. Lingen condemned this *per se*, but emphasized that, given the linguistic problem, the only effective method of teaching reading was to discuss the meaning of sentences and whole passages, not just learn individual words off by heart.

In this area, too, there is explicit evidence that Welsh education was not being measured only against wider current practice but against progressive, enlightened ideas. Symons, once again, put the educational case most sympathetically and succinctly:

> If the competency of the Welsh schoolmaster is to be measured by the standard of the popular estimation of his duties, perhaps almost as many exceed as fall short of it. But if it is not an undue expectation that a schoolmaster who professes to teach English should do more than make his scholars pronounce and spell English words without understanding their meaning – that he should give them some degree of mental exercise – inform their minds of the subjects he professes to teach – acquaint them with the rules as well as the practice of arithmetic – and at least endeavour to advance the younger as well as the older classes of his scholars, – if these be not extravagant requirements for the qualifications of a schoolmaster, I have no hesitation in saying that there are very few persons worthy of that title in my district.

What is significant about this blueprint of the good schoolteacher is that it was not a comment arising from the situation in Wales alone; it was equally true of elementary education in England and was what compelled Kay-Shuttleworth to try to improve teaching skills. Symons went on to condemn in detail the rote learning to which the pupils were subjected. He recorded that virtually no effort was made to help pupils to understand what they were learning.

In another telling comment Symons condemned the monitorial system, in which this kind of rote learning was institutionalized, not only from a Welsh perspective but from a wider standpoint, since the numbers in Wales were 'very inconsiderable': 'The Monitorial System exists only in the few National and British Schools, and I have not been led to think more favourably of it from my observation of its operation in Wales.' Monitors were doomed to the drudgery of teaching the alphabet. They therefore suffered themselves and were the 'unfittest of teachers'. There followed a remarkable passage from Symons, who later became an HMI:

> If education involves mental gain and moral culture, and requires skill, gentleness, patience, and kindness in order to gain access to and mastery over the minds it is designed to inform and mould, how is it to be reconciled with common sense that children should be chosen for such an office?

It can be no coincidence that in 1846 Kay-Shuttleworth introduced a pupil-teacher scheme which eventually replaced monitors with teacher-apprentices, some of whom could go on to win Queen's Scholarships and a training college place. At Kay-Shuttleworth's instigation the beginnings of reform in teacher training were taking shape at precisely the time of the investigations of the schools of the poor in Wales.

The refrain of ineffective teaching was taken up only slightly less eloquently by Johnson in north Wales. He stressed the total inadequacy of rote learning of English, mass class readings, constant copying out of copperplate passages of English riddled with mistakes. He cited the teaching of geography as another meaningless exercise in which pupils learned by rote and understood nothing. Welsh pupils were good at finding places on maps, but knew nothing of the inhabitants, the customs, the economy or the climate of foreign lands.

If teaching was so bad, how could it be remedied? As always, there were two answers. Teachers needed to be better trained and better paid. Both these solutions were, by implication, advanced regularly in the Reports. Symons, reporting on Monmouthshire, recorded that 'the teachers are for the most part very incompetent

to teach, and wholly unacquainted with any efficient system of instruction'. Elsewhere, he judged that 'the notion that there is any necessity that a schoolmaster should learn his business is quite in its infancy
in Wales'. He was right, but the generalization applied to England,
too. Johnson reported of north Wales that, of 643 teachers, only 65
were trained, and then only for an average of six months each.

We have already seen that the commissioners commented on the
lowly status and abysmal pay of teachers. Training of teachers was
no solution by itself. Symons argued that if they were trained 'such
training would fit men for employment in other spheres, where they
would realize four or five times the emolument and enjoy a much
higher social position than they can hope for as schoolmasters in
Wales under existing conditions.' He noted the heroic efforts of those
who established and ran the normal school in Brecon, the only one
of its kind in Wales, but argued that normal schools would not succeed without better pay for teachers. The necessary level of wage
would never come from voluntary local effort. In short, 'adequate
instruction, . . . in elementary schools in Wales, is utterly hopeless
by means of local efforts or local benevolence'. Elsewhere there is
specific reference to state aid. He cited clergymen in his district accept-
ing that only the state could supply money on the required scale.
The thrust of Symons's argument is that government aid is essential
for providing salaries for schoolmasters, and would be better used
this way than by providing money for buildings, as present policy
decreed. Symons also instanced Nonconformist ministers who
believed that state aid would be accepted. The commissioner is aware
of voluntaryist reservations but does not accept them as general.

In Wales, for obvious reasons, we see the Blue Books in a Welsh
context. Contemporaries were outraged by the attacks on the personal
morality of the Welsh, the slurs on Nonconformity, bias and unfairness on a massive scale. Welsh historians, concerned with the political and religious fall-out of the Reports, have pinpointed their
considerable impact on the national awareness. The realities in the
Blue Books, and the reality of the myth of the Blue Books, have
etched themselves into Welsh consciousness. It is the contention of
this essay that, however emotionally justified, this has led to a
misinterpretation of what Kay-Shuttleworth and the commissioners, Symons especially, were about. The real insult to Wales lay in
the fact that it was not Wales as such which was the object of their

interest. For them, Wales was a means to an end, and that is a condescension to which the Welsh are far more accustomed.

The bench-mark which the commissioners used was not that of existing education practice for the education of the lower classes in England. The situation there was just as bad. The bench-mark was a vision of a more enlightened education which could only come about if there were better-trained and better-paid teachers. Kay-Shuttleworth had first-hand experience of the normal schools in Switzerland which had been influenced by Pestalozzi and Fellenberg. For religious and political reasons he could not get a state normal school established in Britain, so he set up his own, the famous Battersea Training School, a very few of whose products taught before the commissioners in 1846/7. In 1843 he described, for the Committee of Council, a capitation scheme which would have effectively provided grants towards teachers' salaries. The committee would have none of it. All this was in the context of a climate of discussion about the extent of state aid in which J. A. Roebuck, for example, had presented a scheme to the House of Commons in 1833 in which parents who could not afford an education would be given state aid.

It is impossible to know precisely what influence Kay-Shuttleworth had on the initiation and terms of reference of the inquiry, how far the home secretary was involved, what hidden motives there may have been behind it. There was suspicion at the time, particularly among Welsh voluntaryists, that the enquiry was a ploy to provide a state system of education for Wales. Frank Smith was inconclusive in discussing the mystery of the changed terms of reference as they appeared in print. More recently, David Griffiths has once more highlighted the questions which surround William Williams's initiative. The evidence is circumstantial. However, the educational case, the catalogue of educational woes listed in the Blue Books, is entirely commensurate with Kay-Shuttleworth's believing that the lower classes were being deprived of their birthright by the elementary school system as it existed and that the only answer was a system of teacher training and pay financed by the state. In hindsight, he and the commissioners of 1847 were right. And Charles Dickens was just as apt and pungent a critic of the education on offer in England.

3
Education in Glamorgan since 1780

Educational provision in Glamorgan in 1780 was of marginal significance to the people. What little education did exist was the preserve of the Anglican Church and any system divorced from it was scarcely conceivable. Already there were economic developments in train which were to provide a base for dramatic change. The industries clustered around Glamorgan's valley tops and the Swansea area, making increasingly anachronistic an ecclesiastical organization based on an agricultural economy, eventually rendered antediluvian an education system based largely on the parish school. But, for decades yet, education would remain conditioned by the fusion of Church and charity, Sunday school and self-help.

For fifty years after 1780 education remained almost totally charity-based, although there were increasing numbers of private-venture schools which sprang up where there was sufficient demand to be met by minimal provision in often bizarre accommodation. Organized education was in the hands of the National Society and the British Society operating, until 1833, wholly outside the orbit of the state.

The conditioning topographical division in Glamorgan between *Bro* and *Blaenau*, accentuated with increasing industrialization, was inevitably evidenced in education. In rural Glamorgan, in parish after single-school parish, the Anglican charity-school concept was at work – catechism and Bible, an education for basic literacy and numeracy, the inculcation of the social virtues of deference, humility, hard work and honesty. As industrialization brought change in patterns of settlement, that hegemony came under threat – hence the National Society for the Education of the Poor in the Principles of the Established Church. As a major educational sponsor it trod the perennial tightrope – sufficient instruction for the salvation of the individual soul and social harmony, not so much as to raise the poor from their station. The education provided was sectarian, though

Dissenters had access if they attended church, and it was cheap, this deriving from the monitorial system. The Society's objective, simply, was to provide an Anglican school in every parish but the financial constraints were formidable. The schools were funded by individual patrons or diocesan committees in poorer areas. Such efforts varied substantially from area to area. In Bridgend, a progressive local committee opened boys' and girls' schools in 1812 and trained apprentice teachers. National Society efforts mounted in the 1830s, with the spectre of state funds being channelled into burgeoning Nonconformity. Results were mixed. By 1846–7 there were more Anglican schools in Glamorgan (113) than in any Welsh county save Monmouthshire. Only thirty-seven of these were in union with the National Society, and Glamorgan's grant (£1,194) ranked sixth in the league table for Welsh counties, despite population changes. This money was supplemented in a variety of ways: in Barry by fees from parents able to pay, in Margam subvention from the wages of employees of the English Copper Company.[1] In return, monitors passed on a minimum competence, a little knowledge, and virtually no understanding. Lack of money, untrained teachers, shortage of books, absenteeism and a short school life ensured this.

The British and Foreign School Society, providing elementary education on non-denominational lines, was founded in 1814 but its principles had already governed the establishment of boys' and girls' schools in Swansea. The boys' school was the first such school after Joseph Lancaster's original venture in London and led to his visiting Cardiff, Neath and Swansea in 1807. Once more, educational developments reflect economic changes in Glamorgan. The county's gentry grudgingly supported Anglican endeavours; but there was a new source of patronage now, however limited. So, in 1808, the Harford family started a Lancasterian school for their employees at the Melingriffith tinworks near Cardiff. Even more penurious than the National Society, the British Society had its successes. The girls' school in Swansea defected to the Anglicans before local Quakers built another, but over 3,000 boys were educated free in the town's Lancasterian boys' schools which became the training ground for all Lancasterian teachers in Wales.[2] Fee-paying crept in here, too, and accentuated the ubiquitous educational problems of short school life and absenteeism. Conceived by middle-class philanthropists and imposed from above, this education met no intrinsic needs.

Ministering more nearly to the linguistic and religious susceptibili-
ties of the inhabitants of Glamorgan, young and old, were the Sunday
schools. Probably the first Sunday school in Wales was established
in Cardiff in 1786, perhaps resulting from the county's links with
the west country, by which means news of Robert Raikes's pioneer-
ing efforts spread to Wales. One of the Sunday school's earliest
advocates in Wales was Morgan John Rhys, born at Llanfabon on
the borders of Glamorgan and Monmouthshire. The movement
spread rapidly in Wales from about 1798 and the schools, in two
hours or so each week, taught pupils to read their native language,
normally Welsh, as a means towards imbibing denominational
religious knowledge.[3]

As each denomination spawned its schools, and elements of
competition and socializing were built in, the system took firm root
in the county. Here were schools of the people for the people which
would prosper with the denominations, though in industrial
Glamorgan it is doubtful if half the children attended. There was no
training for teachers and the educational objectives were limited,
yet they, mainly, created the reading public for the eight weeklies,
twenty-five monthlies, and five quarterlies published in Welsh in the
1860s. Here lay danger, of course. While education was inspired by
religion, the Sunday schools were in the mainstream. Once the day
schools became the repositories of a secular education, increasingly
functional, Sunday schools lay outside the mainstream, vulnerable.
Their language became that of the day of the week which was different. For much of the nineteenth century it seemed to matter little
that they coexisted with a functional, English-language educational
system. In the end it did matter.

Early in the nineteenth century there were indications of the way
economic and social change fed through into the education system
in the growth of the works schools. Between 1806 and 1808 came
a copperworks school in Kilvey and a tinworks school at Melingriffith. Between 1816 and 1834 ironworks schools started at Neath
Abbey, Hirwaun, Dowlais, Wenallt and Pentyrch. Schools were
attached to collieries at Hirwaun, Llangyfelach, Dinas, Penllergaer,
and Cilybebyll.[4] Whether it is appropriate to call some of these
works schools is dubious, in that they were traditional schools
established by industrial entrepreneurs. Distinctions are indeed blurred
in the early days but, in embryo, these schools signalled a new
Glamorgan.

In the 1830s and 1840s the context of Glamorgan's education changed. Most significant, in 1833 the government injected £20,000 into the system nationally. The grant was for building new schools and the state distanced itself by channelling money through the voluntary societies. But the one inexorable upward curve on the graph of the history of education, that of state intervention, was beginning to be plotted. State money meant accountability. A central body, the Committee of Privy Council on Education, followed in 1839. Immediate local impact ensued as the National Society plunged into school building to take advantage of the 50 per cent grant, though efforts were more successful in north Wales than in Glamorgan. All this sharpened the edge of the educational problem for Nonconformists. Most, including the Independents, who were strong in Glamorgan, insisted on a holistically religious view of education which rejected state interference and money. The inadequacy of voluntaryist effort soon became clear but in the meantime diverted state-subsidized effort. Only two places in Glamorgan benefited from state help from the British Society between 1833 and 1840, Morriston and Mumbles.[5] Social convulsions – the 1831 Merthyr rising and Chartism – helped highlight educational shortcomings. Government linked the two; and Tremenheere's Report of 1840 had already highlighted the social strains in industrial Glamorgan. In the midst of this, denominational wrangling focused on Graham's Factory Bill of 1843, which linked state intervention with Anglican education and led to protest meetings in Neath and Swansea.

The report of the education commissioners published in 1847 is redolent of all these stresses in the system. It reveals a society in transition; but it does not show Glamorgan's educational provision as any worse than that of the rest of Wales. Taking the three counties of Glamorgan, Pembrokeshire and Carmarthenshire, 11.4 per cent of those aged under five attended school in Glamorgan, compared with the three-county average of 8.8 per cent. For the age-group five to ten, the figures were 43.5 per cent and 36.5 per cent respectively, and for ten- to fifteen-year-olds, 21.6 per cent and 23.3 per cent. Because of industrialization and the existence of works schools, Glamorgan had begun to diverge from rural Wales in education patterns. There were more trained teachers than in the western counties (13.4 per cent) and a smaller percentage of pupils in Anglican schools – 33 per cent in Glamorgan, nearly 50 per cent in Pembrokeshire. As many as 18.6 per cent of Glamorgan's scholars

attended works schools compared with 1.3 per cent in Carmarthenshire and none in Pembrokeshire.[6] However, the Guests' provision
in Dowlais is offset by the fact that 'for the children of men employed
at the Cyfarthfa, Plymouth and Pen-y-Darren works, no provision
has hitherto been made, further than some trifling subscriptions by
the proprietors to the National Schools . . .'[7]

The mythology of the 1847 Report has clouded the relative
insignificance of its educational impact. It reiterated condemnation
of educational provision in the county. Voluntary effort provided
minimal facilities in rural areas and was overwhelmed in industrial
parts. The Sunday schools provided basic literacy for about a fifth
of the population of Glamorgan, Pembrokeshire and Cardiganshire.
They were praised, but were hardly relevant to the commissioners,
who had been briefed to investigate 'the means afforded to the Labouring Classes of acquiring a Knowledge of the English Language'.
Dissent did not much dissent from the notion that this was the path
to be followed. Here the kaleidoscopic pattern of Glamorgan's schools
was almost uniformly deficient. Of the 327 schools, 173 were dame
schools, almost invariably grossly inadequate. There were
denominational schools, workhouse schools, and works schools. If
Glamorgan's school buildings were better than those of its western
neighbours they were still deficient in fabric, equipment and furniture.
In essence, as R. R. W. Lingen realized full well, economic change
had seen age-old patterns modified irrevocably. The works were to
industrial Glamorgan as the manor to the parish, ruminated Lingen.
The works school must now be the parish school. The implication
was clear. There must be new forms of education, since these iron-
working areas neither accorded with the social structure deemed
necessary for social stability, nor fostered the language by which it
might be altered: 'the elimination of a middle class is rendered still
more complete when, to the economical causes tending to produce
it, is superadded the separation of language.'[8]

For the moment, the 1847 Report revealed Glamorgan schools in
which low-status, untrained teachers provided a most rudimentary
education with the aid of wholly inadequate equipment in the midst
of interdenominational wrangling, lack of patronage from the wealthy,
and profound social change. In other respects the Report depicted
two Glamorgans. In Merthyr there were forty-two schools; eight
Anglican, two Nonconformist, thirty-one private adventure, and the
Dowlais works schools. The Dowlais schools showed, uniquely, what

was possible – wide syllabus, high standard of equipment, trained teachers, and many pupils staying beyond the age of ten. In Cowbridge hundred, there were twelve day schools, seven of which were Anglican, with one affiliated to the National Society. In Dinas Powys hundred, all but two of the sixteen day schools were Church schools providing the only education in their parish.[9]

The Anglican educational effort was inadequate. Nonconformists dissipated their energies in wrangles over the role of the state. The vacuum was being partly filled by the private-adventure school. There was an organizational demarcation line between rural and industrial Glamorgan. Lingen saw some of the ramifications. And there was a further complication. Lingen appreciated that because of internal migration there was sufficient 'common character' to allow for generalization. That common character arose out of a common language, and it kept the Welshman at the bottom of the social scale: 'his language keeps him under the hatches, being one in which he can neither acquire nor communicate the necessary information.'[10] By now, of course, the necessary information was no longer that knowledge of the Bible still provided in the Sunday schools in the language of heaven. It was the information required to climb the career ladder in Victorian industry. It is doubtful if Lingen or Welsh parents ever conceived that the Welsh language should be adapted to this function. The pedagogic implications were beyond Lingen, when teachers 'are often most inadequately acquainted with English themselves . . .'[11] and derived pedagogical skills from such life-experience as serving in the artillery or lime-burning. Yet ironically, Lingen, the product of the kind of public-school classical education which has been seen as central to Britain's industrial decline, appreciated the wider implications of the Welsh situation. He was complimentary to the Welsh and 'the efforts of the mass of a people, utterly unaided, to educate themselves, upon their own model'.[12] What was at fault was the religious base of the model – and not only in Sunday schools. There was nothing to support the full-blown utilitarian, capitalist ethic: 'whether we look to the agricultural or to the manufacturing quarters, there is but little trace of that education which affords a sound, sober, practical rule of life, and qualifies men to do the best for themselves, and therefore for society . . .'[13] Inexorably, economic change dictated that there would be a move towards this new model. For the moment neither employers nor workers saw the necessity. The former had insufficient foresight to create the demand so, as one Glamorgan schoolmaster put it, the Welsh 'will not . . . make sacrifices until it shall be more plainly shown to them how great an advantage will be gained'.[14]

So the ground-rules remained the same after 1847, though there was sporadic activity. By 1865 there were over 2,000 day-school pupils in Guest-sponsored schools and the Dowlais system catered for a range from infants to adults. After the 1847 Report revealed how meagre had been their contribution to education the Vivians opened their Hafod Copperworks school that year with 350 pupils, rising to over 1,000 by 1878. The changing pattern of economic activity in the county was reflected in the thirty-two colliery schools which opened after 1850, the most ambitious opening at Dyffryn in 1857.[15]

The problems remained. The lack of synchronization between the education on offer and the society it was intended to serve, and the disparity in education for the lower orders as perceived by the providers and the recipients, meant that length of school life and irregularity of attendance were basic flaws. There was no compulsory schooling, effectively, until 1876. Even in Dowlais many pupils had only one year's schooling. The 1847 Report had shown the swift decline in proportions attending school in Glamorgan after the age of ten. Why should parents forgo the extra wage? Indeed, how could they, often? That is why the Sunday schools catered for so many more scholars. Absenteeism meant, in practice, 25 per cent of pupils in twenty schools in Neath attending for fewer than fifty days.[16] Evening schools had to counteract physical exhaustion. Just occasionally there are glimpses of future controversies; it seems to have been the 'relevance' of draughtsmanship and mathematics which was the key to the relative success of Cwmavon Company school and the schools of the Neath ironworks.[17] It remains that, for the moment, Lingen had misread the situation; the range of occupations which required education in industrial Glamorgan was limited. In rural areas, in a society of landlord-tenant deference, the time-honoured rituals prevailed. What schooling was required by the labourer, the blacksmith and the seamstress? Indeed, the pressures on children to work on the land increased in the second half of the century as the industrial areas sucked away the population.

State intervention, through education and factory legislation, starting so modestly in 1833, constantly modified the situation thereafter and eventually revolutionized it. Glamorgan, particularly, was a county which demonstrated the inadequacy of that voluntaryist philosophy which was, paradoxically, strong there. The religious 'question' again demonstrated the significance of economic change within the county, and between Glamorgan and much of the rest of Wales. For example, proprietors like Vivian in Hafod and Guest in Dowlais founded their schools on Anglican principles but bowed to the religious predilections of their workers, who paid for the schools out of their wages, and made them non-denominational, serving a secular purpose. Here was a microcosm of state dilemmas. Voluntaryism could not be the answer, especially in a county like Glamorgan, because of increases in population and, more fundamental in the end, because the education which was required in an industrializing society inexorably became more sophisticated. Soon it was not the voluntaryists who wondered where the money would come from but the state – another constant theme. The government's reaction was Robert Lowe's Revised Code of 1862 and the Education Act of 1870.

Inevitably, a similar battle raged over the training of teachers. Since an elementary education was regarded as the lowest form of enlightenment and the status of teachers was commensurate, their training needed to be safe rather than informed, appropriately again left to the voluntary societies. In 1845 a Congregational conference at Llandovery decided that a normal school be built to supply teachers for the principality. By 1848 this college had moved to Rutland Place in Swansea, though it collapsed in 1851.[18] Here was a graphic refutation of David Rees's argument that the college should be supported by voluntary subscription. Non-Anglican Welsh students had to go to Borough Road College, mainly to have any Welshness knocked out of them. Contemporaries endorsed Hugh Owen's belief that English students had a 'more lively mental attitude'.[19]

It was clear before 1870 that the training system, like the elementary system it served, could not cope, and the battle for education's soul was joined. A Welsh Educational Alliance was established in Cardiff in 1870 to campaign for a national secular education system, but the 1870 Act clung to the notion of denominationally informed education wherever possible. In rural areas of Glamorgan, Church schools remained predominant. The Welsh Educational Alliance, defeated in 1870, now turned its attention to gaining control of school boards. But even in a county like Glamorgan, with its bewildering new frontiers, the scale of change in the structure is easy to exaggerate. School boards tended to be patriarchal and middle class. In some rural areas they were merely the instruments for perpetuating the status quo. In Gower they, and the schools, chose to be dependent on the local gentry, especially the Mansel Talbots, to the extent that HMI Williams commented in 1884: 'Matters in this locality are not in a satisfactory condition. The majority of the Board are completely in the hands of the great landowners of the neighbourhood, and seem disinclined to act contrary to their personal interests ...'[20] When a school board decided in 1896 that the catechism should not be taught at Oxwich during school hours, Miss Talbot would have none of the idea. By 1899 the school-leaving age had been raised to twelve but potato-picking was still of more economic significance than an elementary education.[21]

There is still no denying the profound modification of the system as the school boards catered for the children of Glamorgan's demographic revolution which saw the county record a net gain in migration in every decade between 1851 and 1911. In Merthyr a school board was elected in 1871. It immediately took over three British schools and, in 1875, Cyfarthfa ironworks school. In the 1880s the board built three new schools and, by the time it had taken over the Dowlais schools in 1892, three-quarters of Merthyr's children were being educated under the board's aegis.[22] In tapping in to another money supply, that of the Science and Art Department, school boards such as those in Merthyr, Cardiff and Swansea contributed to the beginnings of higher elementary education, the national implications of which were not long in becoming apparent. In general terms, the state was being forced by economic imperatives to educate more of its population to a higher level, so widening the provision of both technical and more conventional education. This involved tolerating a degree of economic and social mobility wholly unwelcome to the governing classes. By the 1890s the situation was getting out of hand and the attempt at containment took the form of Morant's machinations and the 1902 Education Act.

In Wales the issue was complicated by the political domination of radical Liberalism, a cultural nationalism which focused on the Nonconformist/Anglican rift and the resurgent debate over the Welsh language. All fed in to the education debate. All were manifest in the peculiar complication in the Welsh education system, the schools which were born of the Welsh Intermediate Education Act of 1889. The intention behind the schools was to cater for that middle class which had not existed in sufficient number to generate its own schools. The 1879 Schools Enquiry Commission listed only two classical schools for Glamorgan, both of which had long ceased to cater for foundation students. Cowbridge alone qualified for first-grade status, while Bishop Gore's foundation in Swansea had closed for a decade after 1842.[23] Influential Welshmen were convinced that national advance required an organic middle class in Wales, manufacturing its leaders through a radically redefined educational system. The Aberdare Report advocated schools intermediate between the elementary schools and the first-grade classical schools. The Report shared current English thinking that such schools were not appropriate for an industrial working class. For them higher elementary schools were suitable. This judgement was significant for Glamorgan because after Mundella's Circular 213 higher elementary schools were founded by Boards in Cardiff and Merthyr (1884), Dowlais (1884) and Rhondda by 1893, orientated towards the technical and scientific subjects sponsored by the Science and Art Department.[24] Here was another wedge between Glamorgan and rural Wales. The schools were progressive in that they integrated with the county's economic base and provided some modest social mobility.

Eventually, Glamorgan's intermediate scheme was approved in 1896, the last in Wales because of tortuous negotiations over Cowbridge school, which was excluded after all. But the same mentality which gave rise to higher elementary schools in Glamorgan ensured that provision of schools under the 1889 Act was the least satisfactory in Wales. The average size of intermediate school districts in Wales was 8,000: Glamorgan's was over 35,000. Porth's school served a population of 88,350.[25]

What ensured that the dichotomy between different types of non-elementary schools did not last was that Welsh educational change now became enmeshed with wider class and political struggles. The blurring of distinctions between higher elementary schools and other forms of secondary education was intolerable to a Conservative government and led to abolition of the school boards in the 1902 Education Act and rigid demarcation of schools under the 1904 regulations. Secondary education was, as far as possible, to be preserved for the middle classes in fee-paying schools under the aegis of the safer county and county borough councils. From a Conservative viewpoint they were safer in England than in industrial Wales, where Glamorgan's secondary education was now to be in the hands of the county council and the Cardiff, Swansea and Merthyr (from 1908) borough councils. Urban district councils in Aberdare, Mountain Ash, Pontypridd, Neath, Barry and Rhondda were intended to control only elementary education, though Rhondda, uniquely, acquired control of its secondary schools also.[26] The 1902 Education Act permitted local authorities to open new secondary schools. Many of the higher elementary schools in Glamorgan were transmuted into municipal secondary schools, so introducing a dual administrative system in secondary education and the striving of yet more schools for that academic respectability and house and prefect system which characterized the English public schools. Technical, and especially vocational, education, in this context was anathema. The lack of synchronization between a still-prosperous Glamorgan and its educational system was yet more marked. By 1920 there were twelve municipal secondary schools in the county, re-emphasizing differences between Glamorgan's secondary system and that of most of the rest of Wales. Additionally, the dual system was often the focus of unedifying dissension between Central Welsh Board and Welsh Department of the Board of Education.[27] A more sinister duality was institutionalized, as the mass of Glamorgan's children attended elementary schools, while an élite minority profited from a secondary education which, alone, allowed a degree of occupational mobility. In the interwar years the Glamorgan authorities, Labour-dominated, devoted themselves to widening access to this select area. They did so in the context of increased state intervention inaugurated by the 1902 Act as government dictated the areas of control which should be allowed the seemingly powerful local education authorities. The scene was set for conflict between state and local authorities in Glamorgan, where political persuasions were normally diametrically opposed. The state had dictated that the school boards had become too dangerous to existing social stratification. Many of the schools they had created, technically and vocationally orientated, were sucked into the intermediate school slipstream. The highest achievement for a pupil from the mining valleys was to become a teacher. Initiatives of the type which, in Merthyr, had led to a relevant curriculum of drawing, geometry, machine and building construction, mathematics, chemistry, mechanics and engineering being developed in the 1880s and 1890s at day and evening classes in Penydarren, Treharris, Abermorlais, Caedraw and Dowlais, could no longer be channelled direct into a secondary type of education.

Although not all was lost there was a hiatus as evening continuation classes ceased in Merthyr in 1906 for two years.[28]

The Aberdare Report of 1881 had not only recommended a new school system in Wales but also a new pattern of provision of higher education. Civic pride in Cardiff and Swansea was aroused in competition for the new south Wales college. Despite the reluctance of the 147 benefactors to honour their pledges, the University College of South Wales and Monmouthshire opened in Cardiff in 1883.[29] It reflected genuine pride and self-confidence in town and county. Its first, outstanding, Principal, Viriamu Jones, determined to develop scientific and technical education and, jointly with the county borough, a technical school was set up within the college, attracting over 2,000 students in 1903–4. Another vital feature was that the college served local needs. In 1900, 83 per cent of the students came from Glamorgan and Monmouthshire. The pattern continued; in 1938–9 817 of the 970 students came from within thirty miles of Cardiff.[30] Again, access patterns to the college confirm that Wales was a meritocracy and, as such, markedly different from England. There was virtually no independent school sector, with the partial exception of Cowbridge. Eighty per cent of Cardiff's students came from Welsh secondary schools which, themselves, took over 90 per cent of their pupils from the elementary schools.[31]

For the moment, Swansea had to be content with its technical college which resulted from the 1889 Technical Instruction Act, though it was to become a university college in 1920 after the Haldane Commission's Report. From 1916 the technical school within the Cardiff university college took on a life of its own and, just before the First World War, the Treforest School of Mines opened,[32] to remain, rechristened, to the present day. The lack of state concern for technical education, despite claims made for the efficacy of the 1889 Technical Instruction Act, is epitomized in that the school of mines was opened by the coalowners. In 1916 Treforest's principal suggested to the Haldane Commission a plan for a faculty of technology to co-ordinate local authority and university provision. It never materialized.[33]

The transformation of Glamorgan's education system in the second half of the nineteenth century from largely voluntary enterprise to a state system catering, to some extent, for secondary, technical and higher educational needs, had taken place in the context of economic prosperity and expansion. When Glamorgan drew up a blueprint for educational development under the terms of the 1918 Education Act[34] it reflected the confidence of a county still at the height of its prosperity and motivated by the notion of an education fit for the families of heroes. The local education authority now had massive responsibilities in catering for 207,000 pupils aged between five and sixteen, funded with the help of a 50 per cent state grant. The differences between provision in Glamorgan and rural Wales were now apparent. Not only was there a substantial non-intermediate secondary sector but six of the municipal secondary schools charged no fees, in contrast to all the intermediate schools. There were other lines of demarcation. Whereas in Montgomeryshire, for example, nine secondary schools catered for 570 pupils, in Glamorgan county alone thirty-seven secondary schools catered for 7,827 pupils in much larger units. The population invasion of Glamorgan was reflected in the scale of opportunity for secondary education. Whereas in 1917 19.75 per 1,000 of the population gained access to the secondary sector in Montgomeryshire, only 6.92 per 1,000 did so in Glamorgan. This represented considerable educational disadvantage for Glamorgan's working-class population, with its 273,972 men working in the mining, metal and transport industries and the dominance of domestic work and dressmaking among the female population.

The main plank in the 1918 plan was highly ambitious and nationally significant. It constituted doing away with the parallel system whereby the great majority were restricted to an elementary-school education and the chosen few proceeded to secondary school. In a plan prefiguring the Hadow recommendations of 1926 and, in some respects, even the post-1944 pattern, it was postulated that all pupils should transfer to secondary schools, some created from higher elementary schools, for a free education from twelve to sixteen. Intermediate-type schools would continue to prepare pupils for university and the professions. The other secondary schools, thirty-three of them, would provide 'a good progressive course of general education up to a standard approximating to that of matriculation'.[35] This was both ambitious and radical, so that if it had materialized it would doubtless have brought confrontation with the government. The practical plan was reinforced by an educational philosophy in a debate which rages still: '[the authority] have no intention of giving vocational education in their Secondary Schools . . . they are, however, agreed that . . . in an agricultural area the . . . curriculum should have especial regard to some subjects that an agricultural community should . . . be educated in. Similarly, in industrial areas teaching of some subjects will . . . bear . . . upon the . . . industries of the area.'[36] Such theories have never worked in British education. But there were possibilities in Glamorgan that the academic/technical divide might have been blurred by plans to link engineering, mining and metallurgical laboratories with intermediate schools.

Further education, too, reflected a county in good heart in 1920. In 1912 Welsh local education authorities took over the school of cookery in Cardiff. In 1913 Swansea's training college transferred to the local education authority under the terms of the 1902 Act, and in 1914 Barry Training College opened with 120 Glamorgan women students and forty from Monmouthshire. So, by 1920, the local education authorities had become, in their short existence, the focus of local educational activity. Great plans were afoot. The limitations of local initiative became painfully clear only with the Depression. The tragedy of the interwar years in Glamorgan is compounded in education because we know what might have been. Education in Glamorgan in 1920 was beginning to reflect a society which was Welsh, relatively prosperous, and politically influential. In the succeeding two decades not only were there no new initiatives but also the creative energies of the county were channelled into resistance. This led to heroics, but it also compounded the waste.

The 1920s and 1930s in Glamorgan saw economic disaster reflected in every aspect of society. In education the plans of 1920 came to nought. There were countless individual tragedies as university and college places were not taken up and career ambitions remained unfulfilled. The secondary school loomed even larger in community life, providing the ticket to something better. The exodus of the more talented from Glamorgan was accentuated. Teaching, usually in England, became yet more the summit of ambition. Not only was there no secondary reorganization after the 1920 plan, there was very little after the Hadow Report of 1926, though this was partly due to traditionalist directors of education like W. J. Williams of Cardiff.[37] There were only nine central schools in the county by 1936.

The mass exodus of the Depression years, coupled with great efforts to expand the secondary sector, paradoxically meant a dramatic improvement in secondary education opportunities, rising to proportions hitherto seen only in the most sparsely populated rural counties; 20 per 1,000 in Rhondda, 19.9 per 1,000 in Cardiff County Borough, 16.9 per 1,000 in Glamorgan county by 1938.[38] This was far above anything available in England. Paradoxically, too, the centrality of the humanistic, academic, 'grammar' type of education brought community and education more closely into mesh, to the benefit of individuals if not to the county and the Welsh nation. If the educational system had adapted more successfully to the ambience of thriving industry before 1920 the tragedy of the inter-war years would have been compounded. The system geared to the successful, based on competition and results, was consolidated. The pre-First World War clash between O. M. Edwards and Major Edgar Jones of Barry County School, a debate over the soul of Welsh education, was finally resolved in the latter's favour.[39]

In a changed context Glamorgan, with Monmouthshire, remained different from the rest of Wales. Labour-controlled councils fought back against attempts by London governments to undermine hard-won gains. Immediate clashes meant that the Merthyr authority, committed to as much free secondary education as tradition allowed, was unable to open Quakers' Yard as a free secondary school until a Labour government came to power in 1924. Cardiff, similarly, had to wait until 1924 before Sir Charles Trevelyan allowed free education in its municipal secondary schools.[40]

There were no concessions to a Wales wracked by disaster. In 1932 the government decided to impose drastic economies. Glamorgan local education authorities had tried to maximize the number of free places in intermediate schools and provide free education in municipal secondary schools. On 15 September 1932, the Welsh Department, following the Board of Education, stipulated that free places in secondary schools were to be replaced by means-tested special places. There was an outcry, but the official line was that the 'poor folk' of Wales could not really appreciate the intricacies of government policy. Glamorgan local education authority, under one of its formidable chairmen, Sir William Jenkins, carried the fight furthest, putting up a totally unacceptable plan to make all the county's secondary education free, then, alone of the Welsh authorities, claiming that the relevant costings could not be provided. Glamorgan was forced into submission, although it secured 100 per cent special places, ensuring that access to secondary schools was wholly on merit. Swansea secured a similar concession.[41] So, out of a squalid exercise the Glamorgan authorities made a leap towards a secondary system based on ability rather than the ability to pay.

The Glamorgan authorities chose to concentrate on expanding the career-enhancing secondary schools in the inter-war period at the expense of modern or central schools. Their achievement was dramatic – twenty-two schools built or taken over, a secondary school population up from 7,827 in 1914 to 22,149 in 1939, though this still represented only 20 per cent of the age-group.[42] Despite the special-place system, well over 60 per cent received their education free because of the economic state of the county. Access was by merit. In Glamorgan the much-vaunted 1944 Education Act was putting into effect much that already characterized the system.

In the university colleges the Depression also reinforced humanities at the expense of sciences, in turn consolidating traditional Welsh employment priorities. Swansea University College soon had more arts students than combined numbers of science and applied science students. In 1937 65 per cent of arts students and 45 per cent of science students wished to become teachers.[43] The proportion of arts students in Cardiff University College was even higher.[44]

Economic devastation in south Wales led the second Labour government to commission a committee, chaired by Caerphilly MP Morgan Jones, Parliamentary Secretary to the Board of Education, to report on 'The Educational Problems of the South Wales Coalfield'.[45] It condemned the inadequacy of technical education and led to the establishment of the Advisory Council for Technical Education in South Wales and Monmouthshire. There were other initiatives after 1929. Between 1929 and 1931, five mining institutes opened in Glamorgan, fed by 84 junior centres, providing over 350 separate classes. In Rhondda two additional centres served fifteen junior feeders. From such institutes students could proceed to technical colleges in Cardiff or Swansea, or the School of Mines at Treforest. Nearly 40 per cent of the institutes' students were under twenty-one, but again many were forced to leave Wales for work.[46] There was some attempt to relate training to patterns of employment for girls. Domestic employment was the destination of most girls (46.8 per cent leaving school in Aberdare in 1937 intended doing such work) but cookery and needlework were low-status subjects. Eight of the thirty-three day centres for women's training in England and Wales opened in Glamorgan. There was no plan, just an ad hoc response to local tragedy: 'government assistance is more easily obtained in the Special Areas by associating with unemployment what should be regarded as educational work of first importance'.[47]

Indeed, there seems no doubt, then as now, that unemployment gave rise to off-the-cuff policies in education and training which proliferated bewilderingly. There was no coherent national policy and little attempt to integrate educational and economic priorities, though this should not detract from the efforts of extra-mural departments, WEA, local authority camps, and 'settlements'. Fundamentally, though, some government conscience money did nothing to disguise the complete lack of co-ordination among the providers of vocational and non-vocational education. Precious resources were frittered away.

The Second World War solved Glamorgan's unemployment problem in the most tragic fashion. Disruption in education was countered by what, in this context, were wholly justified ad hoc solutions. One thousand, one hundred and twenty-three evacuees had to be dealt with; schools denuded of male teachers had to employ married women; and air-raid damage had to be countered. Immediately, thoughts turned to the better society to be built after the war. The 1944 Education Act is one monument to that conception; but far too often that has disguised its essentially conservative nature.[48] Civil servants had already decided in 1941 that there should be no multilateral system of secondary education. This prompted confrontation with Glamorgan's politicians, dubbed 'left-wing' by Wynn Wheldon during the war, as significant as any in England or Wales. The history of that confrontation explodes the cosy notion of educational partnership in postwar years, which has found favour in education texts. It also highlighted, again, the political and social demarcation line between industrial and rural Wales.

The 1944 Act required local authorities to submit development plans. A major concern was how the authorities would provide secondary education for all children over the age of eleven. Cardiff's plan was so orthodoxly tripartite that it caused no problem, though HMI castigated it for lack of imagination.[49] Merthyr, under the influence of D. Andrew Davies, was equally orthodox.[50] Glamorgan County Council's plan caused problems.[51] There were to be two types of secondary school, certainly, but in the first instance pupils would go to their nearest secondary school and remain there to School Certificate stage. There would be no eleven-plus examination. More controversially, because curricula had always been used as a means of differentiating schools, and therefore social classes, there was to be a common curriculum up to the School Certificate stage. The plan was submitted in June 1947 and turned down flat by the Ministry of Education. It was 'seriously detrimental to the brighter pupils . . .' The ministry's tactic, as with all disputed plans, was to conduct a war of attrition. Mr Weston of the Welsh Department minuted: 'I have always intended to be tough with this Authority.' Both Ministry and Welsh Department thought they could rely on the director, Dr Stephens, to support them. By September 1949 Glamorgan had backed down. Most of the grammar schools were to remain. Controversy still surrounded the plan to convert Barry and Penarth schools into comprehensives. The ministry insisted, in effect, that such 'well-defined residential areas' must have grammar schools. Comprehensive schools could be allowed on new housing estates. Here was a blatant class judgement. The plan had still not been approved in 1954. When another delegation trooped to the Ministry in October 1954 its leader, Llewellyn Heycock, caught the civil servants out in a variety of contradictions. It served no purpose. In March 1955 Glamorgan surrendered over its Barry and Penarth proposals. In December 1956 the county's plan was approved.

Swansea County Borough's plan was as radical as any in England or Wales.[52] It involved replacing all existing provision, including the grammar schools, with multilateral schools for those aged eleven to eighteen. L. J. Drew, the director of education, carefully distanced himself from the plan but 'the Authority consider that a unique occasion is offered for experiment in their area'. The Welsh Department was only prepared to allow an 'experiment' of one such school for boys, one for girls, to serve new estates. Here was a head-on challenge to the Ministry of Education. The usual tactics were employed; 'the least said the better', delay. By September 1949, nearly three years after the plan was submitted, there was still no official reaction from the Ministry of Education. But then Swansea caught the habit. Asked for a revised plan, none was submitted until 1953. By 1955 Swansea still had 'about the best tripartite organisation of secondary education in Wales'. So much for the concept of partnership. David Eccles insisted in 1955 that Swansea's grammar schools should stay, though this decision was withheld from the council until after the 1955 general election because of its political sensitivity. Swansea had to be content with its two bilateral schools at Penlan (1956) and Mynyddbach (1957). Swansea's development plan was approved eleven years after submission, duly doctored. David

Eccles had argued that Swansea's politicians wanted change for social not educational reasons, yet Eccles was not normally naïve. In all these joustings, technical 'streams' just became expendable, to be fastened on to whichever school, mainly modern, happened to be politically convenient.

With hindsight, the time and effort expended in heading off threats to government policy were colossally wasteful. The climate in which educational politics operated in the late 1950s had changed dramatically. Under the mounting pressure of pupil numbers, due to 'bulge' and 'trend', the restraints so rigorously imposed in the 1950s gave way to expansion and the heady days of the 1960s.[53] Circular 10/65, backed up by the threat of financial sanctions, helped to transform Glamorgan into a county of comprehensive schools. Only in the county borough of Cardiff was there real political opposition.[54]

Demographic pressures helped transform the rest of the education system, too. Barry and Swansea Training Colleges took 200 students each in 1958, over 700 each a decade later. Cardiff Training College grew from its emergency roots to become Wales's premier college by 1969, with over 1,000 students.[55] Intake remained localized but the colleges were training teachers for England. The most talented of Glamorgan's young people left their native county in droves.

Dramatic expansion was followed a decade later by spectacular contraction. Nemesis befell the college in Barry while in Cardiff and Swansea there were mergers with other institutions. Here again the role of central government, the Department of Education and Science, in procuring its preferred solutions, is evident.

The university colleges in Cardiff and Swansea underwent more dramatic social transformation. As late as 1949 they served Wales. By 1970 only 43 per cent of students in the university were Welsh, though the highest percentage of Welsh undergraduates in a constituent institution was the 49.7 per cent for Swansea.[56] With the Robbins Report (1963), residence and mandatory grants irrevocably changed the relationship between university colleges and the community.

Scientific and technical higher education expanded commensurately, as the School of Mines became the Polytechnic of Wales in 1968 and Cardiff Technical College progressed first to College of Advanced Technology (1957), then University of Wales Institute of Science and Technology. There was a considerable expansion in technical colleges, too. None of this amounted to a co-ordinated policy in Welsh terms involving a marriage of Welsh education and training with the economic priorities of the country. The Advisory Council, in 1945, wished to see university and non-university technical education organized collaboratively.[57] It was not to be. Local initiative, like Merthyr's wartime plans for a technical college,[58] were allowed to mesh haphazardly with government policies. Present TVEI initiatives are built on time-honoured shifting sands.

Glamorgan's educational history over the last two hundred years has a far wider resonance. A superficially uniform educational structure across Wales adapted to a changing balance of population and wealth. This echoed eventually in divisions between Liberal Wales and Labour Wales as Glamorgan's politicians groped their way to a more egalitarian education system. This in turn brought Glamorgan's policy makers into conflict with central government. The county's aspirations assumed a British significance in 1932 and in the wake of the 1944 Act. Such conflicts illustrate the most significant of themes, the inexorable process of centralization in the administration of education. A county as powerful as Glamorgan had to bow the knee if it attempted to break the centrally moulded consensus. Finally, then, the paradox of centralization. It has been more in evidence as devolution has increased, from Welsh Department of 1907 to Welsh Office of 1960. The devolved bodies have faithfully followed government policies in education, yet one of those causes which has been allowed to flourish, especially in recent decades, has been that of education in the Welsh language, in Glamorgan as elsewhere, often in the face of parental apathy. Centralization has meant that Glamorgan's education system, academic and technical, has inexorably anglicized in conformity with state policy while allowing recent significantly accentuated manifestations of Welshness.

4
Pembrokeshire education, 1815–1974

The nineteenth century saw the transformation of educational provision. The underpinning of this revolution came with the intervention of the state in providing some education for all its citizens. However reluctantly, however slowly this was conceived and executed, it amounted to an unprecedented entanglement which governments of the future either could not or would not unravel.

State involvement fed through into all the counties. Throughout the nineteenth century, and arguably well into the twentieth, it reflected a belief that a proper education was one to be paid for, either in the great public schools which were reformed in the first half of the nineteenth century, or in the grammar schools which educated the middle classes. These were naturally in areas where there was some concentration of population, as in Haverfordwest which had a grammar school. For those unfortunates who could not pay there had to be charity.[1] A mixture of genuine philanthropy and self-interest decreed that there had to be a minimal education for the poor, but it should be limited in scope.

Most of the philanthropy which fuelled a variety of educational initiatives before 1815 was religious. The Welsh Trust of the seventeenth century had been successful in Pembrokeshire partly because the language difficulty, which affected so much of Wales, was less in evidence. This, together with the influence of Sir Erasmus Philipps of Picton Castle, resulted in fourteen to sixteen of the eighty Trust schools in Wales in 1675 being in Pembrokeshire.[2] The work of the Society for Promoting Christian Knowledge in Wales was also hampered by its emphasis on English, the reluctance of contributors and religious and political sensitivities. Once again a Pembrokeshire man was a leading light and Sir John Philipps helped in the foundation of twenty-two SPCK schools in Pembrokeshire. There was no demand from below for the education on offer. Not only was there no obvious gain from a Trust or SPCK education, there was the positive disincentive that the pupil's labour was unavailable. Sporadic attendance was the besetting evil of Welsh education at all levels until well into the twentieth century. Such problems were in evidence in eighteenth-century Pembrokeshire when Sir John Philipps gave a compensatory 20*s*. a year to parents of pupils in Rudbaxton.[3]

There were elements of continuity between the charitable efforts of the Welsh Trust, the SPCK and the most significant of Welsh educational initiatives of the eighteenth century, the circulating schools. Again the connection with Pembrokeshire was important. Griffith Jones was supported by Sir John Philipps, his patron and, from 1720, his brother-in-law, as well as by Madam Bevan of Laugharne. David Howell[4] notes that there were twenty-five circulating schools in Pembrokeshire in 1772–3. A major reason for their success across much of Wales was the willingness to conduct them in Welsh. In parts of Pembrokeshire it was the flexibility to conduct them in English which was important and this was apparent in at least some instances.[5] However, vital to the success of the circulating-school movement were their highly limited aims, which allowed them to operate in the most rudimentary of premises, and the pittances they paid to itinerant masters.

By 1815, therefore, there was a substantial legacy of educational endeavour in Pembrokeshire and it was this which provided the template for effort in the early decades of the nineteenth century. The main thrust had been the charitable efforts of the Anglican church. Parish schools and those supported by the Madam Bevan charity were central, but there were also schools helped by private charity, for example by Lord Cawdor in Stackpole, by private venture, and by Nonconformist congregations. Highly significant also were the Sunday schools. Such provision was nothing like enough. Richard Brinkley has shown just how far short of ideal was the provision in many rural deaneries in Pembrokeshire in the early eighteenth century, with whole swathes of parishes without a school.[6]

Voluntary effort

Despite increasing national disquiet, reflected in parliament, over the fate of young children condemned to infant labour, grinding poverty and widespread illiteracy, the period to 1833 saw a continuation of the charity and self-help ethos in education. For the moment the religious bodies tried to cope.

They tried to do so with the aid of two national societies. The British and Foreign School Society was founded on the inspiration of Joseph Lancaster, a Quaker, in 1814 and relied on the monitorial system of instruction to bring an elementary education to the labouring classes. It had no denominational flavour, though it relied on the Bible as the textbook.[7] The influence of the British Society on Welsh education was sparse indeed, at least until the 1840s. When Lancaster visited south Wales in 1806–07 he seems to have got no further west than Carmarthen, and most early activity was centred around Swansea and Cardiff. There is no indication of a British school having been opened in Pembrokeshire up to 1833 when state grants first became available to the society. Even then, Wales profited little. In 1834 a letter arrived at the society from Templeton bemoaning the fact that there were more than 200 poor children requiring instruction, but there is evidence that the society provided £125 out of building costs of £450 for a school at St Dogmael's that year. The British Society seems also to have paid for a teacher and materials at a school in Sealyham near Haverfordwest.[8] Haverfordwest itself received a substantial grant of £125 towards a new school costing £400. The contribution of the British Society to Pembrokeshire education was extended in the period 1835–40 by grants for schools in Templeton, Narberth and Reynoldston.

The National Society for Promoting the Education of the Poor in the Principles of the Established Church, founded in 1811, entertained the hope of providing a church school in every parish. Against a background of substantial Nonconformist religious loyalties among the Welsh its activities were sporadic. In 1815 an affiliated school was opened in Pembroke. Other schools, already operating, entered into a connection with the society, such as that in Tenby which was held in the old castle.[9] However, by the beginning of 1817 there were only twenty-three affiliated schools in Wales.

The first state financial contribution to the societies was made in 1833 and this resulted in increased interest in their work. By 1836 there were sixteen schools in Pembrokeshire in affiliation with the National Society.[10] They offered a very rudimentary education. Given the expense of the schoolmaster's salary, the monitorial system furnished a feasible method of providing some rote learning of the three Rs and instruction in the principles of the Church of England.

The schools shared the universal problems of elementary education – grossly inadequate funding, untrained and amateurish teachers and a clientele which was not at all convinced of the necessity for the little amount of schooling which it was being offered. However, state intervention, particularly state money, complicated the religious issue dramatically. The fundamental issue was the extent to which state funding should be allowed or encouraged to support denominational education. It was to remain a fraught issue in Wales, at least until 1944. But the situation in Wales, as in England, was deeply worrying when viewed from above if not from below. A select committee report of 1816 revealed that only about 7 per cent of the population went to day schools. This situation was regarded as socially dangerous as well as demoralizing. Bentham, for example, argued that personal ignorance, dirt and squalor could only be countered by a national system of education. But all such efforts came to grief because of basic religious disagreements, as when Brougham's Parish Schools Bill of 1820 had to be withdrawn because of Nonconformist opposition.

Anxieties grew in Wales and about Wales in the 1820s and 1830s, mainly because of apprehension over the social disorder in Merthyr and the south-east of Wales. Ideas of action nationwide were always thwarted. Kay-Shuttleworth, first secretary to the Committee of Privy Council, wanted to disburse money outside the two educational societies for normal schools and the non-denominational training of teachers. There were immediate protests and his plans came to nothing. There is circumstantial evidence that the educational enquiry of 1846–7 in Wales was less intended as an indictment of education in Wales specifically than part of Kay-Shuttleworth's design to provoke central government into some activity.[11]

In the late 1830s and the 1840s there were more manifestations of social unrest in Wales. In the east there were the Merthyr Rising and the activities of the Chartists; in the west the Rebecca Riots. Government enquiry became more urgent but attempts at action always ran up against the religious difficulty. In south Wales, the stronghold of voluntaryism and so resistant to the British Society even, Graham's Factory Bill, which involved the appointment of Anglican schoolmasters to new schools, served to arouse emotions. Protest meetings were held in 1843, one in March in Haverford-west.[12] The main result in north Wales, spurred on by Hugh Owen, was the opening of British schools. In south Wales the voluntaryists rejected this solution and founded their own 'South Wales Committee of Education' to establish schools of their four denominations and open a normal school in Brecon to train teachers. However, there was some help from the British Society in this venture and British schools were opened in Pembrokeshire in late 1846.[13] By this date there were eighty-four schools in the county which were associated with the Established Church.[14] This provision was substantial compared with the other Welsh counties. In terms of grants from the National Society, also, Pembrokeshire came out well. The county received £1,663, compared with the highest amount of grant to a Welsh county, that of £2,073 to Denbighshire. Yet the inquiry of 1847 was to reveal just how deficient was this level of provision.

The Blue Books

The 1847 investigation into Welsh education has become part of the mythology as well as the fact of Welsh history. The Pembrokeshire investigation was in the charge of R. R. W. Lingen, the most formidable and least sympathetic of the commissioners. He was generally more impressed by the schools in the English-language areas of the county. His investigation revealed that there were 211 schools of all types in Pembrokeshire, to serve a population of 32,578 in the age range from birth to under fifteen.[15] Of these it was calculated that 20,847 were aged between five and fifteen. Some 35.9 per cent of children between the ages of five and ten attended school; 29.3 per cent between ten and fifteen. In both age-groups there was a far higher percentage of boys in school than girls. 64 per cent of the schools were in good school buildings, 17 per cent in 'indifferent' buildings and 18 per cent in 'bad' accommodation. There were 3,597 pupils on the books at these schools, and generally they were not too far from their nearest school, only 12 per cent travelling more than one and a half miles. But the problems of providing anything other than the most rudimentary education are graphically illustrated by the fact that just under a half of pupils had been in school less than a year. Only 13 per cent had been at school more than three years. These statistics provide stark evidence that parents regarded day-school elementary education, if it were warranted at all, as something to be tasted before the real business of life proceeded.

Many of the schools in the county were small, privately run institutions, with instruction provided by the teacher alone, while 19 per
cent were run on the monitorial principle. In the monitorial schools
there was an average of twelve pupils to a monitor; in the non-
monitorial schools there were twenty-eight scholars per teacher.
Despite our concept of education being so intimately connected with
religion, fewer than half the schools opened the day with a hymn or
a prayer. The language of instruction in all elementary schools in the
three counties of south-west Wales was substantially English but the
anglicized nature of Pembrokeshire is evident in comparison with
Carmarthenshire, especially. In 76 per cent of Pembrokeshire's schools
English was the only language used, compared with 29 per cent for
Carmarthenshire. The education available was rudimentary – reading (usually based on the Bible), writing and arithmetic, with a few
schools providing extra subjects such as geography or vocal music.
These subjects were taught by teachers who had taken up teaching
at an average age in Pembrokeshire of thirty, and had been in teaching for about ten years. These averages were similar across south
and west Wales. Very few, only 13 per cent, had received any training in a model school or a normal school, and these had had an
average of eight months' training.

Pembrokeshire's schools were even poorer financially than those
of Carmarthenshire, and certainly those of Glamorgan where the
average was boosted a little by the incomes going to the works
schools. The average annual income per school in Pembrokeshire
was £18 11s. 1d.

The main provider of the county's schools was the Church of
England, either by means of parish and National schools or schools
still run under the Madam Bevan charity. Church schools provided
places for just under half of the scholars in the county, a higher
proportion than in Carmarthenshire or Glamorgan. Private adventure
schools accounted for nearly a third of pupils. In two respects the
differences between Pembrokeshire and both Carmarthenshire and
Glamorgan emerge in school provision. Since Pembrokeshire had
none of the heavy metal industries associated with east Carmarthenshire or Glamorgan there were no works schools in the county. There
were very few British schools in Pembrokeshire by 1847, as one
would expect given the society's impact in south Wales, but
denominational schools reflect an interesting pattern. Nearly 5 per
cent of the county's scholars were in schools provided by the

Independents. This compared with over 8 per cent for Carmarthen-shire, where the denomination was particularly strong, but only 2½ per cent in Glamorgan.

The commissioners of 1847 were scathing in their denunciation of the day-school system in Pembrokeshire, as in all the Welsh counties, though we would do well to remember that contemporary descriptions of schools for the working class in Kay-Shuttleworth's Manchester depicted a system at least as bad.[16] Even so, the catalogue of unsuitable teachers, and schools which often lasted a very few years, and an education of such short duration for most pupils, amounted to a damning indictment. Thirty-five per cent of schools in Pembrokeshire were in a poor state of repair.[17] Yet Lingen commented favourably on one aspect of Pembrokeshire's initiative which was not paralleled elsewhere. This was an alliance of 992 subscribers from the labouring and middle classes who had established the Pembrokeshire Educational Committee.[18] This committee struck a chord with Lingen in providing some degree of that self-help of which middle-class Victorians were so beloved.

The commissioners were far more favourably disposed towards the Sunday-school system in Wales than the day schools. They were genuinely impressed by the efforts and achievements of the Welsh in creating the system on such a scale, putting such creative effort into it and reaching out to adults as well as children through it. The pattern of Sunday-school provision is most interesting in the county. This was remarkably uniform, in percentage terms, in Pembroke-shire, Carmarthenshire and Glamorgan for under-fifteens, with 35 to 36 per cent of the whole of the relevant age-group attached to a Sunday school. Pembrokeshire reflected the substantial adult membership, with 34 per cent of all scholars being over fifteen. However, this varied substantially between denominations, with 80 per cent of Anglican scholars being under fifteen, while only about 60 per cent of Baptist, Independent and Calvinistic Methodist scholars were under fifteen. In all, in Pembrokeshire, there were 223 Sunday schools, teaching 11,418 pupils below the age of fifteen and 5,998 over fifteen. They were taught by 2,675 teachers, two-thirds of whom were male, and eleven of whom, all Anglicans, were paid. One of the most interesting statistics provided by the commissioners, though it has to be treated with extreme caution, is that 6,322 of the scholars were 'said to attend' day school. This was something over half only of the Sunday school scholars under fifteen. The Sunday schools, providing a yet more rudimentary education than many of the day schools, were contributing substantially to the population's ability to read. Of Pembrokeshire's total number of scholars (17,566), both over and under fifteen years of age, 11,232 were recorded as being able to read the Scriptures. They were taught to do so mainly by laymen, though Independent ministers made far more effort than those of other denominations to teach in their Sunday schools. It may be no coincidence that a higher proportion of Independent Sunday school pupils in Pembrokeshire (70 per cent) were able to read than the scholars of other denominations. The least literate were the Anglicans, but of course they had the fewest adults among their number. This measure of literacy, reaching to so many people untouched by day schools, was a formidable achievement. But its limitations, by any enlightened standards of formal education, were enormous. In almost all the schools scholars learned parts of scripture off by heart, they were catechized on scripture and in the majority they sang hymns. Later in the century the Sunday schools became far more, providing the opportunity for parades, teas, festivals of hymn singing and competition. Their educational role was limited, but it did have a purpose. The objective was to enable scholars to read the Bible and so derive moral enlightenment and salvation from it. In this it had a far clearer objective than so many of the providers of day schools.

The language in which pupils were instructed in Pembrokeshire strongly reflects its linguistic difference from Carmarthenshire especially, but also from Glamorgan, because the strength of the Sunday schools was that they were usually held in the language of the hearth. In 75 schools Welsh was the language used; English alone was the language of instruction in 102 and in 46 both languages were used. In Carmarthenshire, on the other hand, only 19 Sunday schools were held solely in English, while 140 were held in Welsh only and a very significant 149 in both languages.

The commissioners' judgement was that the best elementary education in Pembrokeshire was provided in the hundred of Castlemartin.[19] This hundred, together with that of Roos [sic], was 'little England beyond Wales' and Lingen equated the higher standard of educational provision with the 'greater number of resident gentry and proprietors than in the purely Welsh parts'. The commissioners also commented on the 'strangers' who either lived in Tenby or 'frequent it as a watering place in the summer' who 'help by their presence to break through that feeling of isolation in which the lower orders of Welsh throughout remoter districts too complacently hug themselves'. It is obvious that the commissioners were more at home in English Wales which housed recognizable philanthropists like the Earl of Cawdor. It is also true that some of the resident gentry were highly perceptive in the judgements they provided for the commissioners. M. A. Roche of Pashiston [sic], Pembroke, argued that 'the parents seem to consider education – or, I should rather say, the mere prelude to education, such as reading and writing are – rather as an accomplishment, as a rich person would regard German or Italian, than as a necessary thing; so that very little excuse is sufficient for their negligence in not sending their children, and a very little affront sufficient for their withdrawing them'.[20] There could hardly be a more succinct statement, by implication, of the dilemma confronting educational providers, including the state, in the Victorian era. Working-class parents saw no particular advantage in sending their offspring to school when this served no obvious extrinsic purpose, but deprived the family of a possible wage. The government, reflecting the interests of the middle classes, was increasingly convinced of the necessity for education as an instrument for securing social cohesion through implanting an acceptable value system among the lower orders. Parents were often not convinced – and gentry, middle class and industrialists were not sufficiently convinced – to provide a voluntary system which would meet the need if parents had been prepared to send their children on a voluntary basis. The only answer to state need was state provision – compulsory schooling in state-provided schools. Yet this was not only to fall foul of religious pressure groups, but also all the *laissez-faire* instincts which informed Victorian statecraft.

In contrast to the Castlemartin area the north-west of Pembrokeshire came in for much scathing criticism, both on educational and social grounds. The area was Welsh and so warranted a blast at Welsh morality:

> Little care is taken to separate the resident male and female servants properly in the farm-house at night; but further than this, the system of bundling, or, at any rate, nightly visits of the men to the women, prevails extensively. The unmarried men-servants in the farms range the country at night; and it is a known and tolerated practice, that they are admitted by the women-servants at the house to which they come. I hear the

most revolting anecdotes of the gross and almost bestial indelicacy with which sexual intercourse takes place on these occasions.[21]

Morality and education were inextricably linked in the Victorian mind.

Dewisland hundred also had its examples of worst practice. Goodwick day school, for example, was kept in a room in an ordinary house. The room contained two tables and three benches, all in a poor state. The teacher was a one-legged retired sailor of seventy years of age. The pupils 'read very badly and were excessively ignorant'. None knew who had written St John's gospel, nor the fact of the crucifixion of Jesus. The pupils knew the name of the parish in which they lived, but not that of the county or country.[22] On the other hand some schools earned high praise. For example, the National School at Uzmaston, near Haverfordwest, overcame its accommodation in a 'thatched mud hovel' to provide a good standard of education in scripture knowledge, the geography of the Bible, some history and arithmetic. Generally, however, it was only the occasional Sunday school and National school which came in for praise.

The crucial element for the day schools was external funding. Cresselly National School, for example, was held in a purpose-built stone schoolroom. It cost £75, of which £42 had been given by the Committee of Council. Its running costs were partly met by a local landowner, Seymour Allen, but the pupils paid 1*d*. per week. There were desks, benches, calculating boards, maps, prints, a blackboard and a paper clock for teaching the time. Pupils were able to read well, their general knowledge was good and they could do arithmetic to a reasonable standard. There were few such schools in the county.[23]

It is interesting in the light of subsequent events that some of the most stringent condemnation was reserved for Tasker's charity school in Haverfordwest. It was held in 'a ruinous garret'.[24] The plaster in the roof was cracked and the sky could be seen, the floor was covered in sawdust 'and also spit over in all directions'. In this extraordinary setting 'the boys sat at long desks round the room, wearing a prescribed uniform – long blue coats with red collars and cuffs, red waistcoats, corduroy breeches, worsted stockings and laced boots'.

From Blue Books to school boards

We have seen that Kay-Shuttleworth was convinced that only state schooling could minister to the ignorance among the working class all over England and Wales, an ignorance which he regarded as a social evil. State subsidy did rise steadily, sufficiently for governments to start worrying, as they have never ceased to do since, about educational spending. The result was Robert Lowe's Revised Code of 1862 which restricted and constricted elementary education into a 'payment by results' system. Apart from building, all state money now depended on attendance (4s. per pupil) and success in the three Rs (8s. per pupil). Costs were cut and the curriculum pared down. The code was enforced. In 1868 the British School in Pembroke Dock had one-tenth of its income deducted because 'the elementary subjects are imperfectly taught. The writing is particularly defective.'[25] This system did not solve the problem caused by the demands of a rising child population and increasing necessity in an ever more complex society for a more literate and more numerate population. In 1870 the government accepted the inevitable and inaugurated substantial direct state provision of elementary education.

The 1870 Education Act ensured that the state would 'fill in the gaps' in the elementary school system once the voluntary societies had had time to try to fill the gaps themselves. There was immediate reaction in Pembrokeshire where denominational rivalry, financial fears, and community clashes were all evident. Representatives of the Established Church and the gentry gathered in Haverfordwest in November 1870 to set up 'a special fund for those parishes where School accommodation is deficient'. These were the people 'who desire to have schools built on the voluntary principle as opposed to the schools supported by the rates'. God and Mammon were allied in argument as Earl Cawdor, Archdeacon Clark and others demonstrated that 'the voluntary principle would be superior to that of rating the parishes for the support of Education, inasmuch as it would be far more economical, and ensure the teaching of the Bible'.[26] The *Pembrokeshire Herald* offered staunch support to the Establishment: 'we have carefully perused this Act . . . it is, in our opinion, a bad Act . . . it has this one dark blot upon it – in that it casts a slight upon the Christian religion, and is in plain and direct contradiction to the principles inculcated by the inspired word of God . . . it affords a kind of legal recognition of every form of unbelief, and even of Atheism.' Equally reprehensible to the editor was that the Act entailed in 'every parish or district in which it is brought into operation, all the detestable evils of a contested election'.[27]

The efforts of the denominationalists did not quash demands for

school boards. A special meeting of Haverfordwest Town Council
was called in December 1870 to consider setting one up. W. Davies,
supporting the idea, gave 'instances of children who do not go to
any school, but are kept away from it because they earn 1*s.* 6*d.* for
their parents but the time has now arrived when this will be put an
end to'. In a particularly telling sentence he made the implicit connection which underlay the whole concept of elementary education
throughout the nineteenth century and, arguably, well into the
twentieth: 'We have no more right to resist a fair rate for the education of children than we have to resist a rate for the maintenance of
the poor.'[28] Haverfordwest got its school board in January 1871.[29]
Llanstadwell ratepayers decided in December 1870 to apply for a
board, having had a remarkably amicable interdenominational meeting. They started off in the British schoolroom but found it so cold
they transferred to the National schoolroom. St David's held its
meeting to discuss applying for a school board in January 1871.[30]
Steynton and Narberth, too, later got their school boards.[31]

Some of the machinations surrounding the creation and working
of the school boards are excellently exemplified in the cases of St
David's and the Pembroke and Pembroke Dock areas. At St David's,
dispute arose at the ratepayers' meeting over the proposition that
the proceedings should be held in Welsh. There was anxiety within
the Nonconformist ranks that the presence of so much of the cathedral
influence would affect the result. Nevertheless, both the ratepayers'
meeting and a subsequent poll of the parish resulted in large majorities in favour of the establishment of a board despite active canvass-
ing by a number of the cathedral clergy.[32]

In Pater (the name for Pembroke Dock until 1850) there was a
National school and a British school, the latter having been built in
the 1840s as a direct response to the former. In the 1850s a vitupera-
tive rivalry developed between Bonnewell, the secretary of the British School, and Canon Kelly, vicar of St John's, Pembroke Dock. It
led to a vitriolic slanging match in the pages of the *Pembrokeshire
Herald*. But it was also evidence of an attempt to increase
denominational educational provision. A church school opened in
Pembroke in 1855 and a second British school for the Pembroke
and Pembroke Dock areas opened in 1861. The Anglican response
to this was a new building for the National School.[33]

Dispute between backers of the British and National causes
plumbed new depths in the 1860s as a ludicrous correspondence

was carried on in *Potters' Electric News* between a local printer, T. Ward Davies, and the master of the National School. It was a debate marked by no particularly elevated moral or intellectual grasp of the issues. One called the other 'a numbskull'; the other coined a picturesque and original term of abuse: 'huge, petulant dunghill cock'.[34]

Given the implications of the 1870 Act it is hardly surprising that religious rivalries were exacerbated. Backers of the voluntary organizations scaremongered about the potential rate contributions, as we have seen, but superimposed on this was the rivalry between Pembroke and Pembroke Dock.[35] All agreed that there was under-provision, even when the private adventure schools were taken into account, but the voluntaryists argued that it could be met by two new voluntary schools. They lost the argument. Voting in favour of a school board for the Pembroke/Pembroke Dock area was thirteen to nine in favour.

School boards produced the opportunity for the first substantially democratic elections in England and Wales, with women eligible to vote and to stand as candidates. In fact there were serious attempts in both Pembroke and Pembroke Dock to avoid an election but the interest aroused is indicated by the fact that there were seventeen candidates for nine seats. The only female candidate came bottom of the poll. But dockyard planning for the election had worked excellently; all six dockyard candidates were elected, five of them taking the top places. The Pembroke area school board election was, therefore, a fascinating one in that, despite considerable interdenominational bitterness in the 1850s and 1860s, it was intercommunity rivalries which dictated the pattern of the first election. This was not to last. By 1880 the school board elections had reverted to type, with sectarian rivalries dominant. In 1880 five of the retiring members were defeated, six of the seats were won by Nonconformists and three by churchmen. By the 1889 election there were only two dockyard members.[36]

The activities of the Pembroke and Pembroke Dock School Board may also be taken to exemplify some important elements in the role of boards from 1870 to 1902 when elementary education was once again remodelled. First, there was the provision of accommodation. Within three years the board had taken over Monkton Pembroke British School and Pembroke Dock British School as well as enforcing attendance in those areas in which there was sufficient accommodation. In 1874 the board opened a new school in East End,

Pembroke, and another in Pembroke Dock. In 1877 yet another board school opened, in Albion Square.[37]

Second, the history of the Albion Square School links the Pembroke Board with strands in national politics which led, eventually, to the 1902 Education Act. In 1886 the board decided to use the Albion Square School for classes which would earn a grant from the Science and Art Department.[38] The money administered by this department came originally from the profits of the Great Exhibition of 1851 and was intended to foster industrial, scientific and technological education. By drawing on this money, ambitious school boards could develop subjects outside the Revised Code and keep pupils beyond the school-leaving age. So it was that in 1887 Albion Square School got its higher grade section and set out to teach mathematics, chemistry, agriculture, shorthand, book-keeping, magnetism and mechanics. The section was a great success and Pembroke East End School joined it as a higher grade school in 1891. Both schools also offered evening education by means of continuation classes.[39]

The Pembroke and Pembroke Dock School Board was still expanding its activities in 1901–2 just as the axe of the 1902 Act was about to fall. From the perspective of central government this school board in Pembrokeshire, like so many others in England and Wales, had grown too big for its boots. It was providing an education which might educate people beyond their station in life. This working-class trespass onto middle-class territory had to be curbed. Pembroke and Pembroke Dock School Board was abolished in 1902 for being too successful in answering some of the demands of an increasingly industrial society. Robert Morant, at national level, was determined to reinforce the distinction between elementary and secondary education which the more progressive school boards were blurring by their higher grade schools.[40] National legislation accomplished this after 1902 as control over the newly corseted system passed to central government and, to a far lesser degree, the Pembrokeshire County Council.

The school boards had accomplished much, but the education provided in elementary schools for the mass of children remained restricted and mechanical. There remained many school buildings which were dirty and poorly ventilated.[41] The most intractable problem remained that of the parental poverty which made the child's wage an essential component of family solvency. Under Sandon's

Act of 1876 parents were liable to incur penalties if they did not secure adequate education for their children and there was a spate of cases against parents in Pembrokeshire's courts.[42]

Fining parents for not sending their children to school was hardly an effective method of dealing with such cases as that of John Jenkins of Slade, charged at Roose [sic] Petty Sessions with neglecting to send his three children to school. At the court Jenkins's wife said that eight persons lived on her husband's wages of 8s. a week, and she could not afford boots for her children.[43] It was in such cases that the activities of the school attendance officer were least effective.

The problems of non-attendance, or sporadic and seasonal attendance, survived the demise of the school boards and the legislation of 1902 but were less in evidence. Parent power now sometimes exerted itself in rather different ways, and a Pembrokeshire elementary school provides one of the more bizarre examples. The story is reported in an unpublished volume, but its main details are corroborated in press accounts in a variety of newspapers.[44] In April 1915 a girl pupil in Rosemarket school kicked over a lighted stove and was smacked. The girl, who reputedly suffered from fits, vomited and was kept away from school 'suffering from shock'. The teacher responsible was the unqualified wife of the school's headmaster, Bruce Cattanach. Parents of pupils at the school then 'went on strike', as the log book has it, and the atmosphere in Rosemarket became very bitter. The girl's parents lost a case of assault against the teacher but many parents tried to send their children to other schools (not all of which were prepared to accept them) and others held an unofficial school in the chapel vestry. Twenty-two parents were fined 5s. each and eventually the dispute petered out as the children drifted back to school. The elementary schools of Pembrokeshire were not without their problems in these war years and in the decades to come. Fortunately they were usually less colourful.

Secondary education

One of Lingen's many perceptive comments dotted through the 1847 *Reports* was that the mining communities in industrialized areas had no middle class and 'the diminution of a middle class is rendered still more complete when, to the economical causes tending to produce it, is superadded the separation of language'.[45] This absence of a middle rank in society, so central to Victorian concepts of social cohesion and stability, exercised many Welshmen in the second half of the nineteenth century, especially, perhaps, Hugh Owen and H. A. Bruce. Owen concerned himself first with the problems of elementary education but soon turned his attention to the creation of some kind of Welsh middle class by means of schools of higher rank – secondary schools – in Wales.

The only two schools in Pembrokeshire recorded in 1847 as being outside the run of normal elementary provision were Haverford-west Free School and Pembroke Free Grammar School. Neither was very effective. As Lingen records of the Pembroke school, 'so small an endowment as £11 3s. 4d. is utterly useless'. In Haverfordwest, there were twenty-eight pupils, none of whom boarded, and only three of whom paid fees. These pupils entered as early as eight years of age in some instances. Some left very soon; some stayed years. They were taught English grammar, history and geography, Latin and Greek. The master recorded that the object was to provide a cheap classical education and it would help if the corporation stopped 'send[ing] boys of so low a station in life'.[46] The two 'grammar' schools were of singularly low standard and generally ineffectual.

They shared this low standard with most of the other grammar schools in Wales, although the main problem was less of standards than of lack of any provision at all. Victorian Welshmen, often having made a mark in England, shared the fears and the vision of their English compeers. In Wales, which still reflected the social structure delineated in the 1847 Report – the paucity of the middle class – the situation was yet more urgent. If Matthew Arnold was constantly concerned about the cultural capacity of the English middle class to govern,[47] there were more primitive fears in Wales. How could society exist there without this social cement? The lessons of the Blue Books were obvious – social cohesion required a middle class. The elementary schools were an irrelevance in this context – they were the schools of the working class. Therefore the secondary schools which were the concern of the Taunton Commission of 1864 had to come to Wales at some time. There was at least one important Pembrokeshire voice raised in support of the secondary schools movement – that of the Revd Dr Thomas Nicholas of Solva, though he was a tutor in the Presbyterian College in Carmarthen at the time of his proselytizing in favour of a blend of liberal and scientific Welsh secondary education.[48]

The Aberdare Committee (1881) noted very little educational activity in Pembrokeshire. They mentioned the school in Pembroke which had once been a grammar school but whose endowment had been discontinued in 1838.[49] The only real secondary school in Pembrokeshire was Haverfordwest Grammar School. We noted that it was not treated in particularly complimentary fashion in the 1847 Report. However, its fortunes improved with a new scheme and syllabus in 1855 and an increase in its funding when half of the income of the Milward property in Birmingham was devoted to it. At this time there were forty-one day boys and ten boarders on the roll. There remained a narrow ladder of opportunity for poorer pupils, by means of the twelve Milward scholarships and the two governors' scholarships available to pupils from Haverfordwest's elementary schools. However, it is obvious that a problem which was to plague the intermediate schools in their early decades was entrenched in the Haverfordwest system in the 1880s. This was early leaving, with many of the boys only staying a year or so. Still, the school was extended in 1887 and was teaching a full grammar-school curriculum of the time – Scripture, history, geography, English literature, English grammar, French, mathematics, Latin, Greek, chemistry and drawing.[50] In Taunton Commission terms, however, it was a second-grade school.

The other relevant charity mentioned in the 1847 Report was that of Mary Tasker, endowed in the seventeenth century to provide uniforms and an elementary education for seventy boys. The Charity Commissioners, however, decided that the money should be devoted to providing secondary schooling for girls. In 1892 the school became a Girls' High School, and became integrated into the county scheme for intermediate schools.

The situation in Pembrokeshire in 1880, therefore, illustrates at county level the dramatic inadequacies of secondary education provision throughout Wales. Given the scale of the shortfall, and the financial implications, there could be no solution from within Wales alone; only central government intervention and Treasury money could meet the case. That this eventually came about was a minor miracle; that it took eight years resulted in other initiatives.

The most interesting of these was that of A. J. Mundella, whose Circular 213 of August 1882 provided incentives for school boards serving populations of over 5,000 to establish higher grade schools. But the class implications of this, so often the key to understanding educational history, were well brought out by Robert George, mayor of Pembroke, in giving evidence to the Aberdare Committee who were in favour of higher elementary schools. George thought that such a school in Pembroke Dock might have some attraction for the lower middle class, but 'the upper middle class parents . . . would not want their children to mix with those attending board schools charging fees of 2*d*. and 3*d*. a week'.[51]

Party co-operation and Treasury acquiescence combined in 1889 to produce the Welsh Intermediate Education Act. It provided for a system of secondary education in Pembrokeshire and the other Welsh counties which, much transmuted, leaves many traces. The response in the county came quickly. At the first meeting of the joint education committee charged with overseeing the birth of this new state system there were requests to be considered from local committees in Fishguard, Narberth and Pembroke Dock for intermediate schools to be established in their localities. This was no small commitment, since the building costs of the schools had to be raised locally. In 1890 the joint education committee finally decided to set up intermediate schools in Pembroke Dock, Tenby, Narberth or Whitland, St David's and Fishguard. The original plan was for the Narberth/Whitland school to be shared with Carmarthenshire, and to share the costs and facilities of another school in Cardiganshire's county town. Most tardy in displaying any interest were the inhabitants of Milford Haven, but eventually they, too, were drawn into the scheme. In view of the attitudes displayed for so much of the nineteenth century it is significant that all the proposed schools catered for boys and girls.[52]

In another respect the committee, like its counterparts across Wales, made what, in retrospect, was the wisest of decisions. It decided against the establishment of two or three large schools in the county which would have necessitated pupils boarding. The reasons given were that pupils would not thereby be deprived of the good moral influence of their homes or their Sunday schools. Such high-mindedness did not come unaccompanied by some worldliness – the notion that a number of smaller schools would more adequately spread the financial burden among more ratepayers.

The Pembrokeshire scheme under the Intermediate Education Act eventually passed into law in 1894 and within a few years the county had its network of county schools – schools which continue to form the backbone of its secondary system. The scheme provided for schools at Pembroke Dock, for ninety boys and sixty girls; Tenby (forty boys and thirty girls); Milford Haven (forty boys and thirty girls); Narberth (fifty boys and thirty girls); St David's (forty pupils all told); Fishguard (also forty pupils) and Cardigan (eighty boys and fifty girls) shared accommodation with the neighbouring county. There was more complexity in Haverfordwest since Haverfordwest Grammar School for Boys was substantially outside the county scheme but the Tasker Milward School became part of it.

The kind of school envisaged by the joint education committees was a day school (though the possibility of boarding was not always ruled out) with a graduate head, and pupils aged between ten and seventeen. These pupils would have to pay fees of between £3 and £8 per annum, unless they managed to win a rare scholarship. The exclusivity of the schools was ensured by all pupils, even the fee-payers, having to be at Standard V of the elementary school at entry. Once at the school it was intended that they would study a curriculum which blended the tradition of the middle-class grammar schools of the nineteenth century, epitomized by the inclusion of the Classics, with the more mechanical traditions of the higher elementary schools – metalwork or dairywork for example. The curriculum in Milford Haven County School is illustrative of the general trend. Its syllabus at the start consisted of English, history, geography, Scripture, arithmetic, algebra, Euclid, Latin, French, drawing, geometric drawing, domestic economy for the girls and chemistry for the boys.[53]

Such schools were conceived as hybrids indeed. What the committees did not appreciate at this stage was that it was highly unlikely that graduate headmasters (for there were few women), moulded by a classical tradition, would allow such a blend, with its implicit devaluation of the traditional secondary education. It turned out that they did not. They concentrated on academic subjects.

The recent centenary of the 1889 Education Act was, quite rightly, widely celebrated in Wales. The intermediate schools were a unique achievement, which, because of their economic and sociological significance for individuals and the Welsh nation, have become part of the folk memory, with the details fused into a collective genuflection. In fact, the Pembrokeshire schools, like most in Wales, got off to an inauspicious start. They were plagued with financial difficulties, with the majority of landowners and industrialists refusing to provide the money or the land which might have eased the schools' birth. According to the chairman of the Pembrokeshire Joint Education Committee:

> The rich and great of the county had not helped to any great extent . . . and . . . one leading landowner had replied thus to an appeal: 'I cannot subscribe to the school. In my humble opinion there is too much education at the present day for the good of the County.'[54]

Most of the schools, Milford for example, opened in temporary premises, though Pembroke Dock's temporary accommodation was spacious and the school had new buildings in 1899. These consisted of a staff room, five classrooms, an assembly hall, a girls' schoolroom to assist the attempts at some segregation which characterized all the intermediate schools, a large 'Chemical theatre', a kitchen and laundry for the girls, and a carpenters' shop for the boys.[55]

In most of the Pembrokeshire schools there seemed to be no great difficulty in getting pupils. The problem lay in keeping them for the four-year course leading to the School Certificate. The main impediment was that the majority of Welsh parents were poor. Numbers of scholarships were raised to a minimum of 25 per cent by McKenna's Act of 1907, but the free place was only part of the solution. Parents still had to provide uniforms and books. More significant, once pupils had reached the age of fourteen they were entitled to leave school and earn a living. Staying on meant forgoing the possibility of a wage. This was the hidden cost of education and many parents could not afford to meet it. Girls were especially vulnerable to the early-leaving syndrome. Between 1895 and 1902 a total of 292 girls attended Tasker's school. Some 140 of them stayed less than two years. Whatever the intrinsic merits of their education, in terms of the School Certificate qualification it was wasted. The Board of Education and the Welsh Department attempted to control the situation by requiring parents to sign legal agreements to keep their children in school for the four-year course. There was a steady improvement, though the legal agreements were rarely enforced.

Overall, numbers rose gradually, then, following the national pattern, rose rapidly in the period during and immediately after the First World War, when some of the increasing prosperity of the population was siphoned off into secondary education. For example, in 1906 there were 172 pupils enrolled in Pembroke Dock County School, a number which rose to 339 by 1922. Tenby's sixty-five pupils in 1911 expanded to 189 in 1938–9.[56] This brought about a change in the method of payment of headteachers. At the start they were paid on a commission basis – basic salary and a per capita sum for pupils. For example, J. W. B. Adams, first headmaster of Tenby County School, was paid £120 per annum and £2 per pupil. Milford's head fared worse, with a similar fixed sum, but only £1 per pupil. After the war the local education authority introduced fixed scales, and the headmaster of Pembroke Dock County School earned a very respectable £600 per annum.

As numbers increased so did the pressure on space. In Pembroke Dock temporary huts were brought in after the war before more permanent additions could be provided in 1935. Part of the reason for this expansion was the growing tendency for pupils to stay on into the sixth form, a trend which increased in the 1930s. So Pembroke Dock, for example, had thirty-six sixth formers in 1931. The normal course in the early years of the county schools was of four years, leading to the School Certificate which, at credit level, provided university matriculation. However, from 1917 the Board of Education provided extra funds for Advanced courses for pupils who had completed School Certificate.[57] The competitive nature of this allocation of funds provided yet another élite of schools and pupils in Wales. However, numbers in some schools remained very low. Between 1902 and 1931 only four Higher Certificates were awarded to pupils in Milford Haven County School.[58]

These sixth forms provide yet another reminder of the way in which the Welsh county schools were moulded in the tradition of the English public schools. The headteachers of the Pembrokeshire schools, at least the earlier ones, had to come to the county with much of their undergraduate and teaching experience having been gained outside Wales. Even those like T. H. Jones, headmaster of Pembroke Dock County School for over thirty years from 1906, came from Cardiff Boys' Intermediate School whose first headmaster, Findlay, had modelled that school on the great English first-grade schools.[59] So Pembroke Dock got its school uniform, its prefect system and its house system, though it lost its Saturday morning school in 1910. However, T. H. Jones also introduced the school eisteddfod, which certainly had no precedent in the English schools. Underpinning the competitive element, and the organized games, was the even odder house system, something which came to characterize all the county schools, originating in the boarding arrangements of the English public schools.

Organized school sport was another vital aspect of the county schools, and school teams were crucial in the development of games like rugby and hockey among the adult population of the different towns. There were hockey, cricket and football (soccer) clubs in Tenby County School virtually as soon as it was founded. Again there were problems of provision. Milford Haven School had no sports field as late as 1928. The school shop window, and another ubiquitous tradition in the county schools of Pembrokeshire and elsewhere, was the school prize day, with its guest speakers from the great, the good and the self-righteous, and the slow snail of pupils who had succeeded in obtaining those precious certificates which would allow them, often, to leave Pembrokeshire either to continue their education or to work. The justification of prize day by the headmaster of Milford Haven County School is illuminating in its insights into the attitudes of those heads who moulded the second-ary system, especially when, like Lowther and many of his Welsh contemporaries, they served for such long periods of time, in his case twenty-nine years. He argued that

> Something was necessary to bring together parents, pupils and employ-ers. Employers should know what is being attempted and how far it is possible to modify the curriculum to suit the various needs of industry. On the other hand . . . it is no part of our work to turn out clerks, artisans and tradesmen. It is our duty and privilege to endeavour to lay the foundations for public service, good citizenship and high moral standards.[60]

The Pembrokeshire school which best epitomized changes in attitude towards secondary education was Haverfordwest Grammar School for Boys, the one endowed grammar school in the county. We have seen that reference to it in the 1847 *Report* was scarcely complimentary. But with the new importance attached to education it achieved a greater degree of prosperity. It was by no means a front-rank grammar school compared with its English counterparts. It had financial worries which lasted at least until the end of the First World War. It charged low fees; indeed, at £4 per annum for the basic curriculum in 1897 they were at the low end of those charged in the intermediate schools. The school paid its staff badly. Yet, in so many ways it represented what the intermediate schools were trying to be and was an influence in steering them towards what many critics regarded as an overriding concern with things academic, an examination orientation and an aping of the English grammar-school traditions. There was a concentration on the Classics. The curriculum consisted of Latin, Greek, French, mathematics, Scripture, geography, history, English, drawing and shorthand, with chemistry being introduced in 1891. Sport featured strongly, with cricket, athletics and soccer, swimming and cross-country running. Soccer was a sport not entirely befitting a school with pretensions and in 1930 the more 'public school' rugby was introduced. Heads were translated to public schools – Mr Tombs to Durham Cathedral School in 1906 accompanied by parting gifts which included a purse of gold coins (a recognizable equivalent of today's cheque), Munro's *Lucretius* in three volumes and the *Dialogues* of Plato in five, more elegant stylistically, and in terms of binding, than volumes of the National Curriculum Statutory Orders which are now more likely to accompany heads on their travels.

Haverfordwest's pretensions were at their apogee from 1927, fostered by a governing body which effectively excluded any mere graduate of a Welsh university college from applying for the post of head. In turn the new head, Lang, stocked the school with Oxbridge graduates. He concentrated on examination results, especially at Higher Certificate level, and achieved his true reward by being made a member of the Headmasters' Conference.[61] The other Pembrokeshire heads of county schools did not achieve that, but they generally shared a similar vision of what their schools were about throughout their first half-century.

Between the wars

The state had determined, at least by 1902, though in effect some years before, that it was responsible for the education of all its citizens to a minimum standard. That standard was what could be achieved in elementary schools between the ages of five and fourteen, with the leaving age being determined by the 1918 Education Act. This was a limited education which did not lead to any examination, and therefore no ticket to higher education or a job. That kind of currency was provided, in Pembrokeshire as elsewhere in Wales, by the county schools. Victorian casts of mind were still prevalent among government ministers and senior English civil servants who administered the system. Elementary education was a kind of charity, on a par with other forms of compensation for inadequacy. The only education which was really worthwhile was that which was paid for, and the more it cost the more prestigious it was. The Welsh county schools were some way down the scale.

There was blurring at the edges of this philosophy, provided by the free place system which did provide some outlet for talent. But given the exigencies of the economic situation in the late 1920s and especially from 1929, even this degree of charity was deemed far too generous, particularly when it was being used by the talented poor to circumvent the cherished hierarchies of the class-based education system. This mentality emerges most strongly in the May Report of 1931:

> Since the standard of education that is being given to the child of poor parents is already in very many cases superior to that which the middle class parent is providing for his own child, we feel that it is time to pause in this policy of expansion, to consolidate the ground gained, to endeavour to reduce the cost of holding it, and to reorganise the existing machine before making a fresh general advance.[62]

Costs were to be reduced by making free scholarship places subject to a means test, so aligning it with other 'benefits' to be doled out and reinforcing the notion of financially assisted education as charity. The financial return of this policy in Depression-ridden Wales was derisory, but Wales was dragged along on England's coat-tails. Some of the Welsh local authorities were defiant but even Labour-dominated Glamorgan's opposition crumbled, as it was bound to, in this confrontation with the might of central government. Pembrokeshire, like most of the rural counties in Wales, put the government's policy into action without demur. Indeed, the LEA was a little too enthusiastic in setting the income level very low at which parental contribution would come into effect, so the Welsh Department raised it. The review of the system had one positive effect in that the Welsh counties used it to increase the number of places which were allocated to pupils on scholastic ability alone, rather than the ability to pay fees. Pembrokeshire LEA wanted to allow only 20 per cent of places to fee payers, with the other 80 per cent allocated as special places. This was going too far for the Welsh Department who beat them down to 75 per cent special places. What was happening in Pembrokeshire, as in the rest of Wales, therefore, was the progressive meritocratization of Welsh education, far ahead of England and much in line with what the 1944 Education Act was to bring about in England. Whatever the mitigating circumstances, the settlement reached over Pembrokeshire's county schools in 1933 did not reflect

well on the county's generosity. In the eight county schools the fees
charged rose from £4 10s. per year to £6 per year, while the number
of 'ability' places rose from 45 per cent to 75 per cent. However,
Pembrokeshire's income limits for payment of fees were among the
most stringent in Wales. To merit a free education pupils had to be
in a household in which the income was below 12s. per week net of
rent and rates if they lived in the county, 10s. per week if they lived
in the town. However, these sums were amended to 14s. 6d. and
12s. respectively. A sliding scale then operated up to 18s., amended
to 20s., at which point parents had to pay full fees.[63] It was only
with the coming of the 1944 Act that the means-tested county school
places were replaced by free secondary education as of right.

The 1944 Education Act and its aftermath

From the perspective of those grappling with the implications of the
1988 Education Act Butler's 1944 Education Act is often regarded
as one of those beacons of enlightenment which heralded a new era
of opportunity, and equality of opportunity, in the postwar world.
For the Welsh historian familiar with the ravages of the Depression,
it is tempting to see it in similar light. Here at last was free secondary education for all, transport to get to the schools, a trumpeted
parity of esteem between the different types of secondary schools, a
raised school-leaving age from 1947, all supported by, and linked
to, the other scaffolding of the welfare state.

Of course the 1944 Act was not like that. It was an improvement,
certainly, but only on a system long discredited, even by official
reports such as that of Spens in 1938. That report, advocating much
of what was implemented in 1944, was a conservative document.
As far as Wales was concerned the 1944 Act had considerably less
practical effect than was the case in England. Driven by poverty, a
substantial percentage of Welsh children already had free secondary
education in the county schools. Furthermore, the great majority of
pupils were admitted by competitive examination, to a far greater
extent than was the case in England. We have seen that this figure
in Pembrokeshire was 75 per cent of the entry and in some areas no
fee-payers had privileged access. The element of continuity after
1944 in Welsh educational provision was, therefore, considerably

greater than in England. The major hurdle in the school system, the 'scholarship', was merely transmuted into the 'eleven plus'.

Each LEA had to submit its development plan for education in the wake of the 1944 Act. Pembrokeshire's plan was submitted by D. T. Jones, the director of education, in March 1947.[64] It had to come to terms with a very demanding situation. Pembrokeshire was substantially populated – nearly 91,000 in 1951 – yet with relatively few towns. None of these – Tenby, Haverfordwest, Pembroke, Pembroke Dock, Milford or Fishguard – was particularly large. In essence, therefore, Pembrokeshire encountered many of the problems of rural Wales and had the additional complication of a linguistic divide between the English-language south and the more Welsh-speaking north of the county. Language posed rather fewer problems of principle or practice at this stage because there was, as yet, little momentum in the Welsh-language lobby in Welsh secondary education. Rurality provided formidable obstacles for the simple reason that the government was, covertly, committed to a policy of tripartitism in secondary education. The senior civil servants at the Board of Education had decided that there were going to be separate grammar schools and secondary modern schools. This policy underlay all negotiations, including those of the Welsh Department, with local authorities in Wales. This was despite the policies of some Welsh authorities to opt for multilateral school schemes and, more relevant in Pembrokeshire, the fact that in rural areas of Wales a tripartite, or even bipartite (grammar/secondary modern) solution was highly impractical. Dogma clashed with demography in Pembrokeshire.

There was least difficulty in the towns. Haverfordwest was to keep its Boys' and Girls' Grammar Schools, and to be provided with a secondary modern school. The intermediate school in Milford was to become a grammar/technical school and the town would have, additionally, two secondary modern schools. Pembroke and Pembroke Dock were to have a grammar/technical school and a secondary modern school. In a planning sense, though certainly not in a political sense as we shall see, the intermediate school in Narberth posed no problems either. It was to become a secondary modern school. In other areas the solutions were less straightforward from the Welsh Department's point of view. According to the development plan the intermediate school which served Fishguard and Goodwick was to become an eleven-to-eighteen grammar/secondary modern school for 600 pupils. The intermediate school in St David's was to be a grammar/secondary modern school. Most anomalous, in terms of government policy, were Tenby, where some kind of secondary school divide might have been possible but the director planned a bilateral school, and the Preseli area where he wanted a multilateral school for 340 pupils.

The Welsh Department of the new Ministry of Education had problems. The civil servants there were inevitably carried along on their policy of imposing a tripartite solution but they could deny neither demographic and geographical constraints, nor local sentiment. The county school at St David's was a major headache. In its proposed two-form entry grammar/secondary modern form it was too small to produce a viable grammar stream. So H. E. Weston, who dealt with all the Welsh development plans early on, suggested hesitantly that St David's sixth formers should go to the proposed larger Fishguard grammar/secondary modern school. This was very tempting because it would then allow Fishguard to be served not by this bilateral school but a separate two-form-entry grammar school and a four-form-entry secondary modern school. In this form the gospel according to the Ministry's civil servants, that wherever remotely possible, there should be a complete separation, intellectual and physical, between a grammar and secondary modern education, might be more extensively invoked in Pembrokeshire. This philosophy led also to the rejection at this stage of the grammar element of the proposed multilateral school in Crymych for pupils from the Preseli area.

The dispute over the Crymych school was one of the most fascinating of the duels between the Welsh Office and a local authority in Wales after the 1944 Education Act – and there is no shortage of these confrontations. It involved a cross-border dispute and an ideological dispute. Pembrokeshire's director wanted a full multilateral school in Crymych on grounds of county pride, and the authority emphasized that it wanted 'a real Welsh school' for 'Welsh-speaking pupils'. The Welsh Department wanted efficient planning and, as far as possible, a strict divide between grammar and secondary modern education. This could best be secured by directing grammar pupils from the Preseli area to Cardigan County School. There would then be sufficient grammar-type pupils to allow the school in Cardigan to be a grammar, rather than a grammar/secondary modern school, and mean that the school in Crymych would be a secondary modern school. From the point of view of the Welsh Department here was the perfect blend of efficiency and sound educational principle. The department believed that if the secondary modern school in Crymych became well-established 'the Ay. will slip easily into our way of thinking & aim at two separate secy. schools' (one grammar and one modern).

However, D. T. Jones, the director of education, was wholly committed to the proposed multilateral school in Crymych, and informed the Welsh Department of the fact in 1950. The Welsh Department fought back. They approved plans for the Crymych school in December 1950, but 'just at present any grammar provision here could not justifiably be programmed ... since the grammar pupils of the area are already receiving effective grammar education [in Cardigan]'. Then, in November 1951 officials of the Cardiganshire and Pembrokeshire authorities met again and the Pembrokeshire director stated that Preseli would open as a bilateral grammar/secondary modern school, conceding only that pupils from the St Dogmael's area might continue to attend Cardigan Grammar School. The Preseli school was due to be built in 1954–5 and the Welsh Department, for once, did not get its way in postwar Wales.

The fate of a long-established school, that in St David's, was also in the balance. Here it was HMI who emphasized the Welsh ambience. They argued that if pupils were forced to travel to Haverfordwest or Fishguard they would move to an English atmosphere. There was also tradition and local sentiment to be taken into account in St David's. Despite the unresolved problems the Pembrokeshire development plan was approved quickly. The Welsh Department had got its way in Fishguard, where there were now to be separate grammar and secondary modern schools, though on the same site. The St David's decision was deferred, but in effect the Welsh Department had capitulated, being forced reluctantly into endorsing a bilateral school there. Over Preseli, too, the director was getting his way.

Then in 1953 events took an odd turn in Fishguard as D. E. Lloyd Jones, principal in the Welsh Department, pointed out that, given the twelve additional classrooms being built on the Fishguard site, it would be much more sensible to have a bilateral, grammar/secondary modern school there. There was only one 'very big snag', he acknowledged. It had been his own former boss, H. E. Weston, now retired, who had persuaded the Pembrokeshire authority to drop its plans for a bilateral school in Fishguard in the first place.

Pembrokeshire provides a classic example, therefore, of the

entanglement and confusion which resulted when a loyal attempt
by Welsh Department civil servants to implement departmental policy
got caught up in the realities of rural Wales. The rigid, fashionable
divide between grammar and secondary modern schools, to accommodate the spurious pseudo-psychology of the Norwood Report
which postulated three types of 'minds', could be implemented reasonably easily in towns. In the countryside it was virtually impossible.
Pembrokeshire LEA, and its strong-minded director, D. T. Jones, in
the end had much of their development plan implemented. Their
original solution carried in St David's, in Fishguard and eventually
in Crymych. Of course in other parts of the county, Tenby and Haverfordwest, for example, the transition from county school to grammar school was accomplished easily.

Another feature of Pembrokeshire's dealings with the Welsh Department was its involvement in cross-border disputes. We have seen
that the county caused problems over the Crymych school but, from
a Welsh Department viewpoint, the authority co-operated to the hilt
over Narberth County School. Again we see where power lay in the
formative years after the war. What emerged over events in Narberth was that parents and the small local community had no chance
when pitted against government department and local authority. In
the development plan for Pembrokeshire, Narberth County School,
the oldest in the county, was to become a secondary modern school,
to the chagrin of the local inhabitants. The governors protested, but
the intractable problem was once again the numbers of 'grammar-
type' pupils necessary to constitute a viable school. Grammar-
school pupils could attend the school at Whitland or the proposed
Crymych school, or Haverfordwest or Tenby schools. The only weak
spot in the Welsh Department's case, which a Narberth delegation
sought to exploit in its interview with officials of the Welsh Department and the local authority in Cardiff in 1956, was that a grammar/
secondary modern school of similar size to the proposed Narberth
school had been allowed in St David's. It had no effect. The Narberth school became a secondary modern school.

Secondary education underwent an organizational transformation after the 1944 Education Act, but it is arguable that in terms of
ideology it was highly conservative. The ethos of the schools remained
unchanged in so many ways. It can be summed up succinctly by
quoting some of the subheadings of chapters in the history of Greenhill School, Tenby. We have 'Greenhill with Gibson', an unconscious

tribute to the prime place in school and community of some of these grammar school headteachers. We then have 'The School Magazine', 'Outdoor Activities', the 'Literary and Dramatic Society', 'School Music', 'The School Science Society', 'The A.T.C. and Duke of Edinburgh Awards', a section which subsumes the school Eisteddfod.[65]

The signal achievement of the 1944 Education Act was to get rid at last of the all-age elementary schools, and, up to a point, the ideology which went with that 'elementary' concept. Effective primary schools became a feature of Pembrokeshire's education system, though we should not forget how much of their energy went into the constraining objective of getting pupils through the eleven-plus. So much of the creativity and enjoyment which we now associate with high-quality primary education is consequent on the abolition of that looming hurdle which dominated so many children's lives at a vulnerable age.

The ubiquity of the eleven-plus for decades after 1944 serves to remind us that, in secondary education, the theme is continuity with the early years of the century rather than dramatic change in pattern and ethos. This was still the case at the time when Pembrokeshire officially, in 1974, nine years after Anthony Crosland's Circular 10/65 which pushed the local authorities towards wholesale comprehensivization, officially ceased to exist. Ysgol y Preseli was, as planned, an all-through bilingual comprehensive school. The bilateral schools at Fishguard and St David's were now full comprehensives. Greenhill School (Tenby) and Pembroke were also comprehensives. But there were still secondary modern schools in Haverfordwest, Milford Haven and Narberth. There were still grammar schools in Milford Haven and two in Haverfordwest.[66] The latter two provide an interesting link with the start of our story. Those downtrodden endowed establishments of the Blue Books of 1847, the boys' school in Haverfordwest and the Tasker charity, were now the élite schools of the county, having preserved their identity for over a century and, under the patronage of the state, having prospered mightily. They were still difficult establishments to bring into line with the philosophy of comprehensive education.

5
The 'Welsh Revolt' revisited: Merioneth and Montgomeryshire in default

The education system in England and Wales at the end of the nineteenth century was in urgent need of rationalization. The Education Act of 1870 had seen a redirection of state effort when a system of government subvention to religious denominations had proved incapable of coping with the demands of an increasing population, a rapidly industrializing society and a ruling class haunted by fears of a working-class superiority of numbers undermining time-honoured hierarchies.

Against a background of continuing industrial development and its social consequences, the system inaugurated in 1870 itself came under strain. Towards the end of the nineteenth century, ambitious school boards, utilizing Science and Art Department grants to foster higher elementary work, constituted another threat to the integrity of that educational and class stratification central to Victorian values. At the same time, the religious denominations found it increasingly difficult to maintain their commitments as major providers of education. For example, the physical condition of many Church of England 'National' schools in Wales was deplorable.[1]

By 1902 both the local administrative framework and the political will existed to modify the system fundamentally. The 1889 Technical Instruction Act and the creation of the county and county borough councils provided the former; the return of a Unionist government in 1895, and again in 1900, the latter. The Bryce Commission (1895) recommended a central authority for education and the Board of Education was created in 1899. This enabled the government to exercise a greater degree of central control. In the meantime, there had already been an attempt to remove local power from the school boards by the education bill of 1896, contrary to the recommendations of the Bryce Commission. This abortive attempt at legislation would have placed control of elementary, secondary and technical education in the hands of the county and county borough councils.[2]

The man behind the 1896 bill was Sir John Gorst, vice-president of the Committee of Council on Education and the scourge of the school boards. By regulation and minute he proceeded to curb their powers, aided by the immense tactical skills of Robert Morant, the eventual architect of the 1902 Education Act. Morant's perception of the function of the education system was as hierarchical as that of the government: 'each . . . type of school may have a presentment before it, both of the function which it is intended to fulfil, of the results it is framed to produce, and of the area which it is created to supply.'[3] Gorst and Morant proceeded between them to engineer the Cockerton judgement of 1900 in the courts, in which the London school board was found to be acting illegally in using rate-aid for the provision of secondary education in its higher-grade schools.

With the system in confusion there had to be major legislation. A comprehensive new education bill was introduced by the Unionist prime minister, Arthur Balfour, in March 1902. Its terms had a particular significance for Wales. The new repositories of that local power still deemed appropriate were the county, county borough and some of the more populous urban district councils. The secular policies which had evolved at local school board level in Wales, in a sufficiently flexible system to allow developments appropriate to Nonconformist allegiance, were to disappear. The demise of the boards, together with the continuation of Anglican educational influence in so many parts of Wales, in a political context of resurgent national spirit channelled into challenge to Anglican hegemony, created a climate in which some kind of protest was inevitable. Wales was a predominantly Nonconformist nation, with the Church of England providing less than a third of the seating in places of worship.[4] Yet a majority of schools were affiliated to the Church of England. There remained at least 300 school districts in which the only elementary education available was through the local Anglican school.[5] These voluntary schools were now to be sheltered under the state umbrella and aided by local authority rates, but would be allowed to offer religious education according to their denominational origins and, indeed, control the running and organization of the schools through a majority of denominational managers.[6] Their financial embarrassment would be substantially alleviated. In Wales this constituted a real offence to the Nonconformist conscience. It only required political leadership to channel protest effectively.

Leadership was provided by David Lloyd George. His initially favourable reaction to the bill was quickly transformed into hostility as he saw its implications and, doubtless, the political capital to be made out of opposition to it.[7] The Nonconformist fight against the bill came not only from Wales, of course, and it was pursued through the Liberal Party in the Commons. This did not prevent the Education Bill becoming law in December 1902. In Wales, initial and unexpected attempts at compromise failed and opposition was cemented at a national convention in Cardiff in June 1903. All local authorities in Wales were urged to resist the Act. Such resistance would fundamentally interfere with its implementation. According to its provisions, schools were to be administered by the county and county borough councils as the local education authorities. They replaced the school boards and the school attendance committees. Boroughs and urban district councils over a specified size were also given the responsibility of administering elementary schools. The local education authority was empowered to establish a local education committee to which it could delegate powers under the Act. However, the committee could neither raise a rate nor borrow money. This had to be done by the authority itself.

The elementary schools were now to be placed in two categories. Former board schools were classified as 'provided' schools and were, effectively, council schools. Voluntary schools, with buildings not supplied by the LEA, became 'non-provided' schools. In such schools the board of managers was to number six, with the majority (four) appointed under the trust deeds of the school. One interpretation of this has been that 'the foundation managers would preserve the denominational character of the school and the presence of two managers representing the public authority would act as a check to innovations in religious teaching introduced by too zealous a vicar.'[8] In the non-provided schools, therefore, religious education was to accord with the schools' trust deeds, although there was a conscience clause which allowed pupils to opt out.

Financial responsibility for the maintenance of elementary schools was to be shared between the local authority and the government. Essentially, both non-provided and provided schools were to receive aid for the day-to-day running of the schools from local rates and central government money. Managers of non-provided schools were responsible for providing the school building and for major repairs. Grant provision was complicated and varied from authority to authority so that areas with a low rate income received commensurately more government aid.[9] This formula was of particular significance for Wales because it meant that non-provided schools, on average, received as much from government grant under the new system as they had subsisted on *in toto* previously. This allowed Lloyd George to claim that defiant Welsh local authorities were within the letter of the law in not providing such schools with any money from local rates because 'the new grants were at least equivalent to the combined total of the old grants and contributions from the rates as a whole'.[10] The Board of Education's refusal to accept this verdict prompted further legislation.

By the end of 1903, all the Welsh county councils, except Radnorshire and Breconshire which had 'sectarian' majorities, had refused, with varying degrees of enthusiasm, to furnish their full quota of rate aid and parliamentary grant to the non-provided schools. The most extreme reaction was in Carmarthenshire where, at first, there was resistance to any co-operation of any kind with the voluntary schools, including the payment of the parliamentary grant element of voluntary school revenue, though in the event parliamentary grant was never actually withheld.[11] Other authorities, such as Caernarfonshire, circumvented school managers and administered the voluntary schools in very similar manner to council schools, but solely on the basis of parliamentary grant. In March 1904, the county council elections saw opponents of the Act win a majority in every county in Wales. In some cases the majority was overwhelming, the most substantial (52–3) being in Merioneth.[12] With most of the councils not in practice providing rate money for the voluntary schools, the government was prompted to act. In August 1904, by virtue of the Education (Local Authority Default) Act, the Board of Education was given power to confirm in office, and deal directly with, the managers of those schools being denied rate aid, thereby bypassing local authorities. There was now a head-on confrontation between most of the Welsh local authorities and the central government. In October 1904, a convention was held in Cardiff at which the local authorities and the Free Churches of Wales were represented. The decision of that conference was that 'when the Default Act was applied, education authorities would refuse to maintain any elementary schools. Nonconformist parents of children at non-provided schools would then withdraw them and they would be educated, out of voluntary effort, in chapels and vestries.'[13]

Five Welsh local authorities were eventually deemed to be in default under the terms of the Act of 1904 – Merioneth, Montgomeryshire, Barry, Mountain Ash and Glamorgan.[14] The process was of particular significance in the north Wales rural counties because default in south Wales took place in the context of there being a substantial, even overwhelming, preponderance of provided schools. By contrast, twenty-seven voluntary schools existed in Merioneth and sixty-six in Montgomeryshire. Between 1902 and 1904 these two counties pursued slightly different policies in response to the 1902 Act. In Merioneth, government money was paid over to the managers of the voluntary schools but there was no further intervention in school affairs.[15] In Montgomeryshire, government money was similarly paid to the non-provided schools, though this was eventually made contingent upon a satisfactory response to demands for school buildings and maintenance being brought up to the required county standard, which was unattainable without further funds.

Board of Education papers survive for the two north Wales defaulting authorities and they provide a unique insight into an extraordinary 'cat and mouse' game. The scale and intricacy of default in the southern, industrial areas of Wales were relatively minor, though certainly in Barry politically sinister.[16] In Merioneth and Montgomeryshire the situation was far more complex and demonstrates graphically the lengths to which the central government was prepared to go to deal with defiance of the spirit of the law by locally elected representatives.

We have seen that the Default Act became law in August 1904. The county which had become the test case in Wales for those authorities not co-operating with the 1902 Act had been Carmarthenshire and it was in the wake of a public enquiry into that county's maladministration of the Act that the Default Act was passed. But Merioneth, too, along with some English authorities such as Cambridgeshire, had confronted the board with its central dilemma as soon as the 1902 Act was due to come into force. C. H. Wynn, a major landowner from Rhug, Corwen, wrote to the board in October 1903, asking for clarification as to the source of authority for action if the Merioneth local education authority moved to levy a rate to support only its provided schools.[17] Indeed, this letter was one of a number from interested parties in the Welsh counties seeking guidance as to what action to take in the face of neglect of their duty by the local authorities. Normal procedure at the board, when such advice was sought, was to send copies to the local authority. In this instance, there was no specific charge of neglect of duty as yet, though the board's officials felt constrained to answer the question. Lindsell, the principal assistant secretary at the board, accordingly drafted the outline of a reply. He suggested that it should

> state that section 7(1) of the Education Act 1902 requires that the L.E.A. shall maintain and keep efficient all P[ublic] E[lementary] schools within their area which are necessary. Section 16 of the same Act provides that if the L.E.A. fail to fulfil any of their duties under the Act the Board of Education 'may, after holding a public enquiry, make such order as they think necessary or profess for the purpose of compelling the authority to fulfil their duties, and any such order may be enforced by *mandamus*'. Before taking action under the last-named section on the grounds stated in your letter, the Board would require to have before them facts showing that the L.E.A. have failed in some specific case or cases to fulfil the duty of maintaining and keeping efficient necessary P.E. schools in their area.[18]

Lindsell's suggested reply was returned to Morant, now permanent secretary at the Board of Education. He agreed with its general tenor but wanted the reference to the threat of 'mandamus' deleted; indeed, he wanted the entire reference to section 16 of the 1902 Act left out.[19] Here was a thorny problem for the board. The Education Act of 1902 did provide redress for non-fulfilment of obligations laid at the door of the local authority, but the remedy of mandamus in response to a common-law writ was political dynamite because it provided for the extreme remedy of imprisonment. Morant's response is indicative of the weakness and inadequacy, from the board's point of view, of the enforcement mechanism of the 1902 Act. It required a public enquiry into each instance of non-enforcement of the Act, the issue of a writ and a draconian penalty. Before this letter was sent, on 9 December 1903, Merioneth County Council had, six days earlier, reaffirmed its policy formulated in June 1903 of refusing to levy a rate for the maintenance of the non-provided schools in the county until such schools were placed firmly under public control and all religious tests imposed on teachers abolished. However, all grants received from the Board of Education would be handed over to the managers.

Merioneth's policy soon began to affect the schools. On 10 December 1903 the managers of Llanfair National School requested advice on what they were to do in the light of the latest resolution of the county council.

They decline to support our school and we have no money to go on. Our teachers are unpaid and our stationery at an end. We have no coal. What are we to do? Are we to close the school? We cannot carry it on without books, paper or ink, and the teachers are clamouring for their stipends.[20]

The ominous message went to Lindsell that this was the beginning of the fray in Merioneth. The board's response had to be discussed at the highest level and, by February 1904, was transmitted to Merioneth County Council. Once more it had no teeth. It informed the council that the board had received correspondence from six National schools, Llanfair, Llanilltud, Tywyn, Tynant, Corwen, Glyndyfrdwy and Corris, indicating that the education committee was refusing to maintain non-provided public elementary schools in the county beyond paying over to them any parliamentary grant due under the 1902 Act. The council was informed of something it knew full well, namely, that under that Act all expenses, save those of managers' expenses, were the responsibility of the council. In the light of the council's refusal to meet the debts and liabilities of the non-provided schools at a level which would keep the schools at an efficient level of operation, 'the attitude of your Council raises issues of a grave character, and suggests that it should be reconsidered'.[21] There is then a tantalizing gap in the correspondence over the entire period which covers the passing of the Default Act in August 1904. Presumably Merioneth was to await the outcome of the public enquiry in Carmarthenshire. It is clear that the passing of the Default Act not only did not result in the county being prepared to conform, but may have prompted a more dynamic interventionist policy. The Merioneth Education Committee informed the board on 9 December 1904 that they were managing the non-provided schools of the county from the authority's office.[22]

The following month, the rector of Llanfair informed the board that the bank wanted repayment of an overdraft incurred by the managers of Llanfair National School. Where was the money going to come from? This request occasioned another top-level conference at the board, and another letter to the Merioneth authority. The council was given fourteen days to inform the board of its intentions towards the non-provided schools. The Merioneth reply was that, while they would consider the letter, the managers of Llanfair National School had failed to carry out repairs detailed in the architect's report, and extensive repairs were necessary. The board was now well aware that Merioneth would follow the well-worn tactic of enumerating deficiencies in the fabric of all the non-provided schools, but still prevaricated. In February 1905, the board informed the Merioneth Education Committee that, under the board's instructions, HM Inspector would investigate the claims of managers of certain voluntary schools in the county against the local authority in respect of maintenance of the schools. This merely prompted a reply in March 1905, relating to the National schools at Llanilltud, Ffestiniog, Llanfair, Bala and Tywyn. The Merioneth authority told the board that it [the Board of Education] was 'under mistaken views of the true meaning of the Education Act of 1902 and the Education (Defaulting Authorities) Act 1904'.[23] The authority maintained, yet again, that it was not in default of any obligations under the Acts because the managers of the relevant non-provided schools had not complied with requests to improve the fabric of the schools in response to the county surveyor's demands. Therefore, the board was wrong to suppose that managers of these schools who had incurred 'alleged' expenses had done so because of any action by the Education Committee.

Only at this stage did the board decide to use the legislative powers given to it under the Default Act passed seven months previously. On 31 March 1905, the board told the Merioneth Education Committee that it was not satisfied with the reasons which the authority had given for refusing to pay the managers. The board itself now proposed to refund to the managers those expenses which they had incurred up to 31 October 1904, and these payments were formally authorized by the president of the Board of Education, Lord Londonderry, on 6 April 1905. Merioneth's bluff had been called, since there was nothing to impede the relatively effective operation of the non-provided schools now that the Board of Education met their bills directly. Merioneth operated, to some extent, the 'Cardiff policy' of withdrawing pupils of Nonconformist affiliation from the non-provided schools and opening some emergency schools. But the county's room for manoeuvre with the central government was minimal. The only tactic now was to try to hamper the process by disputing every aspect of the board's actions. Four days later, H. Haydn Jones, an ironmonger from Tywyn, secretary of the Merioneth Education Committee (and later Liberal MP for Merioneth, 1910–45), protested that his committee was being dealt with unjustly because there had been no opportunity to object to the sums requested by the managers. This was, in any case, merely an attempt at delaying the inevitable and cut no ice with the officials of the board. However, the committee was provided with accounts of the payments made to twenty-five non-provided schools. The National school at Maentwrog, for example, received payments for the year to 31 October 1904 of £208 10s. 10d. for salaries, 6s. 4d. for stationery, £12 7s. 6d. for cleaning and £3 9s. 9d. for heating and lighting. The board could now afford to be dismissive of Merioneth's protests. When H. Haydn Jones continued to bombard the board with letters, R. P. Hills minuted to Morant that Jones 'may have some underlying motive, but the terms of this and of his other letters on the subject suggest to me that the reason is to be found in the disputatious tendencies of the writer, rather than in policies.'[24] Sir William Anson, parliamentary secretary at the Board of Education, and Morant, the permanent secretary, agreed that they should adhere to their policy of refusing to continue discussions any further with Merioneth. Morant was also quite prepared to sanction other ways of penalizing the local authority, though, once more, cautiously. The school outfitters and educational publishers, E. J. Arnold, had an exclusive contract with Merioneth Education Committee to supply school books and stationery. The decision to pay some of these schools direct was not to Arnold's liking and the firm wished to know from Morant whether their existing contract still covered the voluntary schools. The internal advice to Morant was that the firm should sound out legal opinion as to whether they could get damages from the local authority for breach of contract. Morant's reluctance mirrored the perennial concern about invoking legal sanctions against local authorities, though he suggested to Anson that this must be the advice the office would have to give to Arnold.

The other complication which arose – though hardly more than an irritant and reflecting rather sadly on a local authority outgunned by the batteries of the central government – was that some of the managers' expenditure vouchers had already been submitted to the local authority, and the authority now refused to yield them up to the Board of Education. H. Haydn Jones was writing frequently in the hope of stalling a little, though in effect merely irritating board officials. By June 1905 Jones had sent up some of the vouchers but by now he had exhausted board officials' patience. Anson and Morant accepted the recommendation of Lindsell that money should be paid out on the basis of bank slips. The local authority had nothing left but bluster: 'My committee feel that the recent delay involving the vouchers has had a valuable result in revealing to what length your Board is prepared to go in order to comply with the demands of the managers of non-provided schools.'[25]

Merioneth had, therefore, followed the conventional policy, advocated by Lloyd George and endorsed at national level, of handing over the government grant alone to the non-provided schools. They were not prepared to provide any rate finance until certain impossible conditions had been met. The Default Act had, however, checkmated Merioneth County Council. Indeed, it was particularly galling for all those Welsh authorities which had backed the 'no-rate' campaign. The Act now meant that, for those authorities found to be in default, rate money would in effect be going to the non-provided schools. Provided schools would receive money from local rates, but part of the central government subvention for these schools would be withheld to finance the voluntary schools. Any shortfall in the authority's schools' budgets would have to be made up by increased rate aid.

Such need not have been the case with Montgomeryshire, where the turn of events was more significant, certainly in the view of the Board of Education. The difference lay in the political configuration of the two county councils. Whereas Merioneth had an overwhelming preponderance of 'progressive' members, only three of the fifty-five being 'sectarian', Montgomeryshire had thirty-seven 'progressives' and nineteen 'sectarians'. Much of the anglicized east of the county, including Welshpool, was Tory territory with Powis and Wynn influence powerful. The passing of the Default Act in August 1904 was bound to meet with some response from the Welsh counties, though the complexities of the legal implications were manifold. We have seen that the Cardiff convention of 6 October 1904 had decided that if the Default Act were operated, then those local authorities affected would no longer maintain any elementary schools. Nonconformist children would be educated by voluntary means, and the Welsh National Council would raise money to make this possible. There had to be some action if any credibility were to be maintained for the Welsh revolt, and officials of the Board of Education were convinced that the Montgomeryshire situation allowed such a response. The Board of Education was informed that, at a meeting of the Montgomeryshire Education Committee on 17 July 1905, it had been decided, by a vote of twenty-nine to thirteen, not to transfer £2,779 8s. 7d. from the elementary education account to the Education Committee to pay the quarterly bill for the salaries of teachers working in the non-provided schools. This was a direct response to the board's threat that 'the Local Authority Default Act provides that the Board may pay to the managers of any public elementary school the amount of any expenses properly incurred for the purpose of maintaining and keeping efficient the school.'[26]

Montgomeryshire confirmed the amount owing to the teachers and, by order of the principal assistant secretary at the board, H. M. Lindsell, Montgomeryshire's unpaid teachers were paid direct on 24 July 1905. On 18 September 1905, the Education Committee discussed the notification from the board that salaries had been paid and the chairman indicated that he, along with the majority of the members, would withdraw from the Committee. Since the remaining six members present that day did not form a quorum, no further business could be transacted.

A week later, R. P. Hills, a barrister employed by the Board of Education to deal with issues arising out of the administration of the Education Act, sent a minute to Sir William Anson on the implications of the Montgomeryshire dispute. He thought that an offer from the Unionist MP for Montgomery District, Colonel Pryce-Jones, one of the rump of the Education Committee, to come to London with a 'prominent radical and nonconformist county councillor (who is an anti-Lloyd Georgite)' to discuss the affair should be taken up, since the board had also to consider when the teachers' salaries for the quarter ending in September 1905 should be paid. Additionally, at a meeting of Montgomeryshire County Council held immediately after the Education Committee had broken up, the full council rescinded all the powers of the Education Committee. Further, the rate proposed by the Finance Committee as necessary for the maintenance of elementary education was not voted.

It is clear from the minute that the board's officials were not certain at this stage what Montgomeryshire County Council's tactics were likely to be, despite the Cardiff resolution, but board officials were not as impressed by the political sophistication of the Montgomeryshire radicals as some in Wales who believed that here was a very clever move indeed. Hills suggested to Anson that it seemed likely that Montgomeryshire would now refuse to maintain both council and non-provided schools, though 'no notices have, so far as we know, yet been issued to teachers in council schools terminating their engagements'. The Education Committee still existed, since the Conservative members – and this made Montgomeryshire unique – were sufficient to form a quorum if they attended in a body. Hills went on:

> The only certain result seems to be that we shall have to pay a quarter's salary to each voluntary school teacher this October just as we did after July. But the question arises whether the Council mean to cease to maintain council schools as well as voluntary schools. Obviously it is quite possible that the whole proceeding is simply a more extensive, because a more elaborate, piece of bluff than anything we have yet experienced in Wales. While legally committing themselves to nothing, the county council have taken a number of steps which can easily be construed for practical purposes as definite measures with a view to complete defiance of government and the Education Act. This, it may be said, is all they intend to do. The case is in many ways the worst they could have to fight because it has hitherto been directed so directly against the teachers and the interference of the Board has so clearly been confined to acts of an entirely necessary character, viz. the prompt payment of teachers' salaries . . . On the other hand there can be no doubt that there is strong evidence of intention on the part of the county council to proceed, ultimately at least, to extremities.[27]

The analysis which went to Anson represented a major statement of board opinion about the situation in Wales. Montgomeryshire was held to be the ideal location for the operation of the 'Cardiff policy', according to which the local authority would refuse to maintain any elementary schools in the wake of the application of the Default Act. It contained large numbers of voluntary schools and few council schools (as the board continued to call them internally). Again, Hills was of the opinion that press and public platform pressure had been such that the leaders of the no-rate movement would now find it impossible to withdraw from entrenched positions.

> Further, there are rumours that considerable pressure has been brought to bear by the English nonconformists as well as by the more militant members of the Welsh no-rate party. The suspicion, made so much of by the unionist press, that the no-rate policy has been all along a farce and that the voluntary schools have been kept going by a surreptitious use of the rates have possibly stirred resentment in the former quarters.

Another reason which Hills gave for the possibility of confrontation was that the board had made it clear that it would not hesitate to use the Default Act and that its use was impending in 'Glamorganshire, Swansea, Carmarthen borough and Barry'. If the Cardiff resolution were not to be proved a complete farce, the no-rate party was obliged to do something 'to answer us'. But Hills was still not quite sure:

> the true explanation may be that the leaders of the no-rate policy still continue to be ignorant of what they mean to do and are only anxious not to be seeming to do nothing. Another more likely variation may be this, that they hope and believe that they will be able to avoid closing the council schools and, owing to the proximity of a general election, to save themselves, but are prepared ultimately to take the fatal step if they find the agitation in Wales getting out of hand or for any particular reason consider that it would be a useful stroke of policy, either for election purposes or for bringing pressure upon the next government to deal with Welsh education as a matter of urgency . . .

Again thinking in terms of the forthcoming election, Hills believed that the Montgomeryshire Council possibly had enough money to pay teachers in council-maintained schools for the Christmas quarter, which would mean that there would not be an actual failure to maintain these schools until April 1906. At that stage, the council could tap the resources of the Welsh National Council, raised largely by chapel collections, and by that means go on until the summer of 1906. What should the board's response be? If, argued Hills, the Montgomeryshire authority was bluffing, then the board need take no action. If, on the other hand, the authority did implement the Cardiff resolution and refused to maintain its provided schools, then the board had to decide on its response. The Default Act provided a way of maintaining the non-provided schools in spite of the local authority; how could the board cope with similar intransigence in relation to the local authority's own schools?

Hills dealt with the alternatives offered. The board could sit back and do nothing. Then, if the schools remained closed, the blame lay squarely on the county council and the no-rate party would experience the kind of bad publicity which they had so far avoided. Hills implied that the Welsh public had hitherto felt no real sense of injury or hardship from the activities of the 'no-rate' party. Only teachers and, in some isolated incidents, a few children had been affected. If all schools were closed then public opposition would be of a kind not yet faced. The difficulty was that this could be turned against the government, and although Hills did not mention an election at this point in his memorandum, it is obvious from earlier references that such thoughts could not have been far from his mind. The problem, he pointed out to Anson, was that the Default Act could not be used against the council's own maintained schools. His concern, therefore, was with the potential political embarrassment which this loophole in the Default Act might create:

> the contention might even be that the failure of government to provide a remedy in the face of failure to maintain a council school was an instance of error . . . if, therefore, the council schools were closed, clamour might arise that the government should provide for the education of the children in those schools.

Hills went on to rehearse the possibilities available for dealing with the situation. The first was to institute a public inquiry and a mandamus under section 16 of the 1902 Education Act, the procedure which had once presented itself for dealing with local authorities not meeting their obligations towards the voluntary schools. The plan was subject to the same limitation as in the former instance. The mandamus and contempt of court proceedings would end in imprisonment of councillors since, argued Hills, there was obviously no defence. The problem, he accepted, was the 'advisability' of imprisonment. The second option he considered was a mandamus without the use of proceedings for contempt of court. According to Hills, this option had been considered as a means of dealing with Carmarthenshire,

> but was not applicable because the default was intermittent, just paying sums from time to time which were just sufficient to maintain the schools. And an order of court could not go beyond a single default so that there had to be a fresh application for a *mandamus* every time a teacher failed to get his or her salary.

So Hills was driven to recommend his third, and preferred, alternative. This was to apply the Default Act. He admitted that it had not been decided whether the Act applied to council schools. The logistical difficulty thus followed, namely, that administration of the Default Act required compliant managers. Obviously in the former voluntary schools the managers were only too eager to co-operate, but how might such managers be secured in the council-maintained schools? Hills believed that precedents from other Welsh authorities might not apply to Montgomeryshire, where there was a 'fairly strong Church and unionist majority'. It might, therefore, be possible to find managers who would be prepared to co-operate in administering funds provided directly to the schools under the terms of the Default Act or, by that Act, to create amenable boards of managers through which payment could be made. So here was a senior civil service legal adviser advocating to Sir William Anson, the parliamentary secretary to the Board of Education, that it might be possible to find a few managers of local authority schools, appointed under the terms of the 1902 Education Act by the local authority, who might be persuaded to co-operate with the central government in defiance of the policy of that local authority; or else to use the Default Act to set up boards of managers by a procedure contrary to the 1902 Act and of dubious legality under the Default Act itself.

If all this went well, there was still the problem of how to recoup money from the County Council for expenditure which the board incurred in paying salaries and in maintaining buildings in the council schools. 'We do not', minuted Hills, 'for instance want to seize the county hall or its furniture if we can avoid it'. So the government department which had shied away from imprisonment of councillors now expressed reservations, in all seriousness, about seizing the seat of local government in Montgomeryshire! But there were other ways open to the central government:

> The obvious way would be to get at the money standing to the account of the council at the bank or any money accruing due to the council and in the hands of persons or bodies known to us. Our obvious resource . . . would be the various public departments who have control of money which is paid to the county council.

As if raising the possibility of seizing county council funds, presumably without any further legislation, were not enough, Hills proceeded to discuss the possibility of contacting the minority party and their leaders in the county.

> There are obviously matters in which they could supply us with useful information and with regard to which we could probably offer them advice which, if carried out, would materially assist us in dealing with the situation. If that situation is one which may develop and direct public opinion in England more than the Welsh revolt has hitherto done it will not be disloyal to take a good deal of time getting confidential information and other assistance from any persons in the district who would be willing to side with the cause of the proper administration of the law.

Here, then, was a policy being put forward at the highest level within the Board of Education which advocated confidential approaches to opposition parties in local government to concoct a policy to outmanoeuvre a properly elected local county council. Even Hills had the grace to contemplate an accusation of disloyalty, only to dismiss it. The reasons he gave for this dismissal are salutary. The Welsh Revolt had not so far had the most serious wider implications. What Hills now feared was that, if Montgomeryshire spearheaded a drive to refuse to administer council schools, and the government were forced to retaliate in the ways he suggested, then Welsh matters would assume a high profile in England, too. The maintenance of schools would have become a matter which involved the integrity of local government.

Unaware of the manoeuvres of the Board of Education, Liberal politicians in Wales were congratulating themselves on their ingenuity. Alderman T. J. Hughes, chairman of the Welsh national executive of the Liberal Party, was interviewed by the *South Wales Daily News* in September 1905.[28] He argued that the 'rump' of Tories left on the Education Committee in Montgomeryshire would doubtless 'amuse themselves' by recommending and conducting correspondence, but the county council comprised the Education Authority under the 1902 Act. He then suggested that it was highly unlikely that the Montgomeryshire Council would levy any rate for elementary education, either for its church schools or its provided schools. This was obviously meant to provoke the kind of confrontation for which the Board of Education was also planning. Hughes argued that, in the absence of a rate, there would inevitably be a financial deficiency in the council schools, since all due government funds had been earmarked for the substantial number of non-provided schools in the county. The government would therefore, according to Hughes, be forced into further legislation 'which will be itself a confession of abject failure' or else have to issue a mandamus to compel the county council to raise a rate. As we have seen, the Board of Education was considering the latter policy but by using existing legislation, the Default Act, rather than contemplating new legislation. There was one turn of events which the board had not contemplated:

> Meanwhile, I hope Montgomeryshire will adopt the converse of our Merionethshire policy, that is to say that so far from withdrawing our children from the church schools they will send our children into those schools, and so compel the enemy so to speak to feed our prisoners.

T. J. Hughes thus continued to fight the battle for non-sectarian education in Welsh schools, but to advocate sending Nonconformist children to Anglican schools must be considered an odd way of going about it. Here was a political, rather than a religious, strategy.

On 21 September 1905, the *South Wales Daily News* exulted in the sophisticated tactics of the Liberals on the Montgomeryshire Education Committee in withdrawing from the committee. In the process they have

> cast the whole responsibility for administering an unpopular and oppressive act upon the clerical party, which demanded and passed the act but while so doing they have in the second place rendered that party absolutely powerless to do any harm . . . the progressives of Montgomeryshire have simply served the clerical party with their own sauce, calling upon them to administer the act under impossible conditions . . . if they throw up their duties in disgust they will simply justify the whole Welsh revolt against the act.[29]

The 'educational expert' who wrote this, obviously one with Liberal sympathies, concluded that, while the Default Act had wrongfooted the Liberals in Merioneth by compelling council schools to earn grants which could then be confiscated for the benefit of the non-provided schools, in Montgomeryshire the Church schools' bill of £3,000, recently presented, could only be paid by the council levying a rate, something which their constituents would not allow them to do. The *Daily News*'s 'educational expert' guessed that Sir William Anson had about £1,000 in unpaid grant to meet the bill. But because the council schools were now placed on the same footing as the church schools in Montgomeryshire, that is they were not being maintained by the council, no more money would be available from that source. So, the analysis went, with no money in the education budget, no prospect of a further rate and no method by which the progressive party could be compelled to attend the meetings of the Education Committee, the only course open to the government would be to proceed with a writ of mandamus. This, as the columnist pointed out, the government had shied away from in the past, and in any case it could not become effective for some months. Readers were then excited with a wordy evocation of the veteran A. C. Humphreys-Owen's plight if mandamus were effected – 'carried on a sickbed at the head of his county council in procession . . . marshalled by police . . . to gaol, an excellent object lesson in Balfourian methods of government on the eve of a general election'. In the eyes of the educational expert, the Montgomeryshire campaign had checkmated the government.

But the Board of Education was, as we have seen, very far from losing the game. On 28 September 1905, R. P. Hills sanctioned a letter to Colonel Pryce-Jones MP and Richard Lloyd asking for a meeting to discuss the Montgomeryshire situation.[30] In October it was indeed confirmed that Montgomeryshire Education Committee had not paid the salaries of teachers in the voluntary schools for their last quarter's work; so the Board of Education proceeded to pay them under the Default Act.[31] Towards the end of October 1905, brinkmanship was taken further when Montgomeryshire County Council intimated that it would not receive the reports of the Education Committee, and the Education Committee proceeded to ask the board what it should do. Since these reports included requisitions for coal, the Board of Education inferred that the county council had virtually intimated that it was refusing to maintain its council and non-provided schools. Once more the board's officials had to face up to the implications of replying to Colonel Pryce-Jones, since the issue was now the applicability of the Default Act to council schools. Officials at the board were extremely cautious, but the potential of the situation was not lost on them:

> As long as teachers' salaries are being paid, and presumably they are, then presumably the schools will go on. The requisitions are mainly for fuel – if this is refused the C. C. are condemning all children attending the council schools to cruel suffering, an act which covers them in infamy even in the eyes of strong opponents of the act.[32]

This attitude reflected precisely what the Tories were now translating into propaganda in Wales. The Conservative *Western Mail* ran a headline, 'Starving the Children – Educational Anarchy in Montgomeryshire – Campaigning Committee to supply Fuel'.[33] The same day the Liberal *South Wales Daily News* reported that Conservatives on Montgomeryshire Education Committee were making capital out of the fact that children and teachers in council schools were to be seriously penalized for the sake of enabling the progressives to carry on the fight against the clerical party in the Board of Education.[34] The chief exponent of the art of highlighting the prospective heart-rending plight of Nonconformist children being faced with starvation during the winter months was the anti-Lloyd George Nonconformist, Richard Lloyd.

Thus, the first recommendation was merely to find out if the teachers were being paid. HMIs were to explore the situation at first hand. Discussion at a higher level also proceeded, if cautiously. On the matter of possible compliant managers in the council schools, Anson reckoned that only in the Welshpool schools, where Colonel Pryce-Jones and Richard Lloyd were managers, would there be consent to run the council schools on an emergency basis. Morant was even more cautious. In his opinion, as long as the schools were open and the children were being taught and cared for, no action was required. Anson endorsed this: indeed, his assessment was that the board had nothing to worry about. He reckoned that board money owing to the council schools was being paid to the voluntary schools as a result of the council's default. The money required to run the council schools was not being levied by rate, certainly, but was coming from the emergency fund set up by the Welsh councils. The Liberals could still claim that no rate aid was going to the non-provided schools either directly or indirectly. But, of course, in practice Welsh voluntary contributions were keeping open the two kinds of schools, which was perhaps even more of an indignity and, fortunately, one of which the Welsh Liberal public seems not to have been aware. As Anson minuted to Morant,

> What appears to be happening is this – the deduction which we shall make [under the Default Act] from the parliamentary grant in order to reimburse the managers of voluntary schools would under ordinary circumstances necessitate the raising of an additional rate for the council schools and thus rate aid circuitously but nonetheless really be given to voluntary schools. Instead of raising an additional rate what we require is to be provided out of the 'emergency' fund and so the rate party will be able to say that no rate is given to the voluntary schools directly or indirectly.[35]

No wonder the board felt constrained to do little for the moment, though Anson did want an opinion from the law officers on the wider applicability of the Default Act. In the meantime, the Default Act was used to pay salaries and other bills in the voluntary schools. It seems that it was at this point that Liberal councillors in Montgomeryshire shrank from the ultimate logic of their policies, with one Liberal member at least stating in November that the council schools would not suffer.[36] The Montgomeryshire revolt, sophisticated as it must have appeared in conception, therefore took the county council out of its depth. When the county confronted the implications of refusing to maintain all its schools, its elected members drew back. In the light of what Arthur Balfour, the prime minister, knew by this time both attitudes were irrelevant: on 4 December 1905 he resigned. The Liberal Party was shortly returned to power with a massive majority and the whole complexion of Welsh politics, including the politics of education, fundamentally changed.

Various aspects of the story of Welsh opposition to the Education Act of 1902 need to be stressed because they have more than immediate local relevance. The first is that the 1902 Act itself had no roots in the Welsh situation. It was a piece of legislation painted in the political colours of the English shires. Wales, as a mainly Liberal, Nonconformist country, was out of step with England and it was the needs of the greater neighbour which dominated. While Wales had a substantial Liberal vote to bolster the Liberal party at large, its outstanding politicians exercised a fragile influence. With the Tory party in power, the political realities condemned Wales to marginality. There can be no doubt that the school boards were working in Wales. They were well adapted to the flexibility required in a country growing at a phenomenal rate, at least in its industrial regions. They were able to provide, in due course, a growing range of elementary, higher elementary and evening education. They were democratic bodies, although naturally not immune from pressure-group politics. Particularly significant was the fact that they provided a way out of the religious complications associated with educational provision which had proved so contentious in 1870. From a Welsh perspective, the school boards provided the best solution to the problem of non-secondary education, while after 1889 there was a specifically Welsh solution to the desperate shortfall in secondary education provision. This provided a perfectly viable, flexible and positive alternative best suited to the political and social realities of Wales, especially if operating under the umbrella of some kind of national council. Of course, it was not to be. While developments in Wales meshed closely with its society, and organic growth, fertilized, it is true, by men like Hugh Owen, filled large gaps in the secondary and training systems, English concerns were that the church schools were tottering, school boards were fostering a system which was undermining perceived class structures, and county councils were at hand to exert some control along politically acceptable lines. The demands of the education systems of the two nations were never more clearly at odds; the political realities of the two countries meant that Wales had to be made to conform.

The second point of significance is the story of how that conformity was secured. Once the 1902 Act had been passed, the prospects of collision with Welsh local authorities were considerable. Certainly the possibilities of an accord with the Anglicans were explored, by Lloyd George in particular, but what is surprising is that they got as far as they did. It seems inevitable, given the religious affiliations of the Welsh, and the pattern of elementary school provision which so often (in the rural areas especially) did not accord with those affiliations, that confrontation should occur. The local government machinery whereby the campaign could be pursued had been created in the 1880s and 1890s. Here was the first major confrontation between that local government and the central government. With local authorities vested with substantial powers, clashes were inevitable. Here was the irony. Having created the school boards by legislation in 1870, the central government found that local democracy was getting out of hand, or getting out of step with the ruling party's priorities. Having invested other local bodies with more authority, some of them also soon threatened the London power-base. A long history of intermittent confrontation had begun. Lord Cawdor saw a long-term danger: 'the growth of the idea that Local Authorities can defy Acts of Parliament'.[37] By incorporating substantial responsibility for the maintenance of education facilities in the local authorities through their rates system, the government endowed these authorities with legal and financial powers – and potential sanctions – which echoed those of central government. Both sides proceeded to exploit their powers with increasing ingenuity. The Welsh authorities succeeded at first, but only in provoking the seeming knock-out blow of the Default Act. Yet Montgomeryshire, through the complex configuration of its local political representation, provided an opportunity for testing the Default Act to the limit. Here, because there were sufficient Conservatives to form a quorum on the Education Committee, the Liberal majority was able to obey the law in every respect, yet make the administration of all the schools unworkable. However, in making the county's own schools share some of the privations of the non-provided schools, and so placing the Board of Education in a dilemma, the Montgomeryshire Council was handing a propaganda weapon to the board and to hostile newspapers which, in the end it seems, restrained the council. Both local and central government responses were of far wider significance than the immediate crisis. What is striking is the range of weapons at the government's disposal in its dealings with local government and the determination with which these were deployed. The board considered using the Default Act in relation to the county council's own schools, it considered the imprisonment of council members, it postulated the confiscation of funds owed to the local authority by other government departments, and it actively encouraged confidential negotiations with local Tory politicians to plan a campaign against the democratically elected local majority. Both sides were not above seeing the privations of children under their care as a weapon in a propaganda war.

Finally, it should be noted that, however the Welsh Revolt was orchestrated, it was pursued earnestly and in a highly complex manner across the counties, with local variations and initiatives essential to it. Indeed, it was the unique situation in Montgomeryshire which posed the Board of Education with its biggest dilemma once the Default Act had been passed. It is notable that there were county councillors who were very reluctant to take on the government, given the array of sanctions available to it. It is equally notable that a central government department was apprehensive, in the light of a possible election, about the chance of English local authorities taking their cue from a policy formulated in Montgomeryshire. The Welsh Revolt was important inside and outside Wales at the time. In that it reveals much about the central government's determination to control the direction of educational change when fundamental issues of social engineering were at stake, it has a wider significance.

6
Those who can, teach:
the achievement of O. M. Edwards

When *Welsh Historian* started a series on major Welsh historians, the subject of the first article was O. M. Edwards (1858–1920), the second, John Edward Lloyd, fellow Welsh knight and doyen of twentieth-century writers of Welsh history.[1] Over a century ago Edwards became a fellow of Lincoln College, Oxford, over the head of J. E. Lloyd. But it was Lloyd, not Edwards, who produced the acknowledged masterpiece, in his *A History of Wales to the Edwardian Conquest*. John Davies's fine vignette in *Welsh Historian* tells us that 'alongside Lloyd's achievement, Owen M. Edwards's works are period pieces'. The *Writers of Wales* series has produced short biographies of some of Wales's literary giants, but as Hazel Davies remarks in her important book on Edwards (University of Wales Press, 1988), 'his voluminous writings do not parade as literary masterpieces'.[2]

So what is Edwards's fascination for historical and literary editors? Simply, he was the greatest teacher that modern Wales has produced. Hazel Davies homes in on many of the paradoxes in Edwards's life – the boy from the tiny tenant farm in Llanuwchllyn whose progress to an Oxford high table was nearly as dramatic in its way as Lloyd George's to Downing Street. And Edwards was at least as comfortable, impressing with his charm and conversation. Then, he spent most of the time between 1884 and 1907 in Oxford 'tutoring privileged students'[3] while working desperately hard to try to ensure the survival of Welsh-speaking communities of the kind in which he grew up. There is a central paradox about his teaching, too. His only regular teaching job was in Oxford and, although his ability to communicate brilliantly with children is well attested, he never taught full-time in a school. But the one point on which I would take issue with Hazel Davies is when she writes that Edwards as educationist was 'a pragmatist, not a philosophical thinker'.[4] Pragmatist, yes – and way ahead of his time in his advocacy of direct-method Welsh-language teaching, escape from the dictated notes which so often passed for history and geography teaching, and endorsement of what are now called in-service training and pupil profiles. But if we take a wider view of Edwards as teacher of children, of adults, of a nation, by means of a whole range of techniques, state schools, magazines, books, then that teaching is informed by a philosophy, or at least a theory of education, which is just as modern. He was no Plato; but the theory, and it was more than the rationalization of a teaching instinct, was there and it was in advance of its age.

It was not a theory of teaching for its own sake, nor was it held in isolation. Edwards believed passionately in Wales, at least his kind of Wales, and in the Welsh language. To preserve these he made some sacrifices. He could have written scholarly history if he had devoted himself to it. There is no doubt that his health suffered from his overwork and single-minded pursuit of this goal of teaching Wales to the Welsh. There is a unity of purpose, then, linking the littérateur, the popularizer of history and the indefatigable editor of periodicals, of which *Cymru* and *Cymru'r Plant* were immeasurably important. Like the contemporary Welsh Sunday schools, that purpose took in children and adults. It was a purpose which was informed by a theory of history and a theory of society, Welsh society; and it was backed up, eventually, by a unique job opportunity.

The theory of history, flying in the face of fashion, was simply that kings and queens and prime ministers were of less significance than ordinary people in the story of Wales. This did not stem from any Marxist notion of the working class being essential to the dialectic of history, but from personal experience and nationalist necessity. Edwards's upbringing – however idyllic and Wordsworthian the communion with nature and wildlife might have been in retrospect – was one of poverty and hardship. It coincided with the decades of political awakening in north Wales, when tenant farmers from his own county of Merioneth fought for, and won, basic democratic freedoms from entrenched landowning privilege. The circumstances of his early years, his personal achievement and his friendship with fellow patriots like Tom Ellis, who helped bring new visions of Welshness to his fellow countrymen, made Edwards's perception of Welsh history a plausible, even ennobling, one. It had two implications, both ahead of their time. First, ordinary people were worth finding out about, decades before historians started rescuing the working class from the 'enormous condescension of posterity'. Second, Welsh history had a purpose. It was no coincidence that J. E. Lloyd's *History* expired at the Edwardian conquest, because the quasi-independent state of Llywelyn Y Llyw Olaf expired with it. But if what mattered was the ordinary people, *y werin*, and Edwards's strange 'Whig interpretation' of Welsh history implied the progress to perfection of the *gwerin*, then Wales had a reasonable claim to being a chosen race and its recent past was worth taking seriously. Edwards did not spell this out – it was not part of his plan to – and in his own history of Wales he made fewer concessions to recent history than he might have done; but the implications were there for anyone who wished to take notice. And eventually, though admittedly under rather different influences, such ideas were to have a dramatic impact on the historiography of Wales and, by today, on the schools.

The theory of society, it follows, was an extension of Edwards's own circumstances and background. The true Wales was a land of Welsh-speakers, religious, serious-minded, cultured, educated farmers and craftsmen. It was far less the Wales of the frontier communities of the coalfields, a Wales of shopocracies, brass bands, accelerating English immigration and, underpinning it all, industry. There is no doubt that Edwards's attitude to industrial Wales was blinkered, both as historian and, more serious, educationist, though he was just as concerned to press the case for the teaching of metalwork and mining in industrial south Wales as to advocate the proper study of agriculture in rural areas. But the reasons for his obsession with the Wales of the countryside make him less culpable on this score than his critics would have it. Edwards was a soul-mate of John Ruskin (1819–1900), writer, artist, art critic and social critic. Hazel Davies, as at so many points in her short biography of Edwards, provides us with vital new information from Edwards's personal papers. Edwards had obtained Ruskin's permission in 1886 to translate three of his books into Welsh. She cites Ruskin's pinpoint response to Edwards's request: 'You have made me as proud as a peacock to find that there is some spirit left in Wales, not crushed out by manufactures and education.'[5] Here, then, is the clue to Edwards's attempts to work out practices integrating Welsh education with the society it was intended to serve; and just as Ruskin is now more fashionable, so Edwards has a lot to teach us still.

Ruskin bucked the trend of glorying in the industrial achievements of Victorian Britain and its unadulterated capitalist, profit-
maximizing ethic. He abhorred the creation of environments of grime
and ugliness which testified to the dominance of these values and
the exploitation of those whose labour created the wealth. His concern
was not that this was economic exploitation but that it meant degradation of the spirit. The spark of creativity, for Ruskin, lay in craft
labour, the ability to conceive of some artefact and to be in charge
of the process of its creation. This was the antithesis of the factory
division of labour. For Ruskin, appreciation of beauty could only
grow from the beauty of the environment. That quality lay in nature
or great art and architecture, the repositories of truth and morality
and feelings. It was this which made the creation of beautiful things
the ultimate fulfilment. Social justice, therefore, lay in providing the
opportunity for ordinary people to escape the mental as well as
physical imprisonment of appalling housing and working environments and poor education, and to have access to creative opportunity
and beauty. Now, whatever qualifications realists must make about
this altruism, however blinkered his historicism, Ruskin's concern
did not stem from condescension towards the working class, but
from what he perceived to be their vitality, that spark of creativity
which alone gave life a purpose.

O. M. Edwards's philosophy of society – and of education –
transplants Ruskin into a Welsh context. There were some slights
upon the industrial working class of south Wales as a result, but
they are not condescending. They could not have originated in a
more different way from those anti-working-class condescensions
all too typical of public school, classically educated, upper-middle-
class educational legislators of the second half of the nineteenth
century desperate to preserve the status quo in the face of economic
imperatives which required some spread of the educational net and,
consequently, some upward mobility. Such an attitude was all too
faithfully reflected in so many of the Board of Education's English
civil servants in the early years of the twentieth century. In the midst
of our growing apprehension since the 1980s over quite where
Victorian economic values are leading us, of concern for the environment, over worries about the effects of a diet of cultural pap, Ruskin
is read again. In these days, when as Welsh people we are wonder-
ing what we are and where we are going, O. M. Edwards's view of
Wales, especially how its social and educational systems integrate, is

as relevant a starting-point (though of course only that) as it ever was.

Ruskin's second telling reference in his letter to Edwards is to education. Edwards, of course, was to become one of Wales's most famous educational administrators – with a difference. The kind of education to which Ruskin referred, and in the context of which Edwards spent his years in school, was a reflection of what they felt industry was doing to the human spirit. It was the educational world of Mr M'Choakumchild, gradgrindery, another quenching of the divine spark. It was Bitzer's definition of the horse as a gramnivorous quadruped. It was facts, to be hammered in, to be tested and to be paid for by results for decades after the Robert Lowe philosophy of education ruled the land. It was about competition, the Samuel Smiles hurdles, the occasional route from poverty to success which Edwards exemplified, and which Palmerston, in the mid-nineteenth century, tried to deceive the British public was within everybody's grasp if they got on their mid-Victorian bikes.

Now, Ruskin, Dickens and O. M. Edwards did not have a monopoly of the truth. Good came out of the Victorian fascination with facts, the collection of which helped to translate a utilitarian philosophy into practical measures in sewerage, public health and schools. But the blasphemy of the gospel of fact, whether enshrined in the Central Welsh Board or any rigid examination system, is obvious enough. If M'Choakumchild quenches any manifestation of creativity, of the imagination, by a regime of facts and examinations, that is the ultimate treachery for children. Edwards's vision, as cultural nationalist and educator, elevated the instincts of the great teacher into a philosophy which informed his writing and his teaching and his administration of the schools of Wales. It is still relevant.

O. M. Edwards became chief inspector in the Welsh Department of the Board of Education from its creation in 1907. What gave all his activities a unity thereafter was that he could try to translate his various analyses of the nature of Welsh society and education into classroom practice.[6] The essential instruments were the teachers of Wales. He believed teachers to be important. This was no trite mouthing of cliché, because he drew attention particularly to the significance of elementary school teachers, at that time in occupations of low status, low salary and inferior qualifications compared with their county school counterparts. As writer and inspector, he took every opportunity to foster the teaching of the literature and language of Wales, its history and its geography, and to stress the organic relationship between them. He emphasized the link between education, including that in the intermediate/county schools, with the community and with the Welsh nation, its language, its crafts and its values as he perceived them. For Edwards, the campaign for metalwork rooms and carpentry workshops in Welsh schools was a moral crusade as well as a pragmatist's good sense.

His major confrontation was with the examining body of Wales, the Central Welsh Board. His contemporaries, and too many historians, missed the point here. The conventional wisdom has been that, because he tried for the job of chief inspector of the CWB in 1897 and did not get it, he pursued a vendetta against the CWB thereafter, especially when, from 1907, he was in a position to do so. Hazel Davies provides highly significant new information in that she demonstrates from Edwards's correspondence that he was particularly equivocal about the notion of returning to Wales at this time. Edwards certainly thought that the job had been fixed, and if this were the case he was not the last to be subject to the idiosyncrasies of academic appointments in Wales. But to personalize the subsequent confrontation, as some historians have done, often to the detriment of Owen Owen, the successful candidate, who did the job capably and for whom Edwards expressed 'the most profound admiration', is misleading. Certainly Edwards was often scathing about the CWB. But all this is to miss the point that if Edwards had become chief inspector of the Central Welsh Board he would have been sucked into an examining and inspecting regime in which he would not have had an iota of the flexibility which allowed him later, as chief inspector of the Welsh Department, to fight for more enlightened teaching methods right across the curriculum, perhaps especially in the language and history which were so central to his work, and to press the claims of the Welsh language and to integrate this into a far more holistic view of Welsh education and society. As it was, he could only make some inroads into the examination-dominated system in secondary schools.

O. M. Edwards was a prolific writer for adults and children in a new style and with a new content which ensured his success as a communicator; he was a unique popularizer of Welsh history; he was a courageous fighter for the educational causes in which he believed so passionately. All these would have made him interesting to know and important to evaluate. What makes him a central figure in Welsh educational history is that when he had to confront Welsh educational problems he did so not only with memoranda and circulars from the Board of Education and the Welsh Department but also, as Hazel Davies tells us in her incisive summing up of Edwards's career, with a sense of mission – 'like every pioneer and prophet, he had a dream . . .' It was O. M. Edwards's achievement that, whatever his failures, elements of that dream became reality, especially for the young people of Wales. That is the consolation for all teachers who care.

7

From intermediate to comprehensive education: a personal view

In the 1950s I was a pupil at Whitland Grammar School. In 1989 it was the only remaining state grammar school in Wales and it, too, is now reorganized into a comprehensive school. By the time I became a pupil there, the school was already more than half a century old. A tablet inset into its front wall records that it was built in 1896, along with some other of those establishments created by the Welsh Intermediate Education Act of 1889. The original building has withstood the weathering of years as if they had never been, at least it seemed to have done so when I last took the half-minute diversion off the main Carmarthen to Haverfordwest road to pay homage to a doubtless sentimentalized memory of schooldays. Indeed, that kind of sentiment to which we are all prone in matters of lost youth has been something of a force in moulding the collective fond folk-memory of communities for grammar schools and promoting adverse judgements of comprehensive schools.

At the time of my last visit the layout of the school had changed substantially since the 1950s, far more than in its first half-century. Apart from the tacked-on, prefabricated canteen-cum-hall, its first fifty years wrought few changes in the building – a single-storey sprawl, walls of a thickness which would not have disgraced a medieval castle, small-paned windows minimizing breakage damage, even if they were expensive to paint, and designed to ensure that pupils were forced, even when their attention wandered, to have their distraction contained by the classroom walls. No German bombs landed in Whitland – indeed it was evacuee country – but only a direct hit would have dislodged this masonry. The woodwork, too, must have been original – in days of seasoned timber why should it not have been? Certainly the large iron bolts with which the prefects secured the doors on the coldest of days against those younger pupils over whom they exercised their petty tyranny might have been designed by Telford to support the Menai Bridge.

The school building I knew encapsulated some nineteenth-century educational philosophies. Outside the bombed conurbations, the Welsh grammar schools had had no trouble in surviving. The layout of the classrooms and the corridors, the scale of provision of equipment, cloakrooms, staffroom and the like reflected an ethic of solidity and functionalism. Curricula and methods of teaching had not altered so much by the 1950s that the internal layout and scale of provision were dramatically anachronistic. There was no hint of the upheavals of the next decades.

The school in Whitland came into existence as an 'intermediate' school, a term included in the Aberdare Committee's terms of reference and incorporated into the famous 1889 Act. The stage of schooling to which it referred resembled more that christened 'secondary' by the Taunton Committee in 1866 to denote a level between elementary and public school education than anything which appeared to provide a link between elementary and university education.[1] And, for the most part, the Welsh intermediate schools were at the lower end of this 'secondary' spectrum, brought into being so reluctantly to reach the parts which endowments could not reach.

That these schools had the right to 'secondary' status is indicated by the fact that they charged fees for all but some scholarship holders. These fees were relatively low but they were an essential means of defining the scope and function of the schools. Indeed, the scale of the fees sheds much light on our interpretation of this word 'intermediate'. The celebration in 1989 of the centenary of an example of unique legislation is entirely appropriate, but it should not blind us to the low status of the proposed creations in contemporary esteem, nor their reflection of a poor and relatively backward society, hampered, it appeared to so many, by the Welsh language. Ironically, partial remedy required something distinctively Welsh, and a recognition of Welsh needs by a Westminster government. In some ways it was a minor miracle, since it extracted money from the Treasury to help finance a Welsh post-elementary system. In doing this, it breached a basic premise of Victorian attitudes to educational provision. By the last quarter of the nineteenth century it was acknowledged that it was the responsibility of the state to ensure that all children were educated to a minimal level and, where absolutely necessary, free or nearly so. This was done as an act of charity; the relief of ignorance resembled the relief of poverty. Conditions in the free elementary schools were intended to provide a level of education inferior to anything which had to be paid for. It was the crime of the school boards in the 1880s to provide a higher elementary education beginning to overlap with that which was available on the market. Any degree of education which aspired to minister to the needs of the lower middle class, or even to the skilled, the respectable, working class, needed to be demarcated by fees. A proper education was one which was paid for, and the best cost the most. That is what, in Victorian England and eventually in Wales, gave it its respectability, its worth and its status. In the Adam Smith society of Victorian Britain how could it have been otherwise?[2]

Notions of self-help, respectability and market forces meshed with practical considerations. There had long been a link between education and franchise reform. John Stuart Mill, when struggling to adapt a theory of utilitarianism to principles of democratic participation in the affairs of the state was faced with a central dilemma. Whatever the prejudices of male-dominated, wealth-dominated Victorian Britain, the philosophy of utilitarianism propelled him in the direction of 'one person one vote', towards the notion of a stake in the state's decision-making for all but those who, for example, were in receipt of charity from the state rather than contributing to it. But the concomitant would be, feared Mill that, because the working class were in a majority, their interests as a group would always prevail.[3] This might be mitigated by providing more than one vote for those either with property or with education. The latter notion informed our thinking for a remarkably long time, given that dual votes for university graduates were last exercised in the election of 1945. The extension of the franchise in the nineteenth century raised questions about levels of education. Where was the educational provision in Wales for many of those respectable, partly propertied male householders, in borough and county, enfranchised in 1867 and 1884?

The appropriate layer of education was missing in Wales. The three commissions of the 1850s and 1860s, Clarendon, Taunton and Newcastle, make it quite clear which schools served which section of society and how they were demarcated. It is equally clear from the Taunton Commission (1864–6) that the structure for educating the middle class was intended to reflect the different strata within that class: there should be three types of school to meet the demands and purchasing power of a class which encompassed those not far removed from skilled artisan to minor landowners. The élite among the Welsh landowning gentry had sent their sons to the great English public schools since the sixteenth century and would not have contemplated such provision in Wales. The thought of a Welsh Eton was an absurdity. Indeed a Welsh Clifton or Shrewsbury was hardly conceivable.[4] There were foundation schools but these were few, relatively poor, compared with their English counterparts and far removed from the main centres of population in the nineteenth century.[5] Crucially, there was an insufficient segment of lower-middle-class clients who could conjure up some fees, yet were not in a position to purchase something socially superior. Hugh Owen and his Aberdare Committee fellows wished to fill this vacuum with schools which provided an education suitable for the children of lower-middle-class and tenant-farmer parents. But here was an odd concept, falling between the philosophies of charity for the poor through the elementary schools, and the basic free-market principle which regulated the provision of secondary education at the level appropriate to the individual purse and which, alone, gave worth and respectability and status to education at various levels between the poorer grammar schools and Eton. The Welsh schools under the 1889 Act fell uneasily into neither category, with their revenues, substantially, an act of charitable subvention from the Treasury together with the product of local effort, the more respectable philosophy of Samuel Smiles in action. At the same time it was inconceivable that any schools which had any pretensions to being for the production of a middle class, be it ever so humble, should be anything other than fee-paying. The answer was to charge low fees, with some scholarships being made available. In that the Welsh schools lay somewhere between charity-based concepts of elementary education and the individual free-market philosophy, they were indeed intermediate. The schools founded under the Welsh Intermediate Education Act were hybrids which existed uneasily for some years, especially as the smaller schools in Wales found it difficult to attract children whose parents were not at all convinced of the economic value of such an education. Yet the intermediate schools were intended for a social stratum above that catered for in the elementary schools. As Samuel Butler, one-time headmaster of Shrewsbury, wrote of the early-nineteenth-century grammar schools:

> there was no exclusion either of the highest or lowest . . . but common-sense evidently points out that the lowest classes would not wish in many cases to bring up their children to liberal professions; and if they had this laudable ambition, would not be able, in many instances, even

when their children had completed their school education, to support them at the universities, or place them out in liberal professions in life.[6]

Butler would have been bemused by the Welsh intermediate schools but Welsh acquiescence in the prescribed social order would have landed 'intermediate' parents with many fewer dilemmas. One of the constant problems of the intermediate schools was the problem of early leaving, as the poverty of Welsh parents in rural and industrial areas manifested itself in the need for the extra wage which could be brought in between the statutory leaving age of fourteen (or even twelve in some circumstances up to 1914) and the age for taking the all-important School Certificate examination at age sixteen. However important practically and symbolically, the Intermediate Education Act of 1889 provided an education system for an intermediate society, an intermediate people.

Whitland intermediate school, like the others in Wales, had formed part of the Carmarthenshire county scheme, so was a county school, and remained so until the 1940s. The county base was reinforced as the joint education committees of 1889 were rendered redundant by the 1902 Education Act which made the county and county borough councils the local education authorities. With that Act, the intermediate schools were drawn into a wider system, as the 1902 Education Act allowed the local authorities to create secondary schools across England and Wales. Carmarthenshire County Council had no need to augment intermediate school provision with municipal secondary schools, like some urban areas of Wales, especially in Glamorgan, Swansea, Cardiff and Merthyr but, eventually, a much more homogeneous system of state secondary education emerged across England and Wales, held together by a common syllabus, laid down by the state for four years after 1904 and bearing an uncanny resemblance to the core and foundation subjects of the national curriculum of the 1988 Act, and the necessity to train pupils for the common qualification of what, after 1917, was called the School Certificate.

So things continued both in wartime and peacetime, in the tragic prosperity of wartime, through the grim rewards of peace in the Wales of the late 1920s and the 1930s. Doubtless Whitland County School, small, quiet, respectable, serving an area dominated by farm and mart and railway, was less affected by the disastrous economic fluctuations of the areas of primary industry, but the knock-on effect of depressed demand affecting the whole range of products in the agricultural areas in school and in the community was a fundamental one. In one study of a rural area in Wales it was found that between 1920 and 1950, 110 people aged between fifteen and thirty left the area because their education gave them job opportunities not available locally.[7] They were individuals whose education had fitted them to leave, to take their talents elsewhere, very often to England. The exodus was even more marked in industrial Wales where a secondary education was yet more highly prized as a means of escape from the depredations of the Depression. This was hardly the stuff of which O. M. Edwards's dreams were made, this diaspora induced by the county schools. Of the sixty leavers from Penygroes county school in Caernarfonshire in 1938, twenty-six went to England – to London, Birmingham, Nottingham, Stafford, Manchester and Burton.[8] Teachers lamented that Welsh chapels were opening in Coventry rather than Cardiff. This was not surprising. The kind of jobs for which the Welsh county schools equipped their products in the inter-war years were not available in Wales – not in the rural areas, with their relatively simple economic organization, nor in Depression-ridden industrial Wales. The community problems arising from the existence of schools such as that in Whitland were recognized in a Departmental Committee Report of 1930.[9] In that year the estimates were that only 19 per cent of boys leaving secondary schools went into farming, 22 per cent took up jobs in industry, building trades and commerce, 21 per cent clerical jobs in the civil service, offices and banks and 16 per cent found work in shops. The professions, and the most significant one was teaching, took 13 per cent of boys and 27 per cent of girls. The report concluded that the majority of pupils from rural Wales left their home communities, although 25 per cent of girls stayed at home after their county school days. Given a similar exodus from industrial Wales due to the Depression, the scale of the social change being wrought in rural and urban communities becomes apparent. The whole purpose of these county schools in the education hierarchy of the day was to produce that solid layer of lower-middle-class professionals who would provide a solid, reliable stratum between the manual workers from the elementary schools, the hewers of wood and the drawers of water as contemporary education reports had it, the 'pedestrians' as they were labelled in the Ministry of Education in the 1950s, and the upper reaches of the governing classes who reflected something of

Baldwin's boast of the substantial numbers of old Harrovians in his first cabinet, almost equalled by the former Etonians. Neither the top schools nor the top jobs existed in Wales. If some might count this a comfort, what was far more serious, from a Welsh viewpoint, was that the kinds of jobs for which the county schools, rural and urban, fitted their pupils were not available in anything like the requisite quantities in Wales either. It has often been fashionable to question the humanistic orientation of the county schools, and their grammar-school successors. Wales was the land of teachers and preachers, peculiarly ill-fitted, it is said, to capitalize on the second and third industrial/technological revolutions. Certainly, the products of the secondary system were destined mainly to take up position either in front of or behind desks. But in the inter-war years it was a very good thing that they were. It was not the county schools which should be blamed for failing to transform the Welsh industrial base. If they had churned out technologists and scientists by the score they would still have ended up in Coventry and the London end of the A40 corridor. They would hardly have revolutionized the Welsh economy by starting electrical industries in Penygroes and Whitland and car manufacturing in the Rhondda valleys. The expanding economy of the United Kingdom in the 1920s, with average earnings going up in real terms by 30 per cent, passed Wales by because it was channelled into new industries which did not depend on those primary nineteenth-century natural endowments which had centred the first industrial revolution on areas like south Wales. The story now was Morris Motors, Boots, Home and Colonial, Pye radios, suburban semis, modest extension of state and local bureaucracies, especially in education. It is no wonder that the Welsh county schools provided teachers and clerks in abundance. It might still be seen as something of a tragedy that those nineteenth-century higher elementary schools were nipped in the bud by Morant and his political sponsors. It would not have made much difference to Wales: off to England the scientists and the technologists and the technicians would have gone. They are still going.[10]

Not a vast amount had changed for many of the products of these schools in the 1950s and 1960s. Of my contemporaries in the sixth form of Whitland Grammar School in the 1950s I can think of very few who live anywhere near the town now. Via university I went off to Croydon to my first teaching post, in common with many another native of Wales. I did not leave from choice but because the first job which anyone offered me was in the south-east of England. It was also the case that in my first year of teaching I was given an O-level class, and A-level and Scholarship work in my subject. My chances of such opportunities in Wales would have been virtually nil. I well remember the advertisements in the *Western Mail* which carried the implicit message 'teaching up to Ordinary level, if you are lucky'. The head of department did all the O- and A-level teaching. He (a lot less frequently she) had been around in the same school for donkeys' years teaching the lower forms and, at last, the elevation had come, promotion internally on death or retirement. At last the chance to do some of the high-status stuff and let the new graduate get on with the lower work. It was an attitude built in to the Welsh system, moulded by the small size of so many of the schools through the decades and, indeed, into the post-Second World War period, and by hierarchies which seemed more entrenched in egalitarian Wales than class-dominated England. So, following in the footsteps of previous generations, off to Croydon I went, teaching history to loquacious young gentlemen from south-eastern suburbs who, while not making Whitgift, the public school just down the road and a cut above us, had passed the eleven-plus and were destined, many of them, for university or apprentice yuppiedom in the City or investigative reporting teams on the *Sunday Times*. I heard far more Welsh spoken in Croydon than I hear in Gower. I joined the Croydon Welsh society, not quite in the class of the London Welsh, but the entertainment was better because it was organized and conducted with an enthusiasm bordering on the frenetic and a talent close to genius by another Welsh teacher far from his roots, Ryan Davies. I have no reason to suppose that my experience differed in essence from that of vast numbers of Welsh people through the Depression years, into the post-war population expansion and the economic prosperity of the 1960s. This is what was happening to so many of the products of the Welsh grammar-school system, something which can hardly have been close to the hearts of the early pioneers, though it is difficult to know whether many would have grieved over it. Probably Lord Aberdare, Viscount Emlyn and the Revd Prebendary H. G. Robinson et al. would have exulted.

To return to matters of organization, the school which made possible such career patterns had been rechristened by the time I was a pupil there. It was a grammar school now, not a county school, within a different educational structure. The 1944 Education Act, hailed as one of the key elements in the new order of the post-war welfare state, changed names but not much else in the Welsh county schools. In Whitland, the grammar school was filled by pupils who passed the dreaded eleven-plus, according to some preordained number, the rest being the also-rans, their prospects blighted at a tender age. The social sieve worked as effectively after 1944 as before, though parents no longer had to pay fees.[11] Whitland Grammar School survived and expanded. But the base from which it expanded had its limitations. The education with its taught and hidden curriculum (though the latter expression had not as far as we knew been invented) on offer in the first half-century of the school's existence was a valued one. It was available to the fortunate few in schools whose teachers were pillars of the community, graduates, well-paid, people of standing often with egalitarian principles within the different hierarchies of which they were a part and into which they were training their charges to go. They organized eisteddfodau and administered rugby fixtures and prefect systems. To do this they wore gowns, most potent symbol of educational apartheid. That was the face which Whitland presented to the world.

It was not what His Majesty's Inspectors of Schools saw in 1949.[12] They saw too many staff qualified in the same subject, Latin, and too few adequately qualified in the various subjects they were supposed to teach. They saw a restricted curriculum, taught with inadequate facilities. They saw, though probably did not use, primitive outside toilets, as well as an extremely cold gymnasium stuck out in the school yard (they were right about that), changing rooms without any facilities for washing after PT or games lessons, inadequate dining rooms and virtually no cloakroom space. The general verdict on my school, not so many years before I became a pupil there, was that this educational pearl in the west Carmarthenshire countryside was a pretty somnolent establishment. And yet, some cautions here for the educational researcher: the frank opinions of HMI provide some of the richest material for comprehending conditions within the county/grammar/comprehensive schools of Wales. One of the strongest criticisms of Whitland Grammar School in 1949 was that the accommodation for the sixth form was ludicrously inadequate. It was. It consisted then, as it did in my day, of one small room which could seat comfortably fewer than a dozen people. Ours was a small sixth form – four A-level historians in my year – but if the scientists had not stuck in their laboratories there might well have been an action replay of the Black Hole of Calcutta. And yet, access to that room could hardly have been a more prized privilege. Hierarchy was entrenched even at our level. We were a select group, having passed a minimum of five O-levels before we were allowed access to A-level courses. Here, in this sleepy rural community, observing still many of the immemorial rhythms of agrarian society, were these incongruous academic hurdles for the youthful population to jump at the ages of eleven and sixteen: the latter, O-level, imposed on a reluctant Ministry of Education by headmasters who wanted to preserve the exclusivity of their sixth forms.[13] They succeeded. We were exclusive; that tiny room was the symbol. That room could hardly evoke more memories if it had been of the dimensions of the floor of the United Nations. We listened there, the French class, to scratched recordings of Baudelaire's poetry on a clapped-out wind-up gramophone with steel needles ripping out the plastic of a 78 as it produced a degree of wow and flutter which would defy classification nowadays. In that room were plotted the downfall of Carmarthen Grammar School's rugby team (though not Gwendraeth's), the casting of the school play, the course of the love-life of all and sundry, including the RE mistress straight out of university, and assignations for Carmarthen's Drill Hall on Saturday night. The HMI report mentions none of this.

My old school had survived the war, the transformation from county school and the far from complimentary HMI report unscathed. It became quite cosmopolitan as a result of the 1944 Act and the transport system. Every morning (except when that prayed-for snow fell) fleets of buses disgorged scarcely willing pupils from the surrounding farms, almost all Welsh, the Proof and Experimental Establishment in Pendine (almost all English) and those strange beings all the way from Carmarthen, fifteen miles away, who for some reason which we hardly fathomed, did not go to their own grammar schools. A few came, as their predecessors had done for decades, all the way from Cardigan on the Cardi-bach. Again we had no idea why. The extent of the cross-border disputes and compromises between the counties of Carmarthenshire, Pembrokeshire and Cardiganshire, necessitated by the great difficulties after the 1944 Act of trying to impose an educationally viable tripartite system on rural areas, are only now becoming apparent. We were conscious that somehow the whole thing meant problems for neighbouring Narberth, another of the oldest batch of intermediate schools in Wales.

Seven miles away from Whitland, it came under a different authority, Pembrokeshire, and met a very different fate. Carmarthenshire's
development plan,[14] called for under the 1944 Education Act,
stipulated that the Whitland district be served by a two-form-entry
grammar school in Whitland and a three-form-entry rural modern
school in St Clears. As far as the Welsh Department of the Board of
Education was concerned this was fine because Whitland Grammar
School would take the 'grammar-type' pupils from Narberth. This
had all been decided by 1948.

The Welsh Department's endorsement of Whitland's continued
existence was made easy because of Pembrokeshire's decision to
change the nature of the Narberth secondary school.[15] This school
was to be transformed into an eleven to fifteen age-range secondary
modern school. Narberth and neighbourhood were not impressed.
Here was one of those sad situations affecting a school which enjoyed
considerable popular support and had an honourable history, but
was difficult to deal with under the 1944 Education Act. Pembrokeshire had its fair share of problems. The Welsh Department was
at a loss as to what to do with St David's county school, for example,
with its annual intake of sixty pupils. By all Ministry logic it should
have been converted into a secondary modern school too, and the
grammar pupils sent to Fishguard. But logic could not always prevail
when there were local authorities, parents and popular sentiment to
contend with. St David's ended up as a bilateral grammar/secondary
modern school. This left the St David's school, even in 1956, with
a grammar stream of 33 per cent of the intake, so that there could
be a class of twenty-eight to thirty pupils, along with two secondary-
modern streams. As the Welsh Department noted, this was not very
sound educationally – that is, given the Government's policies that
there must be strict segregation between pupils of the 'grammar
type' and others.

The snag for the Welsh Department and HMI was that the situation pertaining in Narberth, not alone in rural Wales, was very similar
to that in St David's. Over the period 1951 to 1955 the selection rate
for Narberth Grammar School was over 40 per cent. Why? Not for
any egalitarian reasons, nor the intrinsically greater ability of Narberth pupils to pass the eleven-plus. It was not because Narberth
pupils were over four times more intelligent than pupils in Gateshead
(though they would want to argue the case), but just because there

was no secondary modern school nearby. The local HMI was scathing: 'A two-form entry mixed grammar modern would need to be staffed by a genius of a headmaster and an appropriate number of assistant geniuses if it were . . . to do educational justice to the pupils.' So the Welsh Department endorsed Pembrokeshire's plan for dispatching Narberth's grammar pupils to Whitland, Preseli, Haverfordwest and a few to Tenby. The reverberations of the ensuing dispute preceded Narberth's pupils to Whitland Grammar School.

Certainly the pupils of Whitland Grammar School had as much idea as the governors of Narberth Grammar School that the latter were only being summoned to a meeting with the Welsh Department of the Ministry of Education 'in the interests of good relations'. Poor Narberth's delegation turned up to put a case in terms of transport costs, and the traditions of the school, parental support for the grammar school and community feeling. The Narberth bilateral school which they wanted, would be larger than the St David's bilateral being allowed by the Ministry. This made no difference. On 17 April 1956 the fate of Narberth Grammar School was finally sealed, amid acrimonious exchanges between chairman of governors Idris Williams and director of education, D. T. Jones, Whitland Grammar School profited.

Twelve years after the Butler Act, the system of secondary education around my school was beginning to sort itself out. I doubt if any of the staff, let alone pupils, realized that post-1944 reorganization involving the Whitland school created ripples which spread across the three counties of Carmarthenshire, Cardiganshire and Pembrokeshire, involving calculations of allocations of pupils to schools in Narberth, Haverfordwest, Tenby and Fishguard and, most important, to that showpiece school, the centre of a more ideological debate over multilateralism – the Preseli school in Crymych.

I think we were equally unaware as pupils that we were pawns in a game of social engineering as overt as any in history. In this we were in direct line of succession to those proud scholarship-winners who had gone to the school in its previous incarnation as an intermediate or county school. We were, unselfconsciously, I hope, the 'grammar-school types' so regularly referred to in Ministry of Education documents after 1944, the offspring of government reports from Hadow (1926) through Spens (1938) to Norwood (1943), the last of which so confidently, and so unscientifically declaimed that at the age of eleven it was possible to divide pupils into those who spent their days dreaming up abstract ideas, those who thought technical thoughts and those whose cast of mind was a concrete one. It was a very good thing that so few pupils in Whitland were troubled by technology since there was nowhere for them to indulge their fantasies. Perhaps the nearest properly equipped technical school was in Coventry. So we all fell, perforce, into two categories, though we did not fully realize the implications. Those of us who had been identified as capable of abstract thoughts, thoughts of dubious worth in actually running any aspect of the local economy like its farms, or its railway, or its milk factory, nevertheless had access to subjects inherited from medieval times, begowned masters and mistresses, the smartish school uniform of navy and black, quartered red and black cap set off by a lamb and flag badge which associated us not with some local pub but with the medieval monastery which is still, with Hywel Dda, Whitland's main claim to fame. It tied us in to an examination which, if negotiated successfully, led to the sixth form, thence to another examination and perhaps to university or to training college and out of those communities which had given shape and succour to our existence – the youth clubs, the chapels, the cricket teams, the friends – and all with the community's blessing.

Much of Wales had wanted to go for a multilateral, partly comprehensive system of education after the Second World War, but was denied by its political and civil service masters in Westminster and Whitehall. West Wales did not, but because of its small, diffused communities, various compromises within the western counties and between types of school organization were forced on councils and the Welsh Department of the Ministry of Education. For nine and more years from the time these counties submitted their plans for implementing the 1944 Education Act, central Government grappled with reconciling the constraints of population density in rural Wales, the requirements of secondary education for all laid down in the Butler Act and the private consensus among the civil servants that demarcation between different types of secondary provision was essential.[16] Hardly had the files been closed on the changes stemming from the 1944 Act before the whole system was in the melting pot once more. The Labour government came to power in 1964, determined to implement a policy similar to that which it had endorsed before the Second World War. England and Wales were to become nations of comprehensive schools. This was to happen at the same time as external factors were changing the schools anyway.

Chief among these were the increase in the numbers of the school population – a combination of increased birth rate and a dramatic decline in infant mortality – and the tendency of pupils to remain in school beyond the compulsory school-leaving age, helped by the greater prosperity of the late 1950s and 1960s and the so-reluctant lowering of those examination barriers which had once been intended to ensure the pristine exclusivity of the sixth form. Schools were forced to expand and were made to think about reorganizing. Directors still reeling from directives (in the form of suggestions) from the Welsh Department of the Ministry of Education were now, with Anthony Crosland's Circular 10/65, forced to think again. By this time, it is true, central government had lost some control over the local authorities, which forced Crosland to permit a variety of comprehensive schemes in his circular, a few of which involved dubious interpretations of the term 'comprehensive'. Some authorities, like Glamorgan which, after the war, had proposed radical schemes for secondary reorganization, now took a long time to go comprehensive. The Welsh pattern still managed to emerge rather differently from that in England; Wales became a nation of large, eleven-to-eighteen comprehensive schools.[17] It was the only pattern which made much sense, and still necessitated some grim marriages of convenience between schools on different sites. In many rural areas there were particular difficulties, complicated by growing demands for secondary education to be made available through the Welsh language. Some authorities, like Carmarthenshire, then Dyfed, found it very difficult to convert to a comprehensive system. There were some ironies. Because rural Wales had found it so difficult to provide viable bipartite schemes following the 1944 Act, there was a considerable over-representation of comprehensive schools in Wales in 1964. Thirty-six of the 195 comprehensive schools in England and Wales were in Wales. Crosland's circular still took some time to have much effect, though 47 per cent of Welsh pupils were in comprehensive schools in 1969. The change in the next decade was dramatic as that number climbed to 96 per cent. By 1979 there were only five grammar schools left in Wales. One was Whitland. It has taken another ten years to devise a way for it to go comprehensive, this last, longest-lived of those schools created in the wake of the Intermediate Education Act of 1889.

It has been argued that if Julius Caesar had returned to Britain in

1750 he would not have been too disorientated but, postponing his visit a hundred years, would have thought himself on another planet. If the late-nineteenth-century founding fathers of Welsh secondary education had turned up in Whitland Grammar School in the 1950s, they would not have taken too long to catch up with developments. If they returned now they would be bemused when confronted with the acronymic nightmare of the educational system. Once they had got to grips with the more exotic combinations of the alphabet which comprise educational newspeak, they might struggle with some of the historical ironies within the system they inaugurated. Whitland, like its peer schools, was originally intended to provide an opportunity for fee-payers and some scholarship holders to be separated out from the elementary schools and given a chance to climb at least a few rungs of the career ladder, into the ranks of the lower middle class. Governments clung to the notion of the intrinsic worth of a paid-for education. The social climate is held to have changed with the Second World War. Fees were abolished: the middle class profited most. Ostensibly there was parity of esteem for the over-elevens in their different types of school, but the eleven-plus was now quietly made to take over as the segregating device, tacitly endorsed by the Labour government of the day, its enormous significance reinforced by a unit cost ratio of two to one in favour of the grammar schools.[18] As had always been the case, the superior schools kept their badges, school uniforms, prefect systems, sixth forms, Saturday morning rugby, graduate teachers, different teacher unions and, underpinning all, a different kind of curriculum, an academic curriculum for the 'grammar-type of child'. Any infringement of those curricular distinctions, like those suggested, from rather different standpoints, by Percy Watkins in the 1920s or the National Union of Labour Teachers for much of the inter-war period, or that unacknowledged Welsh educationalist W. G. Cove throughout his career, were violently opposed by the educational establishment, politicians and especially civil servants.[19] Now, a hundred years on from a famous Act, it matters not what the school in Whitland calls itself, nor what its internal organization consists of.[20] A Conservative government is in the process of ensuring that it teaches within the same curricular framework as every other state school in Wales and very nearly the same curriculum as every state school in England. Differentiation of subjects of study has been one of the most pervasive devices for school classification over the last century. With the advent of the

National Curriculum, less subtle hallmarks of superiority will be evident, resting on that competitive ethic so close to middle-class Victorian hearts. For those who delight in the caprices of history, it is a good time to have a centenary.

8
Fifty years of secondary education in Wales, 1934–1984

The story of secondary education in Wales in these years can conveniently be divided chronologically, even if such periodization is artificial. The first two spans must be the years from 1934 to 1939, and the war years. There would be more controversy about the longer periods of 1945 to 1963/65 and 1965 to 1979. However, in 1963 the headquarters of the permanent secretary of the Welsh education office moved to Cardiff while 1965 saw the issue of the circular which symbolizes the change to a comprehensive school system. The year 1979 saw a change of government and a change of direction.

In 1934 Wales had a system of secondary education which had been inaugurated at the turn of the century. As a result of the Welsh Intermediate Education Act of 1889 a network of ninety-five secondary schools had been established by 1902 and this constituted a state system since nearly half the money came from the Treasury. Since government money was involved there had to be a means of inspection and, to this end, the Central Welsh Board was set up in 1896. The new system was remarkably homogeneous since the old endowed schools were largely subsumed under the intermediate schemes. The 'public school' sector was, and has remained, far less significant in Wales than in England.

Organizational homogeneity was rudely shattered in 1902 when the Education Act of that year empowered local education authorities to establish secondary schools. Reflecting current class prejudices of the 1890s and after, substantial secondary school provision for the industrial working class had been deemed inappropriate so that the intermediate schools in Glamorgan and Monmouthshire served absurdly large populations. The pent-up demand was met by municipal schools established under the 1902 Act. In 1907 a dual system of administration complicated matters even further. The Welsh Department of the Board of Education was established in London and opposed any CWB pretensions to speak for secondary education in Wales. This was particularly true during the early days when A. T. Davies, as permanent secretary, was pathologically prone to massage his own ego. The result was an uneasy truce punctuated by bickering, petulance and outright anger, though by the 1930s relations were far easier.[1]

Three more items of background information are necessary to set the 1930s in perspective. First, in 1917, a uniform examination system was inaugurated across England and Wales consisting of the School Certificate, as it came to be known, and the Higher School Certificate. Second, in 1926 the Hadow Report came up with reorganization plans for the elementary sector which had implications for the secondary. It opted for a break at the age of eleven and a variety of post-eleven options, including modern and central schools. Third, the twenties and the thirties, especially the years after 1926, were years of terrible economic depression in Wales. In industrial south Wales in 1929 unemployment was down on previous years – it was running at 20 per cent.[2] A year later it was 31.2 per cent, two years after that 37.2 per cent. There were yet greater localized disasters. In 1930 unemployment in Newport was 34.7 per cent. In 1935 in Merthyr 47.5 per cent of the insured population were out of work. In such circumstances the reorganization of post-eleven education could proceed only slowly.

Industrial depression and rural poverty were not the only reasons why Hadow-type reorganization was slow. There were directors of education, like W. J. Williams in Cardiff, who did not see the necessity for it.[3] But the relationship between secondary provision and the society which saw the need for it before the Second World War was in a constant state of complex tension. The concept of the selective central school, not precluded from taking pupils up to matriculation, was seen as a threat by staffs of county schools. More clearly in hindsight, it was nonsense in much of rural Wales, with its scattered population, to bring pupils daunting distances to two types of post-eleven school. So, a concept not unknown in the 1920s to the Labour Party, the TUC and the NUT – that of the multilateral school – impinged on officialdom in the Welsh Department of the Board of Education. The permanent secretary, in all innocence, suggested that it would be logical to bring all pupils from rural Wales into one secondary school. And if this were to be the pattern for rural Wales it might also be allowed in industrial Wales. There would be a common curriculum for the first two years, then internal selection.[4]

Of course Wales did not get its common secondary schools. The genuine curricular problems which might have resulted were scarcely mentioned. They were as nothing compared with the potential subversion of the existing order, carefully constructed to contain aspirations for upward mobility within strict limits. Working-class pressures could not be thwarted completely in the British system and a freeplace system was gradually extended. But even depression-ridden, marginal Wales could not be allowed to undermine a differential school structure carefully demarcated by a different school-leaving age, differently qualified staff, a different curriculum and, underpinning all, receiving a different level of funding. It cost twice as much to educate a pupil in a secondary school as in an elementary school. In response to the Welsh initiative the president of the Board of Education was informed by his officials that it was not the Board's job to 'satisfy aspirations however praiseworthy, but to recognise facts and take account of real needs . . . the hard facts . . . are that a majority of the pupils over 11 will leave school at 15+ and get their further education by contact with life.'[5]

We have now delineated the main features of the secondary system in Wales in the 1930s. It was distinctively national, in the sense that it was administratively different from that in England. In 1939 there were 103 schools administered under the 1889 Act, forty-two under the 1902 Act. There was only a small direct-grant and independent sector. The secondary school was for the minority, though it was a considerably larger minority than in England, with, in 1938, some 23 per cent of eleven-year-olds admitted. The proportion had always been high in rural Wales. Ironically the ravages of the Depression, the exodus of population, especially those with young families, had lifted the proportion in industrial Wales too. The schools were still fee-paying and capacity to pay was determined by a means test from 1932. Such was the scale of poverty in Wales that over 64 per cent of pupils in 1939 were receiving their education free. Nearly 90 per cent of pupils came in on special places, having earned those places rather than bought them, while 95.5 per cent of them, 20 per cent more than in England, came up from the elementary schools.[6] The schools were, then, far more democratic than their English counterparts yet, in training for university entrance and black-coat occupations, they provided an exclusive education. Perhaps, as in Scotland, there is a paradox here which grows out of rapid nineteenth-century industrialization in Wales.[7] Industrialization occurred in a poor but communally relatively stable rural society. Rapid industrialization created an influential middle class whose needs dominated the creation of the state secondary system in 1889. The secondary schools did not, in such a society, educate only the middle class, but they were modelled on the English public schools which did. For some time the paradoxes, along with the class lines of industrialized society, were blurred by liberal Nonconformity, but they emerge clearly in the end and, at the centre of them, stands the stratified school system, the selective secondary school. The Welsh system, like the Scottish, produced an élite and that élite helped perpetuate the system in its own image.

Increasingly in the 1930s pressures grew for modification of the system and the multilateral school was favoured by involved pressure groups. The Labour Party was committed to it, for example, and prominent among the party's spokesmen was W. G. Cove, former teacher, former president of the NUT and one of the union's sponsored MPs who sat for Aberavon.[8]

The case for the multilateral school was put forcefully to the Spens Committee which reported in 1938. All agreed that it was the only sane method of providing secondary education in the most rural areas. In Anglesey the education committee informed the Welsh Department of the Board of Education as early as September 1936 of their commitment to providing practical, technical and academic education for all the island's senior children in four multilateral secondary schools.[9]

The Spens Report of 1938 came out in favour of a tripartite system of secondary education, with multilateralism accorded experimental status. The editor of the *Welsh Secondary Schools Review* commented:

> The 'parity' between all forms of post-primary education and the proposed existence of three different types of schools has been shown by many to be illusory. What of the psychological needs of the child . . .? Now one of the strongest instincts in a child – and in a parent – is the desire to be treated the same as his fellows: the sense of justice, if you will, or 'parity' again from another angle. How is this profound urge to be met by compulsorily drafting children into three different types of schools as the result of an entrance examination?[10]

Even the Spens prescription was, however, too much for the government who, with the refrain of decades, pleaded poverty. On the day appointed for the raising of the school-leaving age to fifteen, Hitler invaded Poland.

There is no shortage of models by which to gauge the effect of war and there is general agreement on such features as disruption and reconstruction. Disruption of the secondary-school system came in three main forms – destruction, evacuation and enlistment of staff, although building projects such as that for Swansea Grammar School were also held up. Physical destruction was relatively minor in Wales compared with the English conurbations, though there was considerable damage in Swansea and Cardiff. Evacuation caused more problems in Wales because most of the country was a reception area for evacuees coming from Liverpool, London and the Midlands. Secondary refugees provoked few complaints of lack of personal hygiene but they placed strains on the school system. Often there were in effect two schools at work in the same building, one in the morning, one in the afternoon. Examinations were held and the labours of teachers were heroic. They were particularly meritorious in view of the seriously depleted staffs resulting from service in the armed forces. Many schools lost virtually all their male staff, and science subjects, especially, suffered badly.[11] Retired teachers and married women teachers filled the breach, although the Cardiff authority deigned to employ married women only when instructed to by the Board of Education as late as 1943. At least their position was recognized in the 1944 Education Act. War had at least brought about this measure of social change.

Other consequences of the war may have had incalculable long-term effects. Sex education in Glamorgan was given by visiting members of the Welsh Council of the Alliance of Honour. Their secretary wrote to the Neath authority:

> We regret that the lessons that we give in your schools . . . have been greatly interrupted recently by air-raid warnings. In some cases the course has had to be left incomplete; and in other cases lessons have been broken off at a moment when the teachers have been dealing with the most delicate aspects of sex relationships.[12]

Social change did result from the war, partly consequent upon at least a marginally greater sense of equality brought about by shared

danger and equality of sacrifice, partly due to a sharper perception
of the iniquities of the Depression. Earlier than in the First World
War thoughts turned to the better society. The 1944 Education Act
and the Beveridge Report had something in common. In July 1941
a great politician, R. A. Butler, was appointed to the Board of Education as president. Soon a Green Paper was distributed in what has
been called a blaze of secrecy. This was followed by a White Paper
in 1943 and the Education Act of 1944. There were two significant
changes for Wales resulting from that Act, the change in the school
system and the change in the inspection and examination of that
system.

As Butler, with acumen and finesse, reconciled the various pressure groups as they trooped in delegation after delegation to his
office, he had some peculiarly Welsh problems to deal with.[13] The
problem of the precise way in which secondary education might be
organized was not mentioned. The main concern of delegations from
Wales harked back to the old Wales and had little to do with the
new. Indeed this might be said of the Butler Act generally. Prisoners
of the Whig interpretation of educational history, we have been
schooled to regard the 1944 Act as one of those good deeds which
stand out in a naughty world – and of course it gave legislative force
to much that was best about the old system, something which had
been rejected time and again in a prewar society dominated by
financial crisis, Conservative governments and old-fashioned fiscal
orthodoxy. However, Butler's outstanding abilities in the run-up to
the Bill were predominantly devoted to what were essentially –
especially in retrospect – old-fashioned rivalries. Just as the voluntary
organizations – essentially the Roman Catholic and Anglican churches
– had been instrumental in delaying plans for reform in 1929, so
now, once more, they were apprehensive about the financial implications of reorganization, the secularization which would result and
their own loss of influence. Butler's compromise of voluntary
controlled and voluntary aided schools was the solution. In Wales
it prompted reflex reactions recalling a dying, if glorious, past.
The last educational gasp of Nonconformist Wales made its impact
on Butler because of the legally peculiar position of the Welsh
intermediate schools. Under the new order they would technically
be voluntary schools, precisely that category manufactured to allow
denominational religious teaching.

In practice, as Butler pointed out, very few Welsh schools had the endowments to allow for voluntary status in the long term but any suggestion of denominational religious teaching generated apprehension in Wales with its significant Nonconformist establishment. Such concerns indicate that Butler's balm had to be applied to wounds opened up in the nineteenth century. In fact the administrative changes proceeded with ease. The halfpenny rate of the 1889 Act was legislated out of existence in the 1944 Act and, between 1945 and 1947, most of the former intermediate schools were absorbed into the new system.[14]

In other respects the Butler Act may be seen as consolidating rather than inaugurating. The Act made no stipulation as to the pattern of secondary schools but precisely because of this the pressures to endorse what was essentially the status quo were irresistible. The post-war pattern was foreshadowed by the Hadow Report of 1926. The multilateral model had been fully considered by Spens in 1938. Six years later, whatever the impact of war, the essential plank of dividing children into different categories at the age of eleven was as firm as ever. Again, the move to raise the school-leaving age was chiefly remarkable in that this time it actually came about in 1947.

In other ways the 1944 Act merely brought England into line with trends in Wales. Under the 1944 Act secondary education was to be free. This was of course a signal advance, though it must be remembered that it was the middle classes, who had previously had to pay fees, who benefited most. They now obtained an exclusive, that is grammar-school, education free for their offspring. This privileged education could no longer be bought and this too represented progress. But it is interesting that even in 1938 poverty dictated that in Wales 64.2 per cent of pupils in the state secondary schools obtained their education free and no fewer than 88.9 per cent entered on special places, which meant success in a competitive examination.[15]

To question the scale of change wrought by the Butler Act in Wales is not to deny that there were important implications. The Welsh Intermediate Education Act was finally superseded in the wake of the 1944 Act. There was no place for the CWB as an inspecting body. The former was of symbolic significance, testifying to the recognition of Welsh distinctiveness in the later nineteenth century. It was legislation which grew out of a successful, prosperous, politically important Wales. The school system to which it gave birth was integrated with that of England after 1944. The CWB had a chequered history, locked for much of the time in unproductive conflict with the Welsh Department of the Board of Education. But, in the absence of a national council, it was the nearest thing which Wales had to a representative, democratic educational body and it was responsible for a socially significant sector of the education system. Under the 1944 Act a Welsh Advisory Council was to be set up – nominated, of course. Butler was not to know that precisely such a body had been mooted in 1913 to destroy the influence of the Central Welsh Board.[16]

Under Section 11 of the 1944 Education Act and Circular 1 of the Ministry of Education local authorities were required to submit development plans for their areas but none was able to do so in the twelve months allotted.[17] Even by the end of 1947 three local authorities had not submitted full plans. The difficulties facing them were formidable. Some authorities had done little to reorganize along Hadow lines, so making the task of secondary reorganization the more difficult. Cardiff, for example, had made very little attempt to replace its all-age elementary schools.[18] Breconshire reorganization had taken place only in Defynnog and Crickhowell.[19] Now there was the complicating factor of the commitment to raise the school-leaving age to fifteen in 1947.

The Welsh situation was distinctive in that very high proportions of pupils in some counties were already going to secondary grammar schools, as they must now be termed. The proportion varied between 33 per cent and 45 per cent in districts of Breconshire; it was over 30 per cent in Montgomeryshire. Already special provision had to be made for lower-ability pupils because School Certificate work was not appropriate for them.[20]

Despite a situation in Wales in which far higher proportions transferred to the secondary sector before the war, and the potential this offered for imaginative response, the thinking of directors of education, then more powerful than now, was conditioned by the Spens and Norwood Reports, both of which had little to say about Wales. Diversity, or division, of secondary provision was central to both these reports. So, in county after county, reorganization plans based on prewar Hadow thinking were developed. In Newtown and Welshpool the Montgomeryshire Education Committee was so wedded to the notion of maintaining grammar-school education that it insisted on converting the four grammar schools in the towns into secondary modern schools and establishing a new grammar school, divorced from both communities, at a midway point. This was in preference to establishing bilateral schools in both centres of population. It was this latter solution which was favoured by both Newtown and Welshpool councils as well as by the parents. The defence of the county education committee in face of considerable protest is revealing: 'The only place in the county where separate Grammar School provision could be made was the Newtown/Welshpool area . . . two separate grammar schools were not practicable. The only solution therefore would appear to be a Grammar School midway between the two towns . . .' This, of course, was just not true. The rest of this rural county was, perforce, being given bilateral schools. Newtown and Welshpool merely asked for similar provision which, they argued, would provide free interchange of pupils and safeguard them from errors of selection. Further, 'bilateral schools create a healthy democratic community'.[21]

The two decades after the war, then, saw the establishment and consolidation of the tripartite system in much of Wales. The period is, indeed, perhaps best dubbed the 'Raleigh bicycle' era, a time when an increasingly affluent Wales could afford to reward successful offspring richly for their success in surmounting the eleven-plus barrier. In industrial south Wales and, more remarkably, in much of rural Wales – Breconshire and Carmarthenshire, for example, the grammar/secondary modern system became firmly entrenched. Welsh grammar schools continued to take a far higher proportion of pupils than their English counterparts, but this meant the relative neglect of the secondary modern sector.

It is only fair to point out that, in the short term, the logic of prewar reorganization, where it had begun, implied a system of small schools using existing buildings. The first priorities were roofs over heads and attempts to bring down the number of senior pupils in all-age schools. In 1949 about one-third of pupils aged thirteen were in grammar schools, one-third in secondary modern schools and one-third in all-age schools.[22] By 1950 the percentage of pupils in all-age schools was down to 22.5 and this compared with 17.7 in England. The extent of the tripartite hold is evident in the 1951 figures: 54,725 pupils in secondary modern schools, 51,802 in grammar schools, 3,474 in technical schools and 5,183 in bilateral schools.[23] By 1961 there was evidence of some change. In that year there were 88,172 pupils in secondary modern schools, 58,324 in grammar schools and 19,053 in comprehensive schools. There were still 5,107 senior pupils in all-age schools.[24] Yet even this degree of change puts into odd perspective the recommendation of the Central Advisory Council (Wales) in 1947 that Welsh secondary schools should be either multilateral or bilateral, and the official reaction to circular 10/65 that 'no Welsh authority expressed opposition to the comprehensive principle'.[25]

If the distinctive administrative structure of Welsh secondary education disappeared in the wake of the 1944 Act and the tripartite system of secondary education became as firmly entrenched in Wales as it did in England, do we mean to speak of anything other than secondary education in Wales in the postwar period? Just as nationality does not depend on political independence, so an educational system can reflect national characteristics without having a distinctive administrative structure. At the same time there are inevitably many common features between education systems in the industrialized developed world and these are the inevitable concomitants of the economic resources and characteristics of these countries. When such countries – as with Wales and England – share a common central government then the common factors are likely to be most important ones, shaped by common economic and demographic trends.

We are driven, then, to look at the influences which shaped secondary education in England and Wales as a whole in the two decades after the war. First, as far as the organization of the system was concerned, the pressures of the Ministry of Education – civil service and politicians – were towards the tripartite system. By 1955 there were only fifteen comprehensive schools in England and Wales, of which Anglesey boasted a fair proportion. Second, provision was affected by the duo of bulge and trend. The bulge aptly christens the rocketing birth rate, maintained, with fluctuations, long after the immediate postwar period. The trend, that tendency of pupils increasingly to stay on in school after the statutory leaving age, was an accentuation of a milder movement of the thirties. Third, an examination system sharply demarcated the grammar-school sector from the secondary modern, at least until pressure from the secondary modern schools resulted in both the take-up of O-Level examinations and the inauguration of the Certificate of Secondary Education, although that did not get under way until 1965. The institution of this dual examination at sixteen-plus had an incalculable impact. Most significant, it enforced a perpetuation of the secondary modern/ grammar school divide whatever the outward organization of the school. It immediately gave rise to a debate which has not yet been settled. It is salutary now to recall that the examination system was not God-given. In fact it was as ad hoc as so much which has moulded our education system. There is a temptation for the educational historian to compare the O- and A-level system with the School and Higher Certificates which had held sway since 1917. This is misleading since one of the major functions of the prewar School Certificate was to act as a university entrance examination, university matriculation, for those pupils successful at credit level. With the increasing trend in the later 1930s for pupils to stay at secondary school for a sixth-form education, School Certificate became less central in the system.

In 1946 the Ministry of Education reconstituted the Secondary Schools Examination Council.[26] Then, as now, this represented central government control over the shape of education. The Ministry intended that the School Certificate should be phased out and that there should be no external examination before the age of seventeen or eighteen. This was opposed by a minority of the SSEC who argued that external examining was required to maintain sixth-form standards, and the Ministry compromised by proposing the General Certificate of Education. There was a lower age-limit for the examination of sixteen-plus, that is one year over the statutory school-leaving age, and the limit was expected to rise. That hallmark of our examination system, O level, was completely unplanned. Once the examination came into existence the Secondary Schools Examination Council successfully defended it. The Secretary of the Association of Education Committees, Sir William Alexander, led those who saw that the use of O level was not extended. Alexander was also highly influential in securing the eventual adoption of the Certificate of Secondary Education as, basically, a national school-leaving examination. Here again the motives were by no means purely educational and the outcome by no means predestined.[27] That examination system which dominates so much of the work of the secondary school was the brain-child of no more than pressure-group rivalries.

Fourth, at least the second ten years of the two decades after the war were a time of unprecedented prosperity. The 'swinging sixties' were no accident and economic growth, whatever its philistine concomitants, produced a mood of optimism which is perhaps indicated in current manifestations of nostalgia. Such a mood was evident in education. There was growth – there had to be in order to provide roofs over heads and teachers in front of classes; but there was more. In the mid-1950s the share of gross national product expended on education was 3.2 per cent, in the mid-1960s 5 per cent and still rising. Partly responsible for this was a more intangible optimism that education could change society. There was curriculum reform and innovation, a Schools Council and compensatory programmes.

Fifth, connected with educational growth, increased prosperity and a vision of a better society came the accumulation of data coupled with blueprints for action in the form of a series of crucial government reports. In 1954 a report of the Advisory Council on 'Early Leaving' advocated the payment of maintenance allowances for pupils staying on beyond the age of fifteen. In 1959 the Crowther Report advocated a twenty-year programme whereby half our pupils would stay in full-time education to the age of eighteen. In 1963 the Newsom Report, *Half our Future*, advocated the raising of the school-leaving age to 16 and a special programme for the last year of schooling. In 1967, wholly in the spirit of previous reports, committees under the chairmanship of Lady Plowden and Professor Gittins advocated the expansion of nursery education and priority area designation. The common thread in the reports is the stress on social deprivation, and educational researchers reinforced the message that attainment was closely correlated with social background. They catalogued the disadvantages which working-class pupils had to overcome before they could take advantage of the opportunities now theoretically open to them. It seemed that inequality of opportunity remained the hallmark of the secondary system; the difference in the 1950s and 1960s was that educationalists, particularly teachers, thought something could be done about it.

Wales, as part of the United Kingdom, shared in increased prosperity, in educational debate and in implementing new policies. As we have seen, in essence the English and Welsh secondary systems coincided to a greater extent than ever. As early as 1947 the pattern was clear in Wales – 147 grammar schools, twenty-four technical schools and 127 secondary modern or unreorganized schools. The social implications of these figures are readily apparent when we examine the career destinations of the pupils. Of those pupils who left the secondary modern and all-age schools in Wales in 1947, one went to university compared with 826 from the grammar schools. Into home employment, agriculture, mining and manufacturing went 4,713 pupils from the secondary modern and unreorganized schools, 1,295 from grammar schools. Into clerical and professional posts went 722 from the former type of school, 2,277 from grammar schools. The schools were fulfilling their traditional social function of providing personnel for the blue-collar and black-coat jobs in precisely the way in which the elementary and secondary schools had done throughout the century.[28]

By the 1960s these general trends were apparent in Wales. The proportion of pupils staying on beyond the statutory leaving age in 1953 was 34.4 per cent in Wales. This was higher than in any region of England except, by a small margin, the metropolitan area of London and Middlesex. It even exceeded that of the affluent south-east of England, while the comparable figure for the north-west of England was 21.8 per cent. The Welsh figure had increased to 42.9 per cent in 1961, proof enough of the 'trend'. What is significant is that areas of England, including the south and south-east, had now overtaken Wales. So the legacy of advantage passed on from the old county/municipal secondary schools, particularly the high proportion of grammar-school places, was steadily eroded after the Second World War. Given a common system, the affluent regions caught up with Wales despite their lower proportion of grammar-school places. In 1953, 5 per cent of Welsh pupils stayed in school to the age of eighteen, virtually double the proportion in any region of England. By 1959 the figure in Wales had risen to 6.2 per cent but the south and south-east of England, at least, were now catching up fast.[29]

By the mid-1960s a signal change had occurred in the organization of secondary education in Wales. By 1964 there were fewer grammar schools (109), far more secondary modern schools (233) as reorganization of all-age schools had taken place virtually everywhere, and five technical schools. Yet because of the bulge there were over 5,000 more pupils in grammar schools than in 1947, over 2,000 *fewer* in technical schools, while the secondary modern sector now comprised 87,224 when in 1947 there had been only 28,330 pupils in secondary modern schools or senior classes of unreorganized schools. The comprehensive-school sector was more substantial than in all but one English region. Of the 195 comprehensive schools in England and Wales in 1964 there were 76 in London and Middlesex and 36 in Wales.[30] Even so, the hold of the tripartite system was tenacious. There were still, in 1964, four times as many pupils in secondary modern schools as in comprehensive schools. Indeed, the situation in Wales in 1964 was not dissimilar to that in a rural region like the south-west of England. Here there were 21 comprehensive schools compared with 36 in Wales; 305 secondary modern schools compared with Wales's 233.

I have argued that the Welsh and English systems tended to coalesce organizationally after the Second World War. This was because the English regions came to reflect the best pre-war features of the Welsh system – selection by merit, free places – under the legislative impact of the 1944 Act and because the underlying powerful trends at work in both countries were similar – economic prosperity, the tendency to stay beyond the statutory leaving age, the increased birth rate. But it was also because Welsh local authorities chose to opt for a tripartite scheme when a multilateral scheme would have made more sense, and commanded widespread support among headteachers and many of their staffs. While in no way minimizing the practical problems, the predilections of local politicians, local officers or parents, the history of Welsh school organization in the two decades after the war does testify to the influence not of legislation but to the administrative and financial hold of central government depart- ments and the civil service. It is fashionable to contrast the central- izing elements of the 1980s with a more healthy partnership model of the post-war years. The case of Wales brings into question notions of substantial local autonomy in rosier days. The difference was one of style not substance.

Some difference of emphasis, of course, remained. Shadows of the past were evident in the fewer pupils who acquired a technical educa- tion in Wales compared with any English region. Then, the direct- grant sector was by far the smallest in Britain, with only four such schools in Wales compared with twenty-one in the south-west of England, for example.[31] There were three times as many pupils in direct grant schools in that English region least well endowed with such schools, the east midlands, as there were in Wales. Wales had fewer pupils in independent schools than any English region and the Ministry of Education found in 1948 that most pupils in Welsh independent schools came from England.[32] The Welsh system remained more democratic, more the prerogative of talent alone than the English.

If, in the light of history, it is impossible to ascribe this to any inherent virtue in the Welsh it does testify to a less class-ridden society.

The year 1965 inaugurated a decade in which, in the words of the historians of the economics of education, 'the pressure for expansion of education continues, largely of its own momentum . . . but the room for manœuvre has disappeared, since the rate of economic growth has fallen, and the pressure on resources . . . has increased'.[33] How dated even these words now seem. The pendulum which had swung towards innovation and experiment was to swing back by the mid-1970s. The psychological adjustment to the realization that Britain was a second-division economic and political force led to a demand for scapegoats. Always to hand for this role is education because nobody can prove the case one way or the other. But this was only part of the explanation, as a similar cycle occurred in America.

In 1970 Mrs Thatcher's Circular 10/70 reversed Anthony Crosland's of 1965. But the movement towards comprehensive secondary schooling was inexorable. By 1979 Wales was virtually a country of comprehensive schools, with 96 per cent of pupils attending such schools, 13 per cent more than in England. The comparable figure for 1969 was 47 per cent. By 1979 it became easy to reel off the grammar schools left in Wales – Whitland, Gwendraeth, Llandysul, Abersychan and West Monmouthshire. And the comprehensive system was almost dramatically homogeneous in the light of the variety of options listed in Circular 10/65. 184 of the 244 schools were eleven-to-eighteen all-through comprehensives. One of the corollaries was – and is – that Wales is a country of large schools – in 1977/8 14 per cent of secondary schools in Wales had more than 1,500 pupils compared with 5 per cent in England.[34] The 1970s, then, saw an increased number of pupils being educated in fewer schools.

Such changes took place in a wider political setting and highlight again questions about the distinctiveness of the Welsh secondary system. It became increasingly clear that the 1979 change of government was a watershed in the history of education as in so much else. In Wales it was preceded by the devolution referendum, summing up a Welshness which puts Janus in the ranks of the low-achievers. Nowhere, it seems to me, is this better illustrated than in the recent

history of education. Anglicization in the broadest sense, the identifica-
tion of the Welsh system with the English – a similarity of goals
focused so often on examinations, a common ethos, for decades a
mock public-school ambience, a common career structure at the
end from a rather different type of entrant – resulted from a similar
educational system reflecting a society with a common economic
and political base. Yet this has been accompanied, since the war, by
developments which seem to contradict this notion of subtle anglicization. There is no gainsaying that there has been devolution on a
scale which must have Sir A. T. Davies turning in his grave. The
Central Welsh Board disappeared but was replaced with the Welsh
Joint Education Committee in 1949, with its unique place in the
examination structure of the United Kingdom. In 1947 the Cardiff
office of the Welsh Department opened.[35] In 1952 80 per cent of the
work of the Welsh Department was transferred to Cardiff.[36] Here
were battles being won, undramatically, which had once been the
subject of red-hot memoranda. In 1963 the new permanent secretary,
Dr Elwyn Davies, was based in Cardiff, the first time ever that the
office had been located outside London except for part of the war
when evacuated to Bournemouth.[37] In 1964 Wales got her secretary
of state which paved the way, in 1970, for the Transfer of Functions
(Wales) order which transferred responsibility for primary and secondary education to the secretary of state. There was now, and remains,
a Welsh Education Office and an under-secretary of state responsible
for education.[38]

This catalogue of administrative measures forces us to question
whether that familiar scapegoat for many in Wales, that devouring,
colonialist English state machine, was actually responsible for the
linguistic and national ills of Wales. As with Scotland[39] the theory
hardly holds water. There has been no conscious policy of repres-
sion of the Welsh language in Welsh education in the twentieth
century.[40] The Welsh Department of the Board of Education always
encouraged it, as have its successor bodies. So did the CWB and *its*
successor body. In 1953 the Welsh books scheme was adopted by
the WJEC whereby local authorities were to spend £107,000 between
1954 and 1959 on books in Welsh for schools.[41] The Welsh Office
emphasized that government policy was that 'Welsh as well as English
should be taught to all the children of Wales and Monmouthshire,
according to their ability to profit from such instruction', and a
circular of 1953 urged 'Welsh education authorities and schools to

visualise Wales as a bilingual country'.[42] The Welsh Office delighted in recounting that the first bilingual secondary school, Ysgol Glan Clwyd in Flintshire, opened in 1956, to be followed by bilingual schools in Crymych, Mold and Pontypridd by 1962.[43] There was more than a pat on the back. In the wake of the Gittins Report in 1968 Ted Short endorsed the principle of bilingual education in Wales and increased the teacher quota the better to carry out the policy in primary schools.[44]

The 1970s saw a considerable quickening of this process. In 1976 there were seventy-one forms or sets in secondary schools in Wales in which Welsh was taught as a first language, mainly in Dyfed and Clwyd, and forty-seven where Welsh was used for teaching some subjects. In 1980 there were eleven bilingual secondary schools, designated *Ysgolion Cymraeg*. The number of full-time pupils having a bilingual education had risen from 2,017 in 1970 to 7,860 in 1980. Welsh was used as a medium of teaching five or more subjects in thirty-four secondary schools in Wales. Fifty-two schools were offering history through the medium of Welsh. In 1975–80 95.5 per cent of schools in Clwyd, 91.7 per cent in Powys and 95.5 per cent in Gwynedd were teaching Welsh as both a first and a second language. More significant in view of the linguistic and demographic map of Wales, with its massive preponderance of non-Welsh-speakers in the south-east, in only 3.8 per cent of West Glamorgan schools, 9.7 per cent of South Glamorgan schools and 4.9 per cent of Mid-Glamorgan schools was there no Welsh taught. This is to be compared with what might easily have been the case, for in 75 per cent of Gwent secondary schools no Welsh was taught.[45]

Does this level of provision mean that the majority of pupils learn some Welsh at some stage of their secondary school careers? Yes, of course. Does it mean that they have a distinctively Welsh education? This is surely a very different question. If that often perfunctory study of the Welsh language in secondary schools remains unrelated to any study of Welsh history and the Welsh community, indeed of Welshness as a concept and a reality, then studying the Welsh language for a couple of lessons a week for two or three years amounts to little more than trial by mutation. Only if set in the context of the communities which have used the language over the centuries and the factors which have seen its decline can such limited acquaintance even begin to make sense.

*   *   *

I have already encroached too far on the recent past to remain histori-cally respectable. By the time we get to the current decade the historian is transmuted into the opinionated observer. David Smith has a story of the fortune-teller in Pontypridd market whose sign of incitement into the mysterious tent read 'Your fortune told – cautiously'. So, the present analysed – speculatively. I will be brief.

In recounting events since 1979 I need a text from the book of Job. The postwar bulge peaked, if that is what bulges do – in 1963/4. In 1979/80 the secondary-school population began to fall.[46] The proportion of gross national product spent on education has declined in relation to the other big spenders of health and especially defence. We have had our own traumas in Wales. In 1979 the Loosmore report was published and inaugurated a series of investigations which seemed to indicate that Welsh secondary schools were less efficient at producing examination results among middle-ability pupils. It emerged that such blanket criticisms were ill-founded but the sound and fury was real enough – another loss of direction, seemingly, in that year of devolution.

I have argued throughout that the central government voice, sometimes quietly persuasive, gradually more strident, has been crucial in moulding the shape of secondary education in Wales. So no analysis of the current situation can eschew political comment. Since 1979 it appears that, apart from privatization, government policy in educa-tion as elsewhere, has been slanted towards a kind of centralized diversification.

And, despite the fact that policies pour in profusion from central government, it is salutary to recall that one recurring characteristic of state involvement in education is that profoundly important developments are inaugurated by accident. The appalling phenomenon of youth unemployment has spawned a whole series of ad hoc measures which are being hurriedly moulded into a policy reflecting basic political attitudes and prejudices. The secondary school aspect of this is the Technical and Vocational Education Initiative, now taken up by all the Welsh authorities eager to inject some finance into an anaemic system. Is it fair to compare it with the 'whisky money' of the Welsh intermediate schools in Nonconformist, temper-ance Wales? In the perspective of history the education of virtually all Welsh pupils in comprehensive schools is a very recent phenomenon and it seems we are now consolidating something rather like a bilateral system with a division at fourteen. We had our county/grammar schools for roughly seventy years. We have had our comprehensive eleven-to-eighteen schools fifteen or so. Now falling rolls, economic accident and political dogma see a profoundly modified system emerging. The occasion is not appropriate for comment on the rights and wrongs of such change. It is accurate to recall that the secondary system in Wales from 1896 until the mid-1960s was a divisive one, though throughout that time considerably less divisive than was the case in England. In Wales the divisions were based, to a far greater extent, on merit than on class or on wealth.

9
Education in Wales:
a different 'Great Debate'?

In the reign of the first Elizabeth there was a great debate about education. Tutor to the young Queen was Roger Ascham, author of *The Scholemaster*.[1] This book resulted from a long discussion over dinner at Windsor in 1563. Dinner was taken in Sir William Cecil's room and the group included Sir Walter Mildmay, Chancellor of the Exchequer, Sir Richard Sackville, Treasurer of the Exchequer, Mr Haddon, the Master of the Court of Requests, a bishop, Ascham and a few others. Ascham recalled it like this – and it might be salutary to inform some of our present secretaries of state:

> Mr Secretary hath this accustomed manner, though his head be never so full of most weighty affairs of the realm, yet at dinner time he doth seem to lay them always aside; and findeth ever fit occasion to talk pleasantly of other matters, but most gladly of some matter of learning: wherein he will courteously hear the mind of the meanest at his table.[2]

The conversation ranged widely. Cecil himself was a Tory 'wet':

> Diverse scholars of Eton be run away from the school for fear of beating . . . whereupon Mr Secretary took occasion to wish that some more discretion were in many schoolmasters in using correction than commonly there is . . . whereby many scholars that might else prove well, be driven to hate learning before they know what learning meaneth: and so are made willing to forsake their books and be glad to be put to any other kind of living.[3]

Inevitably the hard-liners' wing was represented too: 'Mr Haddon was full of Mr Peters' opinion, and said that the best schoolmaster of our time was the greatest beater.'[4] It may or may not be significant that Ascham records that Sir Walter Mildmay, the Chancellor of the Exchequer, said very little and Sir Richard Sackville, the Treasurer of the Exchequer, said nothing at all. Perhaps, after all, if great debate is not new, the parameters have changed.

Ascham's conversation at dinner focused quite naturally on Eton.

There was no Welsh Eton, nor any education in the 'dominion and principality of Wales' which would have exercised the great minds of state. Today there are commentators whose frame of reference has changed little. Sample the substantial education section in Dillons bookshop in Malet Street, serving London's university. See if you get any impression that the Education Reform Act of 1988 applies to two countries, not one. See if you can find a reference to Wales in the index of the 1,100 pages of the *Encyclopedia of Contemporary Education*. In a collection of essays edited by Moon[5] on the National Curriculum we have, quite rightly, a black perspective on it from Conrad MacNeil.[6] He starts his essay thus 'The proposed National Curriculum is not truly national. The culture reflected in it is no more than prevailing white Anglo-Saxon and totally excludes the significant input from the Caribbean, the African and Indian continents and elsewhere.' There is nothing in the whole book – nor in many like it – to indicate that 'England and Wales' is anything other than a homogeneous mass. Such an attitude is not acceptable.

I want to argue first that, in looking at the wider context of the debate surrounding the Ruskin College speech and its aftermath, we work our way towards a significant Welsh dimension, one which is usually totally unappreciated. Secondly, that focusing exclusively on the one obviously Welsh debate, that over the Welsh language, is wholly inadequate. And finally, that some of the changes which have come about as a result of the Great Debate have given us in Wales unprecedented opportunities to enhance the Welsh dimension of education in its widest sense.

The Ruskin College speech: issues identified

Let me begin by briefly recapitulating the issues which Lord Callaghan highlighted in his speech[7] in October 1976. First, there was concern over 'methods and aims of informal instruction . . .' Secondly, there was a 'strong case for the so-called core curriculum of basic knowledge'. Thirdly, there was the question of 'monitoring the use of resources in order to maintain a proper national standard of performance'. Fourthly, linked with standards, there was 'the role of the inspectorate in relation to national standards and their maintenance'. Fifthly, there was 'the need to improve relations between industry and education'. Finally, there was the problem of the examination system.

It is necessary only to recite the litany of issues to see why it turned out to warrant the epithet of the 'Great Debate'. All have been confronted head-on or tangentially since. It would, of course, be wholly unrealistic to argue that the contexts of the debate in England and in Wales were completely dissimilar. The broad economic and political contexts in the two countries have much in common, inevitably when they share the same central government. But I want to argue that there is many a Welsh dimension to be uncovered if we probe a little below the surface.

The educational context

I turn to just a few of the contexts in which the Ruskin speech was made, beginning with some brief, banal points about the educational context. First, there had been a wholesale change to a system of comprehensive secondary schools in much of England and virtually all of Wales and the consequent liberation of primary schools from the eleven-plus strait-jacket. It carried with it the logic of mixed-ability teaching in primary and secondary schools, and a common examination system at sixteen-plus. This change was, therefore, the catalyst, one of the most significant changes in the post-industrial history of education. Secondly, there continued to be ideological and practical debate over the curriculum, particularly the primary school curriculum, in the 1960s and the 1970s, ranging widely from the child-centred romantics to the 'cultural transmission' conservatives, with some who saw the curriculum as an instrument to enhance the cause of social justice thrown in for good measure. Thirdly, there had been, arguably, a change of orthodoxy as a result of the Plowden Report in 1967,[8] with the child-centred methods becoming the 'accepted' approach. Fourthly, the result was that there was experimentation, and there was, just as important, a rhetoric of experimentation. This resulted in a backlash in the 1960s and 1970s. Some of it consisted of genuine concerns about lack of structure in the curriculum. Some of it, even in the Black Papers,[9] was profound and interesting. Some of it was tabloid-type nonsense. Finally, the response to experimentation and its critics took a variety of forms. There was an attempt to evaluate teaching styles more objectively and in a more conceptually sophisticated way. Neville Bennett's work,[10] for example, was followed by Her Majesty's Inspectorate (HMI)[11] reporting on teaching styles. Another response was the promulgation of the idea of a core curriculum. A third response was to give in to demands for evaluation, with the establishment of the Assessment of Performance Unit (APU) in 1974.

Where was Wales in all this? Very early on, many moons before Plowden[12] – and we tend to forget that there was child-centred life before 1967 – Wales was seemingly set on exactly the same course as England. It is fascinating to contrast the postwar curricular adventurousness, with its emphasis on individual growth born out of the anti-fascism of the war, with later anguished cries of 'back to basics'. In 1949 the Central Advisory Council for Wales[13] reported that:

> Growth implies activity. Activity then should be the pervading quality of school life. The curricula of secondary schools should be based upon activities. Hitherto the tradition of the secondary schools in Wales, and in other countries, has been one of constrained assimilation of knowledge.

The report went on to wax lyrical about there being 'the least impediment to initiative' and that it was in the 'spirit of creative Christian humanism that we wish to approach the curricula of grammar-technical and modern-technical schools in this new era in Wales'. It did not happen in the secondary schools.

How far did such an approach permeate the primary schools of Wales? The basics of reading and writing, the alleged shortcomings of which have produced so much acrimony in England, do not seem to have produced such difficulties in Wales, not even in the last few years. A recent HMI survey[14] reports: 'In a substantial majority of schools (over four-fifths) standards of reading are satisfactory.' 'The early stages of writing are effectively taught and most pupils achieve satisfactory standards'. It is fascinating that it is the imaginative writing and poetry which were inadequate, hardly the stuff of Black Paper and Centre for Policy Studies nightmares. Lest this latest judgement be seen as some kind of reaction to recent pressures we can turn to another HMI (Wales) survey,[15] of 1984. The criticism was that too much attention was being paid to the basic skills: 'In many classes there is a strongly held view that pupils must master certain "basic" skills before they can move on to work which requires independent learning and the use of those basic skills.' HMI summary is unequivocal:

> In most primary schools considerable prominence is given to certain aspects of language and mathematics and much less prominence to most other areas of the curriculum . . . within individual classes the general pattern of organisation is for the mornings to be devoted to work in language and mathematics and for the afternoons to be devoted to the remaining curriculum areas.[16]

Presumably trendy Plowden, even Gittins,[17] fads were being implemented only east of Offa's Dyke.

The political context

It is a truism that educational debate in the 1970s took on an increasingly political dimension and the Ruskin College speech symbolizes this. But I do not accept the historical framework almost invariably erected to accommodate that truism. I have never been convinced by the consensus model of post-1944 educational change, and, equally, I do not really understand the usually accepted notion of the breakdown of consensus since the 1970s. The Black Paper of 1975[18] and the Ruskin College speech raised the same issues – teaching according to set syllabuses and specific standards of attainment and an emphasis on literacy and numeracy. Certainly, partial privatization of the schools in the wake of 1988 has been the result of party political dogma; but in so far as the Great Debate was about, and ended up with, curricular standardization, it represented a kind of consensus among the political parties.

In response to the Ruskin College speech which, for the moment, had upstaged the Conservatives' increased concern to point out that they were the party of standards and excellence in education, they mounted a variety of campaigns to wrest back the initiative. So we have the two parties with not dissimilar concerns, and a general acceptance that the Ruskin College speech was the occasion on which 'the grandiose claims of the sixties were replaced . . . by more sober, pragmatic purposes'.[19] Education was not going to transform the economy or produce social equality. Neither was it, for many commentators, any longer doing its traditional job of passing on the cultural heritage. So, by 1976 the many-pronged attack on the shortcomings, for some the positive harm, of the developments of the 1960s was sufficiently well-rooted to produce a kind of political convergence.

The Ruskin College speech showed Labour's concern. There were other strategies from the opposition, pursued relentlessly by Conservative pressure groups through the 1980s. There were accusations of widespread illiteracy and innumeracy in young employees, for example. The alleged lack of general knowledge provided a bit of light relief. In a December 1987 issue of *The Observer*[20] we were informed that,

> A board (the Associated Examining Board) survey reveals that candidates in previous geography tests put Snowdonia in Scotland, Everest in Africa and Canada in Europe. Asked to name the river that starts near the Equator in melting snow, supplies the Aswan Dam and flows northwards through a desert for more than 1,000 miles, one candidate wrote; 'River Dee' . . . Mr Kevin McGrath, director of vocational education at the Association of British Travel Agents national Training Board (no less) said . . . his criticism was not of geography teachers but of the system [sic]. Geography in school tended to be concept-based, not knowledge-based. Children could tell you what type of soil the Mid-West of America had without knowing where it was.

So the case for devising a national system of testing which would ensure that all children realized that the mid-west of America was in the mid-west of America seemed watertight. But there were problems in devising a fair system. There were some noble attempts to solve the problem, but somehow they did not ring true for England, let alone Wales. When the Centre for Policy Studies came up with specific, national tests for seven-year-olds the questions they suggested[21] did not carry the nation with them – but things are beginning to change. Maths should be questions like

1. Answer, without paper, 9 + 8
2. Calculate, without carrying, 942 + 121
3. Calculate, with carrying, 44 – 26
4. Tell time to nearest hour
5. Start learning tables

In English, they should, for example, be able to write legibly, use a wide range of simple vocabulary, construct sentences in simple syntax, using full stops and capital letters correctly, spell words correctly, know by heart some simple poems like 'I had a little nut tree'.

What, then, of the alleged breakdown of the alleged consensus? There has been a political confrontation, certainly, but less between the political parties than between central government and local government over control of the system. If there had been a consensus here after the war, and based on the Welsh evidence this is highly dubious, it certainly has broken down. And it was this reassertion of central control, orchestrated by the politicians and executed by the civil servants at the Department of Education and Science (DES), who were just as anxious to see central authority reasserted, which has turned out to be of the greatest significance for Wales.

Maclure[22] argues that 'Between 1976 and 1985 – between the Ruskin speech and *Better Schools*, Sir Keith Joseph's White Paper issued in March 1985 – the DES worked through the agenda' laid out in the Ruskin College speech. From a Welsh point of view this reassertion of power at the centre was of enormous import because it was accompanied by a greater degree of devolution of power to the Welsh Office than had ever previously been the case. As a result of the convergence of these two trends there was potentially greater control of education in Wales from within Wales than ever before. And if the DES was, in the 1970s, an 'ambitious bureaucracy', so was the Welsh Office. Successive secretaries of state for Wales, especially recently, have not been slow to assert their leadership and control in Wales. And they are responsible for education in Wales. In Maclure's words, the 1988 Act 'increased the powers of the Secretary of State for Education and Science (and, where appropriate, the Secretary of State for Wales)'.[23] Appropriateness leaves a lot to fight for.

It has taken many forms. Policy statements for 'England and Wales' are now followed up by policy statements for Wales. For example, when the National Curriculum statement[24] emerged from the DES in July 1987 it was followed by a booklet on the National Curriculum in Wales.[25] So, if we do not have the independence founded in law of Scotland, we do have some basic elements of the Scottish system which serve to distinguish it. The elements in Scotland are the Scottish Education Department, including HMI, the Consultative Committee on the Curriculum and the Scottish Examination Board. In Wales we now have equivalents all along the line, the Welsh Office Education Department (WOED), including a far more homogeneous group of HMI than is the case in England, the Curriculum Council for Wales (CCW) and the Welsh Joint Education

Committee (WJEC). There are also in Wales the equivalent advantages of small size and greater community of purpose. In Scotland we read that 'members of HMI . . . have traditionally played a key role in the design, implementation and evaluation of all recent major curriculum initiatives . . . the SED, through HMI, has played a dominant role on all the major committees and working parties responsible for curriculum design and development in Scotland'.[26] In the new centralist climate of control we must look to the Welsh HMI and the WOED to play the equivalent role in Wales. This does not allow for any diminution in the size of the Welsh inspectorate. As is happening in Scotland, its numbers must expand to fulfil this role adequately.

The framework for the separate administration of education in Wales is now complete. For the first time ever, and we go back to battles fought in the period before the First World War, it is intended that Welsh education from nursery to university will be in the hands of the Welsh Office. When the National [sic] Curriculum Council was set up for England it was complemented by the Curriculum Council for Wales. So, the infrastructure in Wales complements the growing responsibilities of political masters in an increasingly centralized education system. Then there has been the practical input on the curriculum, and here we see the realities of Welsh autonomy. On the one prong of the 1988 Act, the devolution of power to schools, there was, and is, no way in which Wales was going to be exempted from the system. On the other, the National Curriculum, the Welsh Office had everything to fight for and, supported from below, it did fight. Given that there is a National Curriculum, Wales has emerged reasonably well, again by being able to get on with the proper job and not being enmeshed in media hysterics. The prime example of this, of course, is the history element of the National Curriculum.

The problem then has been, and to some extent still is, that of defining the Welsh education which we expect these central authorities to implement. By implication there is nothing distinctively Welsh about the theory of the operation of competition between schools, although some in Wales might want to argue that it is less in harmony with our community traditions. The other practical point is that it is irrelevant over most of Wales. We are a rural country, and the free market for those parents without a helicopter who want to see something of their children in their formative years does not actually allow much choice of school. Fortunately, it is what has become centralized that is of the essence to Wales – what is actually taught in the curriculum. That is why, ultimately, the 1988 Act is of such crucial importance in the history of education in Wales.

The language debate

I have, so far, tried to argue that the Ruskin speech and what has happened since, have inadvertently raised questions about the Welshness of education and made possible a liberating degree of independence in implementing it. You may well respond that there have been debates in Wales which have no English counterpart and we ought to concentrate our minds on those. Paradoxically, I would argue that exclusive concentration on these would be dangerous. I wish to raise, very superficially, the issue of Welsh-language education.

Colin Baker has called this the 'gentle revolution'.[27] There was one designated bilingual secondary school in 1945, eighteen in 1988. Welsh is now taught as a first language in sixty-four secondary schools in Wales. Baker also claims that 'the formal subject curriculum, the pastoral curriculum, and not least the hidden curriculum have become progressively more Welsh since 1956'.[28] For many years it was deemed appropriate to teach science and mathematics through the medium of English but that too has changed. The numbers of schools using Welsh for teaching mathematics, technology, PE, physics and chemistry are all up. In 1963 there were ninety entries through the medium of Welsh at O Level. In 1987 there were 6526 such GCSE entries. This is significant because O-Level entries, as they then were, are a measure of the currency of Welsh – its market value.

Such progress has only been possible because of official support – and it has grown steadily. Contrary to much propaganda, the Welsh language has not lacked for state approval and it has certainly not lacked backing over the decades from HMI, since the first chief inspector, O. M. Edwards, set the tone after 1907. What has happened since the war is that this support has meshed with parental support and pressure to an extent unthinkable between the wars. For all those of us who believe in the importance of the Welsh language here has been a real success story. It has been reinforced now by the inclusion of Welsh as a core or foundation subject in the National Curriculum.

Not that we should be lulled into complacency. Any historical analysis shows how fragile the situation is. The population of Wales is over 80 per cent English-monolingual, and just under 20 per cent English/Welsh bilingual. Virtually everyone in Wales now is open to the educational and conditioning influences of the mass media. Nine miles outside Aberystwyth there is a small farmhouse near the village of Llanrhystud on the coast of west Wales, historically the least penetrable by outside influences. It sports a satellite dish pointing skywards. An Australian has brought American English to Llanrhystud. In the age group three to fourteen, nearly 146,000 children spoke Welsh in 1901; in 1971, 69,350. Great efforts are still required if the language is to be safeguarded.

To give just one example of the kind of effort needed, education research into bilingualism has played a relatively small part in the revival. This contrasts significantly with Canada, for example, where research has shown the advantages of balanced bilingualism and strongly influenced Canadian parents' views on bilingualism. The same should apply in Wales.

But concentrating on Welsh-language education is dangerous. Because it is so important it has tended to monopolize interest in Wales. It is all too easy to slip into arguing that a Welsh education is an education in the Welsh language. The majority of the Welsh do not speak the language, however much we hope that number may increase. The majority of the Welsh who speak English have their right to an education which is distinctively Welsh.

The outcome of the Great Debate in Wales

May I then try to sum up my own views as to where Wales stands in relation to some of the issues raised in the Great Debate and the revolution which has followed it? First, I have argued that we are not hamstrung by the dogma of such bodies as the Centre for Policy Studies. There were no Welsh contributors to the Black Papers. There has been no anti-teacher hysteria in Wales. Secondly, there has been no outcry against child-centred excesses in the primary school, because there is no evidence that there have been any. It is inconceivable that, if there had been, the media would have refrained from reporting them. The evidence is that Welsh primary schools have been 'traditional', devoting their long mornings to the three 'R's and their shorter afternoons to the rest of the curriculum. Thirdly, there has been none of the backlash against the General Certificate of Secondary Education (GCSE) *per se* that was evident in England. The recent major survey of all history, geography and Welsh at that level[29] indicated that teachers of the three subjects, without exception, backed the change. Fourthly, we have a practical situation which is more conducive to a common purpose in Wales. We have a country of state comprehensive schools which are now of more manageable size than they used to be, much more capable of forging a common sense of community, far less prone to large-scale opting out. We have no private sector of any great significance in Wales. Fifthly, we have a Welsh curriculum. The essential prerequisite of this was a National Curriculum, but then it was necessary for there to be sufficient of a will in the Welsh Office and a sufficiently well-developed curriculum theory and voice, to press for separate treatment for Wales. We have got that in the language, the history and the geography of the nation. That is by far the most critical achievement. It remains now to ensure that a Welsh dimension should permeate the curriculum, as a cross-curricular dimension, taking in, additionally, other subjects such as music and art and Anglo-Welsh literature. Mediating this to schools seems to me to be a major responsibility of the Curriculum Council for Wales, one which they have been addressing already.

Sixthly, we have an institutional framework. The Welsh Office now has a degree of influence over Welsh education which would have been unthinkable thirty years ago. There is an interesting historical perspective here. In a time of strong cultural nationalism, in the last decade of the nineteenth century and the first of the twentieth, Wales was nearly granted a National Council for Education. What it received from Lloyd George was the Welsh Department of the Board of Education. There is a famous story[30] of how its first permanent secretary, Alfred Davies, asked the 'English' permanent secretary, Morant, for some Board of Education headed notepaper just before he assumed office. He received a crushing rebuke which would have destroyed many a more thin-skinned Welshman. Over the next decades Davies asked for more than notepaper. Not from any Welsh perspective, but from insatiable personal ambition, he was to call for Welsh Department control over technical education, special-needs education, as we would call it now, the school health service and control of university education. He was fought tooth and nail by senior English civil servants. Now, for the first time ever, we have the near prospect of Welsh Office administration of all aspects of Welsh education, including financing higher education through a separate funding council. The symbolic significance of this is crucial. Its practical import is that it is now up to pressure groups in Wales to help influence the measures which they think ought to reflect the distinctiveness of Wales. In practice, we are now nearer Scotland.

Seventhly, I am not arguing for increased Welsh control of education just as some statement of cultural nationalism. I believe that some of the inherent dangers in the 1988 system need be far less evident in Wales. For example, the CCW is in a position to fight for a curriculum in Wales which is more balanced, as reflected in its position over art and music, or less assessment dominated, in which subjects are not reduced to meeting attainment targets. From a Welsh standpoint, cultural transmission is what is vital, while on a practical basis assessment tables to allow parents to make 'rational' choices are just not required over large tracts of Wales.

Eighthly, on the curriculum, sufficient battles have been won to allow us to talk of a curriculum for Wales, not just a curriculum in Welsh. Whatever we may think of the National Curriculum it is for me, at least, more acceptable as such. There has been goodwill in some unexpected places over the inclusion of Welsh at all key stages as a core or foundation subject, despite the problem of supplying the teachers to implement it. It is good to know that the statutory orders for history[31] in Wales have been at least as well received as those for England. There will now be an organic growth as that which was unforeseen becomes the norm, the frame of reference for future debate. Treating Wales as an educational unit is not only recognition of a different heritage, partly expressed in our educational system, but the path to pragmatic advantages. The linguistic, cultural and organizational differences in education in Wales, if allowed to develop, can shed light on the wider picture in the rest of Britain and in Europe. If and when the teachers of Wales, or the CCW, or the research processes come up with more sense in Wales than in England that good sense ought to be allowed to prevail.

The need for co-ordination

Finally, the only way to achieve the kind of integration of effort which is so desirable in Wales is for the present activities to be co-ordinated. How? Wales is full of educational bodies but often the one is not sufficiently aware of what the other is doing. If we think of the varying briefs and overlapping activities of the schools, the university colleges, the institutes of higher education, Pwyllgor Datblygu Addysg Gymraeg (PDAG), CCW, the WJEC, and the local education authorities (LEAs) we get some idea of the opportunity for crossed wires and unco-ordinated initiatives.

The main paymaster, directly or indirectly, is going to be the Welsh Office. It might seem appropriate that from there, from the civil servants and HMI, should come the co-ordination. In practice, this happens to some extent already. But the Welsh Office is in an invidious position, having to interpret policy laid down for England in a Welsh context and ensuring that more local initiatives from bodies which it funds are, on the one hand not stifled, but on the other not incompatible with wider policies. Not surprisingly the Welsh Office has usually to be reactive not proactive. I come inexorably to the conclusion that there has to be some co-ordinated body which has a wider role and a wider remit. I have indicated that in the first decade of this century Wales came close to being granted its own National Council for Education, which would have been a large elected body. An elected body would, at least at present, seem politically unacceptable. In these days an Education Council for Wales would be nominated. Such a body, providing an overview of the whole of education, could be of inestimable value in providing for Wales almost as significant a voice in education as has Scotland. And it would need to be supported by the professional expertise not of a diminished band of HMI, but an expanded group, just as is happening in Scotland now. Of course the Education Council for Wales would have to work within the parameters laid down by two secretaries of state. But within those parameters it would initiate as well as co-ordinate policy and field ideas from individuals and institutions in Wales which would lead to worthwhile practical results. In my view the Curriculum Council for Wales provides the nucleus of such a body and I believe its remit should be extended accordingly.

It was not the intention of the Ruskin College speech to focus attention on Welsh education. On the surface it had no Welsh dimension. But in so far as it has had an impact on later events and legislation, whatever may be the merits and demerits of that legislation on other grounds, I believe that the Welsh have cause to be grateful to a politician who, by interesting irony, waited until his retirement to serve Welsh education by other means.

But I hope that Lord Callaghan will, in the context of this lecture, allow a lady whose sentiments provide me with some cheer in these surrealistic days, to have the last word. On the occasion of a confrontation between Wales and England in educational policy in 1932 she said, on behalf of the Women's Liberal Federation: 'We feel it hard that Wales . . . should be held back by the more backward English.'[32]

10
The curriculum in Wales: perceptions of the 'Welshness' of education

The title of this paper commits me to exploring three themes. First, presumptuously, what does it mean to be Welsh? Second, what have been the Welsh perspectives on the school curriculum in the past? Third, how might these perspectives influence our thinking about the school curriculum in Wales at the present time?

What does it mean to be Welsh? To an influential minority in Wales it is the language that matters above all else. Other dimensions – the religious, social, aesthetic and community life of the people – are subsidiary. This is a persuasive stance since no one can deny either the historical significance of the language and its literature, or that these constitute a fundamental affirmation of nationality. There is a view that the only future for a Welsh identity lies in unity through language. It follows from R. S. Thomas's unequivocal premise: 'When I am asked: what is a Welshman? I unfailingly answer: a man who speaks Welsh ... we have nothing to distinguish us from other people except Welsh.'[1] The fate of the nation without its own language, he argues, is that of Cornwall, 'a spirit hovering above a cemetery'. And yet, even for Thomas, it is not so simple. His vision for the Welsh language is part of his broader view of society – a view which challenges the dominance of the multinational company, questions the capitalistic ethic of the constant maximization of profit, distrusts the alternative viewpoint and political consequences of communism (which he sees as swamping the human spirit), warms to contemporary environmentalist concerns and is suffused by a profound belief in the ultimate spiritual unity of mankind. In this scheme Welshness is, for Thomas, one small manifestation of virtue and wholeness in a world united to work for the common good, a world which is the extension of God himself, 'a great organism in which everything co-operates for the good of the whole; the material, the psychological, the cultural, the social, and so on, as things which are linked together and which influence one another.[2] Thomas's stated recipe for the salvation of Wales is straightforward:

> the first task of the concerned people within our nation is to unite Welsh-speaking Welshmen by virtue of their common tongue. Then let us try to attract the others in our midst and to wean them from the British milk which is by now old and sour. First, we have to win over the English-Welshmen, who have Welsh blood in their veins, always remembering that Britishness is something comparatively new. Less than a century ago, most of Wales was a Welsh-speaking country. Then we must turn to the immigrants, the newcomers, convincing them politely but proudly of the existence of an identity that perhaps they were not too conscious of when they moved to live here.[3]

The educational implications of such a view are seductive. Teaching the language in school, to all pupils, so that they are equipped to communicate in it is the one means to the desired end of recovering and preserving a Welsh identity.

Other analysts of Wales and the Welsh incline to different, more complex, emphases. For Raymond Williams

> two truths are told, as alternative prologues to the action of modern Wales. The first draws on the continuity of Welsh language and literature: from the sixth century it is said, and thus perhaps the oldest surviving poetic tradition in Europe. The second draws on the turbulent experience of industrial South Wales over the last two centuries, and its powerful political and communal formalities.[4]

Williams emphasizes that there are contacts, that both sides 'in adversity ... are now speaking to each other in some new ways', while not attempting to conceal the bitterness of the dispute. But this leads to a central insight which he offers concerning the perspective from which Welshness is viewed: 'perhaps the least known fact, by others, about contemporary Welsh culture and politics is that there are harsh and persistent quarrels within a dimension which is seen from outside as unusually singular.'[5] Whatever our consciousness of diversity within Wales, the existence of that singularity is an essential feature for the Welsh to emphasize to themselves and to the world outside as they work for 'some version of a unifying identity, within and across some of the most radical differences of condition which can be found anywhere in Europe.'[6]

The implications here are that there will be many manifestations of the Welsh identity within the community of the nation, binding the many smaller communities and allegiances which exist within the territory of Wales into a singularity. There is a whole spectrum of loyalties evident among, for example, those who regard the language as the ultimate badge of nationhood, those who work first for political independence, those who want the Welsh to retreat to rural fastnesses, those who identify primarily with the industrial tradition, those 70 per cent or so who just call themselves Welsh. The claims which Rees Davies makes for thirteenth-century Wales resonate in our present condition:

> countries and peoples which lack a common polity and the institutions of unitary governance are not thereby disqualified from developing a sense of national identity. For national identity, like class, is a matter of perceptions as much as institutions. The institutions of centralised authority are by no means its only or most powerful focus. In medieval society, it could also manifest itself in an awareness of the common genealogical descent of a people, in a shared belief in a particular version of historical mythology and prophecy, in an emotional attachment to the geographical boundaries of a country, in a heightened awareness of the distinctiveness of a common language and of common customs, in the yearning for the prospect of unitary rule, in the articulation of a 'we-they' dichotomy to express the distinction between natives and aliens.[7]

It is a source of strength for the Welsh as we struggle with matters of identity that these features of medieval society strike more powerful chords across Europe now than for generations. On 1 October 1989 Neal Ascherson commented that

> every day this week, a European nation has asked for more liberty. East Germans marched in Leipzig, Kasakhs brawled with Russians, Slovenes demanded the right of secession, Ukranians asked for the Uniate church to be legal once more. The Basques went on bombing, the Montenegrins brought home the bones of their last king and buried them in Cetinge, the Scottish National Party held their conference at Dunoon.[8]

He proceeds to quote Erhard Eppler of the West German Social Democrats:

> national identification no longer necessarily connects to nation-States or even aims at the creation of a nation-State, but often roots itself in far older associations . . . you belong to a nation if you acknowledge that you do – but only so long as you do acknowledge it.[9]

Paradoxically, within the European community, it is likely that the smaller nations will find it easier to assert an identity which lack of statehood has previously made problematic. It is no coincidence that one of the essential foundations on which such assertions are to be made, a flourishing and highly regarded historiography, has been one of Wales's proudest achievements in recent decades.

Keith Robbins has shown recently that concern with particularities is reflected in the work of historians across Europe.[10] Among many others he cites the work of that most brilliant of French historians, Fernand Braudel:

> even Braudel has not been able to distil the essence of France. There are many Frances . . . we learn, perhaps without great surprise, that France is a country of diversity and that conventional criteria, such as 'natural boundaries' or language, do not explain the 'unity of France'.

We must allow present tides of politics and historiography to flow freely over into Wales as, for once, we do not have to fight against the current.

The desire for the expression of national differences in national institutions, conferring a variety of degrees of autonomy, strengthens rather than abates in new circumstances, and in turn may be instrumental both in representing and in mediating the uniqueness of that society. It has been argued recently that such institutions in Wales are inadequate compared with those of Scotland and Ireland. Scotland has its courts, its church and its education system, for example. Northern Ireland has a 'ludicrously impressive array of institutions'.[11] Wales, by contrast, had nothing in the way of a separate institutional framework until the later nineteenth century, since when a variety of bodies associated with educational, cultural and welfare measures have been created. Yet it is significant that devolutionary pressures have continued to bear fruit. The Welsh Office employs over 2,000 civil servants responsible for the running of eleven departments, of which education is an important one, and forty-seven divisions of these departments, to implement detailed policies. These policies can be influenced by outside pressure groups. In a matter as significant as the place of history in the National Curriculum we have seen that a widely representative group such as the Association of History Teachers in Wales was able to make a case for separate treatment for Wales, be received sympathetically and see the establishment of a separate National Curriculum History Committee for

Wales. It is true that there have been numerous examples in education of how Anglo-centric policy has triumphed over Welsh wishes – for example much of Wales would have had multilateral schools in the 1950s if Welsh interests had not conflicted with those of Westminster governments.[12] At the same time the judgement that the Welsh Office 'in certain specific areas . . . appears to possess a significant degree of autonomy'[13] is borne out in some recent educational developments. As centralizing tendencies in state education grow so the distinctive role of the Welsh Office Education Department and, for example, the Curriculum Council for Wales become highly significant vehicles for the delivery of whatever we wish to make the Welsh dimension in our schools.[14]

My second question. What have been the Welsh perspectives on the curriculum in the past?

In the nineteenth century such perspectives were marginal, certainly until the last two decades. Wales, as such, hardly figured in the central debate of the century as to what education should consist of for the different classes, though of course from 1847 there was much discussion of how much of it there should be and who should provide it. The aristocracy and the gentry – relatively thinly represented in Wales – attended the public schools and the ancient universities. The dominant ideology decreed that education at these institutions should be education for its own sake; the main content should be classical and mathematical. This was an education for the gentleman, transmuting in mid-century from the Arnoldian ideal of godliness and good learning[15] to the archetype of the boy able to master the Greeks and the late cut, quoting Virgil with a stiff upper lip as the deathless hush fell on the close. Throughout the nineteenth century, in England and Wales, there was a firm dividing line between the classically based, privately purchased education of the élite by means of which high culture was transmitted from generation to generation, and the strictly utilitarian education (what we might call life skills and death skills) dispensed by charity, religious or state, to the masses of the people. The classical bent of the former carried on well into the twentieth century, along with the attitudes and demarcations which it represented.[16]

It is against this historical background that we need to enquire how any perceptions of Welshness may have influenced curricular, as opposed to organizational, developments. There are two broad salient points about the school curriculum in Wales up to 1944. First, there was very little formal analysis of it, merely minimal change by evolution or accretion. Second, the state, the examining boards and the universities between them established the parameters for that curriculum. From 1862 the Revised Code established which subjects qualified for grant in the elementary schools and, from 1904, secondary school curricula were determined by regulation of the Board of Education. Theoretical teacher freedom to control the curriculum was a phenomenon of the 1960s and 1970s; on a long historical view it may even be claimed that it has been a recent aberration.[17]

Given the state's role in determining what should be taught it is not surprising that early interest in the Welshness of the school curriculum should be expressed in terms of pressure-group attempts to influence governments to accord some status to the Welsh language. From the 1880s there was a resurgent Welsh nationalism, cultural and at times political, and it had its moments of considerable influence. One of its manifestations was Beriah Gwynfe Evans's Society for the Utilisation of the Welsh Language which campaigned hard from 1885 to encourage the use of Welsh in schools. The state responded with a measure of indulgence which affected policies in both elementary and secondary sectors. Welsh became a grant-earning subject under the Elementary Code from 1890 and, from the outset, was included in the specification for the intermediate schools' curriculum under the 1889 Intermediate Education Act. As David Allsobrook has told us, much credit must go to the sympathetic Mundella, who summed up contemporary notions of the Welsh element in schools. Future intermediate school teachers should, he said, be in sympathy with the people of Wales and have 'a large knowledge of the Welsh language'.[18]

O. M. Edwards, chief inspector of the Board of Education's Welsh Department from 1907 until his death in 1920, had a much wider concept of the role of the intermediate school in the life of Wales as he pressed for curricular practices in advance of their time. His approach to the secondary-school curriculum stemmed from his distinctive analysis of the needs of Welsh society.[19] I have argued elsewhere[20] that this view was tinged with a romanticism which did not accord with the realities of Welsh society nor with the thrust of Board of Education policies, to the extent that he found himself in confrontation both with the headteachers of Wales's intermediate schools and with powerful English civil servants. Nevertheless, Edwards was the nearest thing Wales has had to a major curriculum innovator.

Edwards had to live with, and was officially responsible for administering in the secondary sector, an education dependent on a distortion of the Platonic tradition of the supremacy of the intellect, epitomizing supreme confidence in the independent status and inherent value of the knowledge to be passed on.[21] At school level this was generally translated into a gospel of fact with its concomitant rote-learning and textbooks like 'railway timetables'. Edwards had to come to terms with this from the standpoint of a Ruskin-influenced, Rousseau-pedigreed Romantic who believed instinctively in the senses as a source of information and understanding.[22] He certainly believed in the importance of pupils in Wales learning about their country through subjects such as history and geography and literature, but with such knowledge informed by a more holistic view of education in which intellectual and craft skills were part of an organic whole. Above all, education should be creative; the burden of his complaint against a rigid examination system was that it stultified that creativity. To Edwards the Welshness of secondary schools should be expressed both in the transmission of knowledge about Wales and in the economic and cultural role which should be played by the products of the schools in their local Welsh rural communities. His philosophy of education was an integral part of a distinctive view of Welsh society:

> Our educational system should strengthen our national life in every direction; it should produce good handicraftsmen as well as learned men . . . We owe much to the influence of England . . . But the belief in personal wealth as against public wealth has come from England also . . . If our rich men do what our poor men are doing – the farm labourer gives a day's wage to a missionary society and another towards a school – we can teach England that it is more important to have a rich people than a collection of rich individuals.[23]

Edwards's ideal was that the education system should reflect the values of community and nation.[24] To Edwards, the Welsh dimension in the secondary schools was to be expressed in Welsh-language teaching throughout the school, the study of history through the medium of Welsh, investigation of the literature of Wales throughout the school curriculum, and the inclusion of craft subjects, agriculture, and navigation to serve the community – all set in the context of a society stressing the virtues of community within the nation rather than the values of individual wealth.

The curriculum which Edwards actually encountered when he was appointed chief inspector at the Welsh Department of the Board of Education had been laid down by the board in 1904 in regulations governing the curricula for secondary schools. After the creation of the Welsh Department in 1907 these were adapted for Wales so that teaching of the Welsh language was included. Then, in 1908, for purely administrative reasons, A. T. Davies, permanent secretary at the Welsh Department of the Board of Education, stipulated that 'in future years the variations between the Welsh and English regulations will be restricted to such *slight* [my italics] differences as may be necessary to meet the special educational requirements for Wales.' The slight variation was that 'In districts where Welsh is spoken, the language, or one of the languages, other than English, should be Welsh. Any of the subjects of the curriculum may (where the local circumstances make it desirable) be taught partly or wholly in Welsh.'[25]

Nothing could demonstrate better the two kinds of forces at work in the world of Welsh education than the approaches of these two colleagues. After Edwards's death in 1920, vision dimmed and administrative matters came to the fore; it was A. T. Davies's priorities, not those of O. M. Edwards, which counted. Edwards's attempts to bring about a greater measure of integration between schools and their communities came to nothing. Regulations and examinations predominated. In the elementary schools, despite the demise of the payment by results system, and whatever praise educational historians choose to lavish on enlightened attitudes which found expression in the 1931 Hadow Report dealing with younger pupils, the tyranny of testing remained in the shape of the scholarship system. This was not regulated by the Board of Education, nor the Welsh Department, but by the local education authorities. In Welsh-speaking Caernarfonshire in the first decade of the twentieth century scholarship examinations were conducted entirely in English, except for Welsh which was an optional subject.[26]

From 1920 there was little effective analysis of the nature of a Welsh schooling, merely discussion of the problem of the Welsh language in education. By the time of the 1921 census, such concern was understandable. The previous decennial census had shown that absolute numbers of Welsh-speakers were still increasing. In 1921 returns indicated instead a decline of over 47,000. Only 39 per cent of the population of Wales now spoke Welsh. The Welsh Department made all the right noises but the secondary schools continued to set Welsh against French and to take the fate of the language less than seriously, especially in more anglicized, county borough, Wales. Welsh had not featured in the CWB's version of its preferred core curriculum as advocated in 1916.[27] In the Bruce Report of 1920 it was organizational problems which predominated. Soon it was the economic disasters of the interwar period, and their social effects, which set the agenda for concerns within and for educational provision, material and curricular. Welsh pupils, prompted by their families, were forced so often to look to England for jobs, the exodus being made possible by precious School Certificates, especially if earned with credit. By 1926 Walter Jones, head of Neath County School, could still argue, at least for the secondary schools, that 'it was to English that all the glory, the culture, the intelligence, the influence, the power, the prestige, belonged.'[28] He believed that schools in Wales should, instead, reflect the special qualities of the country in which they were located. His concern was substantially with the Welsh language but not solely:

> The curriculum of the school should contain more Welsh, ability to speak Welsh or [and that is surely a highly significant qualification] a real sympathy with the Welsh outlook would be regarded as a distinct qualification for any post in a Welsh school. The History, Literature, Traditions and Songs of Wales would be made familiar to the school, and become part of that school life which would inevitably impress every pupil who spent any time on it.[29]

The departmental committee which was established in 1925 to investigate the teaching of Welsh in Wales, and reported in 1927, placed its emphasis on the language, maintaining that the 'history of Wales is the history of the language' and that 'we believe that the Welsh language, Welsh literature, Welsh history, together form the individual heritage of Welsh men and women . . .'[30] Given the terms of reference (the title of the report was *Welsh in Education and Life*), and the fact that in no school in Wales was Welsh the everyday language of the school, it is understandable that there should be no discussion of a Welsh dimension outside that of the language. With hindsight this was too narrow a perspective. Undeb Athrawon Cymreig (the Union of Welsh Teachers), responding to the report, cast its anxieties wider – realizing that there were fundamental forces at work which were, for example, rendering Welsh rural life not only less attractive but, in the eyes of the Welsh, inferior. O. M. Edwards's broad community vision had little place in this world, but neither was pressure for universal Welsh any panacea.

There is an instructive contrast available to us in the Wales of the 1920s. On the one hand we have three official reports – *Welsh in Education and Life* (1927), *Language Teaching in the Schools of Wales* (1929) and *Entrance Tests for Admission to Secondary Schools* (1930), all of which strove to enhance the status of the Welsh language in schools. On the other hand, we have the educational approach of Urdd Gobaith Cymru (the Welsh League of Youth), established according to its founder, to foster in Wales 'its literature, its traditions, its religion and its language'.[31] By 1929 the Urdd movement had integrated its branch structure with a summer camp organization and an annual eisteddfod. The common denominator between the three reports and the Urdd movement lay in the notion that the only conception of Welshness was one in which the Welsh language was the key to initiating pupils into the history, literature, religion and tradition of their country. The difference was that the Urdd movement constituted an educational programme in the Welsh language which was integrated with Welsh communities and a supporting programme of social and cultural events. The Urdd, as befitted a movement founded by Ifan ap Owen Edwards, had far more in common with the community 'Welshness' of O. M. Edwards than did the narrow scholastic and academic focus of the official reports. In the latter the stress was on Welsh in formal education rather than Welsh in life. That success stems only from a fusion of the two was surely the lesson of the activities of the Edwards dynasty.

After the Second World War Wales entered the new era of widening curricular analysis. Soon a duality of effort became apparent which has characterized debate ever since. For those who believe that the essence of Welshness is accessible only to the Welsh-speaking Welsh the thrust has been towards Welsh language schools from infant age upwards. The movement has been very successful – though some of the external reasons for this, the growing economic value of Welsh for employment in the media and the public sector, and the element of inherent exclusivity – have not always merited much attention. But there has been another strand, inevitable as the numbers of Welsh-speakers have declined. It can be found in the last major assessment of the relationship between the school and the community in Wales, published by the Welsh Department in 1952, with its emphasis on 'visualising the problem of language teaching in Welsh schools as a whole, and of associating this with the teaching of history, geography and social studies, particularly in the more definitely English-speaking areas.'[32] An important document, *School and Community in Wales* was, nevertheless, strong on exhortation but weak on the educational theory which, from the late 1950s, was to change the context of curriculum debate.

In this and the following decade it was once more the 'England and Wales' context which provided the steer for curriculum discussion. The nature and direction of curriculum analysis changed for two main reasons. First, for forty-five heady years after 1944, central control of the curriculum disappeared. Therefore, pressures for curriculum adaptation had to be directed away from the centre. Curriculum analysts directed their energies into exhorting teachers to adopt particular teaching approaches and culminated in the notion of the teacher as innovator and researcher.[33] Secondly, and not as paradoxical as it may seem, there was an explosion in the amount of curriculum analysis in America and Britain. Tomes were written on the nature of knowledge, the sociology of knowledge, objectives in teaching, assessment and new subjects (or, rather, combinations of old ones). Very little indeed of this had a specifically Welsh dimension, as all Welsh energies were channelled into the Welsh schools movement.

In the meantime life in schools went on, seven or eight lessons a day of it. What happened? Curriculum planning in schools drew on a strange blend of tradition and ad hoc responses. Pressure groups and fashions all had their impact. For a heady decade in the 1960s the social sciences seemed to be taking over the world, its advocates spurred on by a blend of practical idealism after the Second World War, snowstorms around the two cultures, and the intellectual ambience of *The History Man*. None of this amounted to a curricular blueprint for schools. All that happened was that sociology found a place on school timetables, not long before the bubble burst in university departments. Subject associations realized the threat that the new world posed – history is a good example – and mounted a counter-attack on the ubiquitous, often spurious concept of 'relevance'. Whatever the shape of courses in university education departments, with Peters jostling with Piaget, the 1960s were a period of the pressure group rather than the philosopher of education. There have been no new verities – just the opposite, as we have struggled to come to terms with widening educational opportunity. The strangely named grammar schools of the post-1944 period had a tradition to work with, and made few concessions to the demands of an increasingly sophisticated economy. No one really knew what to teach in the secondary modern schools. Outside their walls, and the homes of their pupils, I wonder how many cared. The comprehensive schools caused a real crisis of curriculum planning because they were the antithesis of all that had characterized school education in England and Wales over the centuries. Should there not be, could there be, a common curriculum for a common school, all pupils learning the same things? Such an idea was quite unprecedented. There were statements from philosophers of education, Hirst particularly, and, as the debate hotted up in the 1970s, attempts by DES and HMI to come to terms with the new situation. There was no consensus. No one said much about Wales.

There were gains and losses as curricular initiatives, especially those of the Schools Council, met with varying degrees of success. There were pressures to come to terms with the demands of a high-tech, multi-ethnic, comprehensive-school society. But in the absence of co-ordinated curricular prescriptions, the state stepped in once again. Now we have a common curriculum informed by no particular philosophy of education, at least none that is worked out from first principles, as opposed to *ex cathedra* statements of what is good for us. And yet there are strange forces at work. One of the more fascinating aspects of the National Curriculum is that the list of subjects it comprises is very similar indeed to that laid down in the secondary regulations of 1904.

Curriculum analysis has become more sophisticated since 1904. For Skilbeck it is axiomatic that the curriculum should initiate pupils into the values and ways of life of a society and provide the knowledge, skills and understanding for social and personal development.[34] The HMI document *Curriculum 11–16*[35] argues that pupils should be introduced to their own cultural inheritance and their world of society and work. Such assertions are significant. First, they focus our attention on areas which, in Wales, are distinctively Welsh because the one area of experience which no one can deny Wales is its cultural differences from England – and these are reflected in the experience of Welsh-speakers and the English-speaking Welsh alike. The second point is that the curriculum, in the end, must embody the value systems of those who devise it. Arriving at a judgement as to what should be taught is not an objective exercise in the sense of being scientifically verifiable. This too is significant for Wales. We cannot teach all there is to know in schools, or even the methods of studying all there is to know. Even if we could, pupils' capacity to master either the material or the methodologies would vary dramatically. Since not everything can be done there has to be selection. The nature of that selection has always been a matter of endless debate and will continue to be so. The introduction of the National Curriculum does not end that debate; on the contrary, it will merely produce pressure groups to work for change.

Discussion will continue to take account of the fact that there are, to over-simplify, two main sets of educational protagonists. First, there is the child-centred, areas-of-experience, education-as-process, education-as-growth school, for whom the notion of an externally imposed curriculum is retrograde since understanding stems from each pupil's personal experience in a unique situation. Second, there are the educational instrumentalists. Instrumentalism certainly can have the noblest of motives – for example initiation into the areas of human experience of intrinsic worth. It is more commonly associated nowadays with politicians, Labour and Conservative, for whom education is a means to a less worthy end, usually, but by no means exclusively, an economic one. The externally determined end leads logically to an externally imposed and tested programme.

Up to a point the instrumentalists have triumphed in the 1988 Education Act and, in a broad sense, the politicization of education is now stark. But it is here that we must be grateful for the separate institutional framework for Wales in educational matters which, I argued earlier, is an increasingly important manifestation of Welsh identity. As the politicization of education has proceeded apace so the existence of the Welsh Office and its education department have provided channels for Welsh aspirations for curricular distinctiveness.

And so I come to the final question: to what horizons might some of these perspectives from the past lead us in contemporary Wales?

I am not convinced of the capacity of schools to be the main agents for change in any society. I believe in comprehensive schools, but I doubt whether they are going to produce egalitarianism. Schools are an element in a system of social conditioning which has always been so complex as to defy analysis by droves of historians and sociologists. If schools are more the creatures of society than its arbiters we need to be careful about exaggerating the impact that a recognizably Welsh curriculum will have on future generations.

A properly educative process, in Wales or anywhere else, under the National Curriculum or any other system, cannot compel. In families or in schools, education must ultimately allow those being educated to make informed choices. The equipoise between what those with power in any society deem to be desirable to pass on to the next generation and the rights of those to whom it is passed on, and their parents, has to be preserved. We cannot live future generations' lives for them, but educators have a responsibility to attempt to provide both information about the society in which young people grow up and ways which have developed of classifying and making sense of that information. Among the most significant ways of doing so have been in terms of subjects now included in the National Curriculum. Essentially we are attempting to pass on, by means of formal education, elements of the ordering of accumulated experience, and the methodological capacity to extend that experience. If that education is liberal, if it is an education rather than indoctrination, it has to consist of experiences which can be accepted or rejected. That acceptance or rejection, in whole or in part, derives its validity from the extent to which the decision is an informed one. Some understanding of their society is essential for all citizens. Education is similar to personal memory, without which we would be disorientated. Obviously it is more than recalled personal experience; it is experience informed by the experience of others, in community, nation, world. The better the quality of the education, the more informed will be the choices dependent on it.

The accumulated experience of those of us who are Welsh is conditioned by our Welshness. I argued in the first part of this paper that the Welsh experience has taken many forms, some shared, some unique. It still does, but I think it has never been argued that it has been expressed distinctively and definitively in scientific form, so there is no point in building in false Welsh dimensions into the heartlands of scientific or technological education.

What, then, *is* distinctive about the Welsh experience? First, there is a sense of place. Since the dark ages the story of the Welsh has unfolded west of Offa's Dyke. The topography of the country has always influenced, and still influences, the pattern of settlement, the way in which Welsh people make their living, whether through agriculture or industry, in the hill country or in the valleys. The pattern of communications, or lack of them, conditions links (or lack of them) between north and south Wales, the relationship between these areas and the English hinterland, for example with Bristol or Liverpool. Topography helps determine economic and occupational relationships within Wales and outside as it has done through the centuries. Much of this dimension of the Welsh experience goes, I believe, under the name of geography and so should form part of the staple diet of pupils in Wales as part of that subject within the National Curriculum.

For well over a thousand years the main vehicle for mediating the Welsh experience, and obviously therefore the most potent element in it, though not in my view the exclusive one, has been the Welsh language. Inevitably, the language is central to the education of those young people in Wales for whom it is the natural means of communication. But the language has been so much part of the Welsh experience that all pupils in Wales should be given the opportunity to learn it, though its teaching as a second language will not be effective until it becomes something more than a school-based foreign language, like French. Language is a means to an end. Part of that end is day-to-day communication, the day-to-day currency of the nation's life. The language provides access to wider areas of the national experience, through, for example, newspapers or television. It provides access to deeper elements of the national experience through its literature, its customs, its festivals. It is arguable that any knowledge of Welsh is better than none. All knowledge enriches. But the element of enrichment is scarcely comparable with that which is opened up by the ability to communicate with people in a language which is a normal part of day-to-day discourse and to be initiated into the culture of the Welsh-speaking nation, whether through the eisteddfod or *Pobl y Cwm*. And here we need to temper with some realism the euphoria which has greeted the publication of the final report of the National Curriculum Welsh Working Group – and not only in terms of financial and teaching resource implications. For how many pupils who study Welsh presently for three years in the secondary school is the end result that they can speak it and read it sufficiently well to make use of it? How many of them want to? Learning Welsh from the age of five opens up far brighter prospects of eventual conversational facility but we should be under no illusions about the number of Welsh learners who will, for example, read regularly in the language. On the other hand we do have a television channel transmitting a wide variety of programmes in Welsh and television, for better or worse, is now the common denominator in our society and our culture. If the medium cannot provide programmes which young people want to watch it has failed. If our education system cannot provide learners with the wherewithal and the encouragement to watch them it has failed. The prominence given to 'viewing' in the attainment targets specified in the National Curriculum Welsh Working Group's final report is highly significant. As the learners tell us, 'language is always a social construction, not a mere mechanical aid. It has to be connected up with the meanings of everyday experiences and ways of seeing the world around us.'[36] Where is the extramural dimension of school Welsh?

It is a fact that the experience of Wales has not been conveyed solely or exclusively in the Welsh language. This is particularly true of the industrial experience of the Welsh of south Wales, the product of one of the swiftest and most cataclysmic changes to have overtaken any nation as parts of Wales were transformed from meagrely populated, rural, marginal parishes into an urbanized, concentrated ferment, coping with social, economic and linguistic pressures of a completely new order. There are still those who echo Saunders Lewis in questioning whether there is, or can be, such a thing as an Anglo-Welsh literature and whether Wales can be bicultural, let alone multicultural. While I do not feel competent to pursue that debate, it seems to be self-evident that some aspects of this urban industrial experience in Wales have been illuminated incomparably in the works of poets and novelists writing in English. This must be incontrovertibly true of the interwar years which affected the psyche of our nation to the extent that some have compared the historical role of the Depression in south Wales to that of the famine in Ireland. That grimmest of Welsh experiences has been recorded by historians, but they would be the first to admit that Idris Davies, Lewis Jones, Jack Jones, Gwyn Thomas or Raymond Williams have been provoked into major literary achievement in response to it. Such literature is the birthright of pupils in Wales. It is central to the nation's cultural experience, it illuminates crucial communal affiliations, class structures, leisure interests and politics in today's Wales. It is the one area in which the National Curriculum has so far let us down, since there is no reference in the report of the National Curriculum English Working Group to the potential of Anglo-Welsh literature in articulating the Welsh experience. It is a recognizable genre and its importance should have been acknowledged in programmes of study for pupils in Wales.

Other aspects of Welsh culture may be less contentious. For example, there has been a strong musical tradition in Wales over the centuries, though a restricted one. It deserves to be reflected in what Welsh pupils learn about their music, despite the universality of the western musical tradition. It needs to be highlighted in the National Curriculum, but to appeal to young people and to reflect the Welsh dimension it will need to be a catholic view of music.

Underpinning any understanding of all these aspects of the Welsh experience must be some knowledge of the main stages of the nation's history. The wide-ranging interests of postwar Welsh historians, coinciding with changing historical fashions which have encouraged a focus on the history of societies and cultures rather than on high politics, have resulted in their work assuming a British and European significance. For reasons with which we are familiar, school teachers of Welsh history have also to be reckoned with, and not only in Wales. Recognition has come in the form of a History Committee for Wales to devise the National Curriculum in that subject. Its existence is crucial, its significance on a par with that of the committee which was established for the Welsh language. Given the subject-based structure of the National Curriculum it will have to provide much of the context for the Welsh dimension of the other subject areas.

I have had little time to analyse the arguments for and against a subject-based curriculum. We now have it, whether we like it or not. In terms of the Welshness of the curriculum it has provided opportunities for subject specialists to make bids for including the Welsh dimension of their disciplines. But this does pose a problem because the Welsh experience is not neatly comprehended in subject areas. That experience has in the past been expressed in, for example, crafts, community distinctiveness, religious affiliation, sport, politics and the media. Historians are best placed to summarize this totality but the major concern about the National Curriculum must be that it will, effectively, allow only discipline-based manifestations of ways of looking at the world. That apart I have less antipathy towards a subject-based curriculum than some recent writers. It does seem to me that when the 'knowledge through reason' and 'knowledge through senses' schools of education are polarized, as they have been in one influential curriculum manual recently,[37] there is a tendency to ignore the revolution in the teaching of these subjects in schools in the last two decades. The subjects listed in the 1904 Regulations are no longer mediated purely in terms of received verities and rote learning. These subject disciplines are an initiation into ways of finding out about the world and rest on epistemological and methodological theories of some force. Indeed, arguing the case for the Welsh dimension in the curriculum must remind us that crude instrumentalism in the curriculum is inadequate, that emphasis on assessment alone is divisive and misconceived. Ultimately, the Welsh dimension, in any worthwhile sense, is not assessable, nor should it be divisive. If it is to be of any value it needs to stress both unity and diversity – a unity beyond that centred solely around the Welsh language and into the unity inherent in the exercise of free and democratic rights in the midst of a common culture and heritage; a diversity reflecting the many manifestations of that national culture.

There is both danger and unprecedented opportunity presented by the advent of a common curriculum in the schools of Wales. So often in the history of education the consequences of government action are unforeseen. Such was the case with so many aspects of the 1944 Education Act, or with the implementation, virtually by accident, of the O-level examination.[38] The 1988 Education Act will be no different. One of the subtle ironies apparent already is that the imposition of uniformity will incorporate some of the best elements of diversity. It is a considerable achievement that we are in the process of creating, for the first time ever, a 'state school' curriculum which is unique to Wales – in content and context. This is a national achievement as important as any in our search for 'creative independence'.[39] To me it is incontrovertible that such diversity of culture, of language, of identity, of community, is of inestimable worth in a Europe in which the tendencies towards uniformity of economic organization, multinational companies and mass culture through television are the norm. We cannot stop this world and get off, but celebration of difference seems to me to be an essential enrichment in its midst. If that assertion be accepted as a premise it follows that its incorporation in diversity in the school curriculum is wholly positive, educational in the profoundest sense of the word.

Above all it holds out the prospect that each new generation of Welsh people will be allowed to make an informed decision about the kind of Wales which can command their allegiance.

11
Which nation's curriculum?
The case of Wales

The historical context

The attitude of the state towards education in Wales emerged in the mid-nineteenth century. In 1847 a government commission produced a massive report on the condition of education in Wales which has become part of national folklore.[1] Its observations, compiled by three Anglican Englishmen, were so condemnatory of all things Welsh, including the language, that they were branded *Brad y Llyfrau Gleision*, the treason of the Blue Books. Yet the report reflected accurately enough contemporary attitudes that English was the language of progress at all levels of society. When the system of 'payment by results' was inaugurated in 1862 Welsh was not included as a grant-earning subject. Indeed, in some schools the language was positively discouraged by the punishment of the 'Welsh Not', a wooden stick hung around the neck of the pupil most recently caught in the act of speaking Welsh. The unfortunate wearer was beaten at the end of the day. Although the state elementary schools established after 1870 do not appear to have imitated this practice, they shared the attitude to the language. Only under the impetus of a resurgent cultural nationalism in the 1880s did Welsh become first a special subject, then a class subject earning grant in the elementary schools of Wales.[2] That apart, there was little to distinguish the curricula of schools in Wales from those in England.

The 1880s also saw the beginnings of a distinctive educational administration for Wales as the 1889 Welsh Intermediate Education Act provided for the establishment of intermediate or secondary schools over a decade before comparable schools were legislated for in England.[3] During the first half of the twentieth century the curriculum for these and other secondary schools in Wales was determined by the secondary code interpreted by the Welsh Department of the Board of Education which was created in 1907. While

Welsh was taught as a subject (through the medium of English!) in districts where Welsh was spoken, and other subjects might be taught wholly or partly in Welsh where local circumstances warranted, the status of the language was low.[4] That other curricular influence, the School Certificate, almost invariably saw Welsh set against French, with French attracting more candidates.

Variety in curriculum practice after 1944

After 1944, determinants of the curriculum in Wales diversified as local authority influence increased, but in terms of 'Welshness' the main preoccupation remained the language. The first Welsh-language school for primary-age pupils had been opened privately in Aberystwyth just before the outbreak of the Second World War and the movement to persuade local authorities to establish similar schools gathered momentum. In secondary education a variety of arrangements met a variety of linguistic situations. The 1951 census revealed a dramatic decline in the number of Welsh-speakers since the previous census in 1931. In much of industrial, urban Wales English was the overwhelmingly predominant language of communication and education. In much of rural Wales, especially the western counties, however, Welsh remained for many pupils their first language and schools reflected this by teaching some subjects – the arts subjects – through the medium of Welsh. Language remained the touchstone. Although Welshness impinged on the curriculum more generally in the form of a ration of Welsh history and the occasional Welsh or local example in other subjects, there was no national policy on how the national heritage and culture should be reflected in the curriculum. This was a matter for schools and local authorities to deliberate, if they were so minded.

The Welsh ethos of schools was manifested in a spectrum spanning near saturation to tokenism. In a small number of schools Welsh was the medium of instruction in the majority of subjects. In others there were Welsh-language and English-language streams. Schools in areas in which Welsh traditions were strong held an annual eisteddfod, or cultural festival of poetry, prose and music. Most primary and secondary schools observed St David's Day in some fashion.

Such variety is not difficult to explain. It echoed the cultural heterogeneity of the regions of Wales. It reflected the distancing of central government from control of the curriculum. It reflected the lack of autonomous Welsh institutions of education. Despite the establishment of the Welsh Office and the appointment of a Welsh secretary of state for the first time in 1964, education policy was determined in London rather than Cardiff, even when, nominally, the Welsh Office became responsible for all educational institutions in Wales other than the university.

Nor was there much debate about the nature of the 'Welshness' which might be reflected in schools. An official inquiry into *Welsh in Education and Life* in 1927 was originally intended to be concerned with bilingualism only. Transmuted into a more general survey for political reasons, it raised fundamental questions about the place of the Welsh language and, incidentally, noted other elements of a Welsh education: 'We believe that the Welsh language, Welsh literature, Welsh history, together form the individual heritage of Welsh men and women.'[5] After the war, despite there being a separate advisory council for Wales, it was not until 1952 that there was a major overview. In that year the Welsh Department of the Ministry of Education published a booklet entitled *The Curriculum and the Community in Wales*[6] which treated the subject in depth and set the debate on a sound theoretical basis, encompassing both Welsh- and English-speakers. The Welsh language, naturally, was the prime inheritance but that inheritance was also mediated in the nation's history. A sense of place was central to pupils' understanding of their environment, so the geography of Wales was another essential ingredient. Welsh children were also entitled to know of the musical, artistic and poetic tradition of Wales. The arguments underpinning these conclusions were subtle and urbane. However, they were far stronger on theory than on practical application. This is hardly surprising since there was no common curricular core across Wales to which practical programmes might be coupled. The weakness of the document remained that there was no attempt to link the theory with exemplar case-studies of good practice in various parts of Wales, which might have stimulated some replication.

Thereafter, apart from a discussion paper produced by the Schools Council Committee for Wales in 1974, there was little guidance from the centre as to what might constitute a Welsh curriculum. 'Secret gardens' were cultivated as luxuriantly in Wales as in England in the context of a common legislative base. Even when it became obvious from the late 1970s that the Department of Education and Science was edging towards reasserting control over the curriculum, the Welsh Office did not take any independent line and produced no major publication which specifically addressed the Welsh dimension. Welsh educationists at all levels had no coherent strategy of response across the curriculum to the revolutionary implications of the 1988 Education Act.

The advent of the 1988 Act

The immediate circumstances in which Kenneth Baker devised the broad outlines of the National Curriculum are not clear. What is clear is that the outcome was a reassertion of subject-based education rather than one based on areas of experience or the interdisciplinary combinations which had characterized so much topic and project work in junior schools and increasingly formed the basis of humanities or environmental studies programmes in comprehensive schools. The core and foundation subjects, technology apart, were very similar indeed to those which were stipulated in the secondary regulations of 1904. However, in the context of the 1980s, the questions raised in deciding the knowledge, skills and processes that constituted each subject were different. The concept of a National Curriculum raised the issue of which nation was to be served; but in the absence in Wales of an autonomous institutional framework or theoretical base the answers were, for the moment at least, ad hoc.

In the crucial area of assessment arrangements there were to be no differences at all. The report of the Task Group on Assessment and Testing[7] was adopted for Wales as well as for England; there was no machinery for a Welsh input into the assessment debate as there was in different circumstances in Scotland. Significantly, while the act established a separate advisory body for Wales on curriculum (the Curriculum Council for Wales), responsibility for advising on assessment was given to a body with an 'England and Wales' remit (School Examinations and Assessment Council). Only in 1994 did Wales, at least nominally, take responsibility for assessment at the first three Key Stages, and probably in the event, for Key Stage 4.

The curriculum for Wales

The content of the curriculum was another matter. There was a Welsh Office parallel publication (*The National Curriculum in Wales*),[8] to the Department of Education and Science's *The National Curriculum 5–16*,[9] a first formal assertion of difference. The Welsh Office accepted – doubtless in the absence of any DES interest – that Welsh language and literature should be a compulsory part of the curriculum and a working group was established immediately. In Wales, therefore, there were to be ten foundation subjects in primary schools and eleven in secondary, one more at each key stage than in England. This prompted discussion of the impact of the extra work on schools. One result was that the Curriculum Council for Wales commissioned a research project to investigate the similarities and differences between the pattern of language development encapsulated in the Statutory Orders for English and Welsh.[10]

Welsh, then, was to be a core subject, on a par with English, for those pupils attending schools in which Welsh was the normal language of communication. In all other schools in Wales, except at the discretion of the secretary of state, Welsh was to be a foundation subject, to be taught at all key stages. Only a very few schools (in south Pembrokeshire's 'little England beyond Wales' and in Clwyd) were permitted temporary exemption, so the teaching of Welsh is now more widespread than it has ever been. In particular, pupils whose first language is English will now be learning Welsh from the age of five, rather than taking it up at the age of eleven as was common previously. However, the problem of the supply of teachers remains and there is constant concern expressed that Welsh-language teaching in the schools, without the reinforcement of greater community usage, is unlikely ultimately to preserve Welsh as a language of common discourse. Recent research indicates that 20 per cent of pupils in Wales receive their education in Welsh in primary schools, while only 12 per cent use Welsh as their first language in secondary schools. The proportion of pupils who take their GCSE examinations in Welsh falls to 3 per cent.[11] On the other hand, the 1991 census revealed that Welsh speaking among the school-age population has increased, so reversing a decline going back to the beginning of the century. This reflects the considerable success of the Welsh-language schools in attracting pupils not only from Welsh-speaking homes but also from monoglot English backgrounds.

That the teaching of Welsh should now permeate the schools was accepted with some enthusiasm and a remarkable lack of acrimony. For many, it was the touchstone of national identity. But what other elements should differentiate a Welsh education from an English? Again, administrative structures impinged on curriculum planning. Each working group established by the secretaries of state for Education and for Wales contained one member, working in Wales, nominated by the secretary of state for Wales. The Wales-orientated input of that nominee varied from group to group. There was considerable disappointment in Wales that the Statutory Orders for National Curriculum English did not reflect the contribution which Anglo-Welsh literature made to the inheritance of Welsh pupils, some responsibility for which must be accepted by the Anglo-Welsh literary establishment who failed to appreciate the importance of the Cox Group. Here was no mere parochialism because, from time to time, the essence of the national experience had been illuminated in such literature – the best example being the 1920s and the 1930s. There was more than adequate material by Welsh authors or on Welsh subjects to provide suitable material for school study – ranging from Gillian Clarke and Harri Webb to Dannie Abse and Dylan Thomas.

Any such curriculum planning – or lack of it – was a matter of chance in the absence of any overview of what should constitute a Welsh National Curriculum. Pragmatism prevailed over history. The Association of History Teachers in Wales was founded in 1982 and established an enviable reputation for its conferences, its journal and its dissemination of information. It carried sufficient weight in Wales to be invited by the Welsh Office to put its case for special arrangements to be made for history since it was a subject so central to pupils' understanding of their national heritage. A delegation, led by the Association's president, Emeritus Professor (now Sir) Glanmor Williams, FBA argued that, ideally, this centrality should be reflected in the setting up of a separate working group for Wales. Failing that, there should at least be double the normal representation from Wales on an 'England and Wales' group. The delegation put its case in a highly constructive encounter, but realized that, with history being one of the major battlegrounds between right and left, political difficulties might surround the establishment of a separate group.

Not surprisingly, there was considerable satisfaction when Wales got its equivalent of a working group to operate in tandem with that of England. The History Committee for Wales's remit clarified further the nature of the relationship between Welsh and English educational systems. It was emphasized that the assessment system underpinning the National Curriculum was to be common to both sets of orders, so the attainment targets and statements of attainment had to be agreed. Fortunately, despite stronger reservations in the History Committee for Wales than in the History Working Group concerning the ten levels of attainment which had to be defined for each attainment target, both groups were able to agree statements. The Welsh group was at liberty to pursue an entirely independent line over content and the final report and subsequent Statutory Orders gave substantial weight to Welsh history in a British and European context. The chronological framework of the core units in the two reports was similar but the particularity of Welsh history was fully reflected in very different programmes of study.[12]

On the relatively rare occasions on which a curriculum appropriate to Wales had been discussed, language and history had inevitably figured prominently. It was usually argued that these must be complemented by a sense of place, but once more the theory was far less prominent than the pragmatism. The Association of Geography Teachers in Wales was of much more recent foundation than its history counterpart and was not in a position to press for a separate working group. Even so, Welsh geography teachers did have an impact on the thinking of the group and the final report recommended that Welsh pupils should study Wales as a separate entity rather than merely study their own immediate locality.

At this stage, Welsh had been recognized as both a core and a foundation subject, while history and geography were rather differently constituted foundation subjects. There was now to be an ideological clash over two of the other foundation subjects, art and music, which had the entirely unforeseen consequence of widening the fissure between the National Curriculum as it operated in England and in Wales. The significant difference now was that this resulted from a strengthened institutional base rather than obvious national priorities. It is true that Wales could claim elements of a musical and artistic tradition different from that of England – for example *penillion* singing, in which a singer follows a melody line different from that of the accompanying instrument, normally the harp – and it was appropriate that these should be reflected in schemes of work.

But due to the growing authority of the Curriculum Council for Wales a different kind of educational tradition also exerted its influence. There has been no manifestation of extreme educational ideologies of either right or left in Wales and the responses to the consultation over the music and art working groups' reports reflected this. Teachers in Wales favoured the original reports rather than those right-wing responses which called for more attention to historical aspects of music and the work of the great composers, for example, and argued for less emphasis on pupils' creativity. The views of the CCW, reflecting Welsh teachers' predilections, prevailed and, indeed, allowed Welsh Office Ministers to emphasize the divergence between the 'English' and the 'Welsh' National Curriculums. This was indeed an unexpected outcome of the 1988 Act.

The flexing of curricular muscle in Wales was even more evident in an issue still unresolved, that of the English curriculum. This has been the ultimate battleground between the die-hard traditionalists and the moderates. The former, having the ear of ministers in England, in 1992 brought about National Curriculum Council proposals for a review and revision of the English curriculum, a review which the Curriculum Council for Wales regarded as unnecessary. The NCC view prevailed. In 1993 both bodies produced proposals for consultation. The NCC insisted that there should be greater use of standard English and a set of prescribed texts for study. The CCW response was significantly different. It was in line with the original Working Party (Cox) Report, did not insist on standard English for infant pupils and eschewed mandatory texts for study. It could be argued that, at Key Stage 1, pupils whose first language was Welsh should be treated differently but this would not apply in the case of more than 80 per cent of pupils in Wales. In this divergence CCW, backed by its masters in the Welsh Office, came of age as an administrative body pursuing an independent line. And Wales has emerged with a National Curriculum in which only science, technology, maths and physical education are likely to be the same as in England. Confirmation of this interrelated independence has arisen outside the National Curriculum proper. In August 1993 it was reported that Baroness Blatch had requested the NCC to recommend ways of raising the standards of religious education teaching in English schools by providing model syllabuses. The Welsh Office indicated that it would not be requiring the CCW to follow suit since the teaching of religious education in Wales was satisfactory.[13]

The role of the Curriculum Council for Wales

The increasing distinctiveness of the curriculum in Wales since 1988 has evolved piecemeal because the institutional framework which might have underpinned a more coherent strategy has developed in similarly ad hoc fashion. Indeed, the independence of the CCW is wholly reliant on the Welsh Office. However, the CCW has increasingly taken policy initiatives. It is arguable that the most significant of these resulted in the publication in 1993 of CCW Advisory Paper 18, *Developing a Curriculum Cymreig*, a curriculum intended to encapsulate 'Welshness' in schools. The document takes it as axiomatic that all pupils in Wales are entitled to a 'Welsh curriculum', which it identifies as a sense of place and heritage, a sense of belonging, a knowledge of the contribution which the Welsh language and Welsh literature have made to life in Wales, an understanding of the importance of the creative arts and an awareness of the influence of religious beliefs and practices on Welsh life.[14] It proceeds to analyse at three levels ways in which schools might meet this entitlement – through the statutory National Curriculum, by means of cross-curricular themes and by fostering a Welsh ethos in schools, whether they be in the rural fastnesses of Welsh-speaking Gwynedd in the north-west or the anglicized industrial and post-industrial valleys of Gwent in the south-east.

At the first level the paper analyses the way in which subject orders in history, geography, art and music differ in Wales, while also arguing that subjects in which there are common orders should draw on Welsh examples wherever these make sense in context.[15] The strength of the document lies in its practical suggestions, derived from actual school experience. For example, one primary school in Cwm Tawe, West Glamorgan, pursuing the National Curriculum geography course, 'attempted to lead the pupils outward from their own school and home area, enabling them eventually to compare and contrast aspects of the geography of their own valley with those of the wider world'.[16] Study Unit 24 in Key Stage 3 history prompted one school to a detailed study of Welsh emigration to Patagonia in the nineteenth century.[17] AT3(i) of the art orders inspired work on film animation, in which Wales has played a leading part in the last decade while, inevitably, there has been music work on the harp and *cerdd dant*, the folk music of Wales.[18] Religious education syllabuses are, of course, agreed by local Standing Advisory Councils, so providing ample scope for the development of Welsh themes.[19]

A second dimension is apparent in detailed exploration of the way in which cross-curricular themes might be exemplified from Wales. Some lend themselves well – community understanding, economic and industrial understanding and environmental education, in particular.[20]

The third level on which the document argues that a Welsh ambience may be developed is that of more extensive use of the Welsh language. For example, 'If all signs and notices within a school are bilingual, the Welsh language will gain in status and impact for the pupils, and this will also remind visitors, governors and parents of the school's policy of creating a positive Welsh atmosphere.'[21]

The work on developing a *Curriculum Cymreig* is set to continue by means of detailed study of the Welsh ethos of specific schools, the conclusions of which will be passed to all schools in Wales. Beyond the statutory requirements it will, of course, be up to each school to decide to what degree 'Welshness' should be imprinted, although the new Welsh Language Act (1993) will require schools to have policies on the use of the language.

Uncertainties and changing scenes

At present, curriculum and assessment, indeed the structure of education generally in Wales, are in a state of flux. The 1988 Education Act revolutionized the role of the state in education, thereby inadvertently raising questions about the relationship between the Welsh nation and the British state in a new context. Issues of cultural and political nationalism coalesced. The ten-subject curriculum inevitably prompted analysis of the distinctive cultural heritage of Wales and the nature of entitlement to it of Welsh pupils. Equally inadvertently, other elements of the 1988 Act led to analysis of the administration of the education system in Wales. For example, common provisions for schools to opt out of local authority control stemmed from a historic unity between England and Wales, but in practice have emphasized differences, in that so little enthusiasm has been generated for 'opting out' in Wales. Again, as the curriculum and testing arrangements envisaged in the 1988 Act have had to be modified, so has the potential for distinctively Welsh provision.

The situation in Wales now reflects additional uncertainties to those which led, in 1992, to the review, spearheaded by Sir Ron Dearing, of the National Curriculum and its assessment.[22] It is likely that no official of the DES in 1988 envisaged substantial divergence between the curriculum in Wales and that in England, yet there are now likely to be differences of content or emphasis in six subjects as well as in religious education. The Dearing interim report has indicated that the subjects of the National Curriculum will be retained, albeit from ages five to fourteen and in slimmed-down form. This has been fully endorsed by the Daugherty Report, the Curriculum Council for Wales's equivalent analysis.[23] So Wales will continue to have its different curriculum. However, the modification of assessment arrangements is likely to undermine the *Curriculum Cymreig*. A hierarchy of subjects has emerged, with the probability that statutory testing will be confined to the core subjects. Apart from those pupils whose first language is Welsh the core contains nothing of the essential *Curriculum Cymreig*. Since statutory testing will have a vital bearing on the status of subjects of all age groups, the most recent developments threaten to undermine some of the progress made in developing a Welsh National Curriculum.

Institutional change may help counteract this dilution. The strange intention in the DES in 1988 was that curriculum and assessment should be administered by separate bodies in England. Since assessment was to be common in both countries there was no need for separate assessment provision for Wales. With the rethink of 1993, a new nominated body came into existence in Wales in 1994, the Curriculum and Assessment Authority for Wales, taking the acronym ACAC from its title in Welsh – Awdurdod Cwricwlwm ac Asesu Cymru.

Conclusions

We have seen that, as a result of the scale of state interference in education since 1988, claims to a separate curriculum in Wales have led to institutional developments of some significance. The whole question of a *Curriculum Cymreig* is bound up with how wider differences in Welsh education should be allowed expression. Broadly speaking, there are now two approaches to the curriculum in Welsh schools, both of which see it as one element, though a vital one, in the debate over Welsh educational autonomy. The purists argue that control of Welsh education should reflect Wales's national status, with at least a similar degree of independence to that of Scotland, with its different arrangements for curriculum, assessment and school funding. Ideally, according to this view, one controlling body for Welsh schools should be responsible only to a democratically elected Welsh Assembly, so having substantial leeway to initiate policies appropriate to Wales on school funding, local authority powers, curriculum and assessment. Discussion of the curriculum for Wales would start *ab initio* to ask precisely how far it should reflect the culture which forms part of the heritage of all pupils. But 'Welshness' would also be reflected in a rejection of much of the competitive, business world, producer consumer, league table model which informs government education policy.

Others take a more pragmatic view based on immediate political realities. Almost by accident the post-1988 educational reforms have resulted in substantially greater educational devolution than was previously the case. Central to this process has been intense, if surprisingly sporadic, debate over the emergence of a distinctively Welsh school curriculum. Any judgements made about what pupils should learn reflect preconceptions about the cultural heritage of a nation and its people. The debate over the National Curriculum has inevitably helped sharpen analysis of Welsh nationality as expressed in the control and constituent elements of its education system generally. Continuation of that incremental devolution so characteristic of Welsh educational history over the past century, and concomitant dissection of the elements of the system, decree an eventual outcome which is tantalizingly opaque.

12
The Dearing disaster: a perspective on recent curriculum change

Any invitation to comment on future patterns of school education in Wales and England is an invitation to foolishness. There are two approaches which might mitigate the folly. Some have a vision of Utopianism in the classroom. It involves better funding, smaller class sizes (despite current political propaganda), less bureaucracy, more rational initial and in-service teacher training, for example. In curricular terms it involves consensus over the blend of prescription and teacher autonomy, and an endorsement of the principles underlying the *Curriculum Cymreig*,[1] that is, Welshness, at a variety of levels, informing an international curriculum which would provide the foundations for the worlds of work and leisure.

That approach is not very helpful. There were elements of Utopianism in the 1960s, but it is not fashionable now. Any vision of the educational future must be founded on hard realities. These can only be understood by seeing how firmly they are rooted in the past. The past will not provide a blueprint but will furnish some clues to the future. At least that gives us some purchase on reality, some chance of avoiding navel-gazing. If we analyse underlying principles in state education, that is the system over the last 125 years, there seem to be some generalizations possible, highly illuminating about the present situation. Let us explore two of these themes. First, the state, through its government, has always had a major concern with what is taught in schools, and has intervened accordingly. The essential reasons for this are the power of education to modify the social order, the impact of education on the economy and the fact that the education system reflects ideological conflicts in a variety of intellectual and organizational forms. Secondly, the state is concerned with the assessment of what is taught, because its preoccupation with the social order, the economy and the potency of ideas all require judgements to be made about individuals and groups.

The state has always had a major concern with what is taught in schools – and has intervened accordingly

The state, through its government, has been concerned with what is taught in schools for a variety of reasons, all of which have some bearing on the present situation, though of course in changed contexts. Underpinning all else is the fact that education has always had too powerful an influence on citizens for rulers and governments to ignore. So, the first reason for state interference is that governments have always been afraid of the power of teachers. Long before the days of state education, in the sixteenth and seventeenth centuries, teachers had to be licensed – and, if it is any consolation, were harried and persecuted. Religion was the problem then, but the underlying reason has always been the power which is conferred by the ability to read and write. Tudor and Stuart governments were well aware of the dangers of mass literacy. People can read revolutionary pamphlets as well as morally uplifting texts.

One consequence of the power to read and write, and such modern equivalents as cruising the Internet, is that it leads to social mobility, another crucial concern of governments. Since governments always represent the interests of particular classes, however defined, they inevitably have a view on a social force which, potentially, can do so much to modify the social structure. In early modern Britain, before the state invested money in the school system, there was relatively little concern. The education system generally reinforced the existing social order according to a time-honoured curriculum. There was an education in university or great boarding school or town grammar school which had to be paid for; it catered for the landed and professional classes and was essentially classical. The justification for the classical curriculum was simple. Classical ideas, reworked in the Renaissance, embodied the learning in literature, philosophy, mathematics, architecture, art, music, even in today's jargon human movement, which was the hallmark of civilization, including enlightened government. So, despite the increasing industrial development of early nineteenth-century Britain, the education of the gentleman in no way reflected that economic change. A classical curriculum provided a superior education for the ruling classes, based on the notion of knowledge for its own sake.

It was a wholly different story for the lower classes. Those who could not afford to pay, the workers on land or in factory, had

available only a charity education and they did not need that education for farm or foundry. So why was there so much effort put into
providing charity education? There were two main, linked, motives.
First, there was the religious motive – that people must be able to
read the Bible and imbibe the correct doctrine. Then there was the
necessity for keeping the lower orders under control in a period of
unprecedented economic and social upheaval. A minimal education, in the three Rs, was deemed necessary for both. But it had to
be cheap.

By the middle of the nineteenth century another central-government
concern became increasingly apparent – another of the themes linking past and present – the efficiency and professionalism of the society
for which government is responsible. In an industrial society based
on competition, especially since there was an empire to run and
exploit, ever higher degrees of education were required. Under the
impact of economic change in nineteenth-century Britain both the
organization and content of education were eventually transformed.
What then loomed large for a government still overwhelmingly
representative of the social élite, was balancing wider educational
opportunity made necessary by the deficiencies of amateurism and
threats to industrial supremacy, with safeguarding the social structure.
The 1851 Great Exhibition summed up increasing complexities – a
celebration of imperial might and industrial superiority but, already,
worries about Britain's competitors – the USA and Europe.

What the middle classes were certain they should not sully their
hands with was anything like applied science or technology. Pure
science, and even activities like photography, were socially acceptable as an amateur activity but anything which smacked of the process of production was anathema. The result was that after the 1902
Education Act the middle-class state secondary schools had an
academic, humanistic curriculum. As the 1888 Cross Commission
had concluded, technical instruction was for the factory, not anything
to do with secondary education. The dichotomy between elementary
education, practical and functional, and secondary education, involving the transmission of a cultural heritage, was a matter of class and
ideology entrenched in state policy by the beginning of this century
and it has cast its shadow down to the present.

By the beginning of the twentieth century, the tension between
government's economic and social priorities was increasingly evident.

After 1889 in Wales, and after 1902 in England, there was state-funded secondary education as well as elementary education, but the two were rigidly demarcated. There were still class divisions, however blurred at the edges, with the upper class firmly ensconced in their private/public schools, the middle class in their fee-paying county schools and the working class stuck with the elementary schools. There was a ladder between the elementary and secondary sectors but it was narrow, and safeguarded by the scholarship examination, a feature which, again, is significant for analysis of the situation today. The curriculum of the public schools and the second-ary schools was traditional and humanistic; that of the elementary schools far more functional. Such divisions have been maintained throughout the twentieth century. After 1944/5 a socialist govern-ment allowed both public/private and direct grant schools to continue unmolested. Whatever the rhetoric, the secondary modern school/ grammar school divide was rigid, and perpetuated the class divide, though with the edges now blurred to a greater extent by a broader ladder and the propaganda of the meritocracy.

This divide continued to be reinforced by the curriculum. From 1904 the curriculum in secondary schools – Latin, Greek, history, geography, English, science, mathematics – very like the subjects of the National Curriculum now, was laid down by the state. It would appear that the state grip on the curriculum loosened in the interwar years. The Board of Education ceased to stipulate the elementary school curriculum in the 1920s and the secondary curriculum in the 1930s. In practice there were sufficient subsidiary constraints to ensure that the curriculum continued to reinforce the organizational divide. Even after the 1944 Education Act primary schools had to concentrate on the three Rs because of the eleven-plus examination. In the grammar schools, some of the rigidities of the old School Certificate did disappear. But the demands of university entrance ensured that the old hierarchy of subjects was maintained.

Against such a background, developments in the 1960s and 1970s were unprecedented. The most remarkable was the change to a comprehensive-school system. This, at a stroke, removed the func-tion of the primary school in the meritocracy, that is sorting out the sheep from the goats, and this allowed a new order of curricular freedom in those schools. But at this point it is vital not to lose sight of another constant theme of state involvement. There was an ideological side to the curricular freedom which resulted from the educational experiments of the 1960s and 1970s, especially the emphasis on the pupil-centred approach to learning. It may have its antecedents in Rousseauist notions of child development but its client-centredness is a central plank in Marxist analysis of teaching and learning. Marxist educators would argue that formal teaching of information within subjects is a manifestation of the inferiority of the learner, an undermining of the autonomy, the rights, of the learner. There are those who would argue that determining what should be taught is an essential part of the way in which the ruling class perpetuates its power. So the implications of the politics of the curriculum debate, and the organizational framework in which it takes place, become obvious.

It is hardly surprising then, that it was not long before government ministers became convinced that this curricular freedom was too great. But against a background of postwar ideological hatred of everything fascism stood for, and relative consensus among the educational politicians, a 'softly-softly' approach was adopted. As early as 1960 David Eccles became convinced that it was inappropriate that such an important area of concern as the curriculum should be regarded as merely the preserve of the professional teacher. The Curriculum Study Group was established, to be superseded by the Schools Council, but the Schools Council never addressed the issue of the curriculum as a whole. Given the ideological debate centring around the change-over to comprehensive education and increasingly strident criticisms from industrialists, it was inevitable that some reappraisal would be called for. The comprehensive schools caused a real crisis of curriculum planning because they had no precedent. At this point, in the early 1970s, another matter of vital concern to governments brought the debate to a head. This was the change in the economic situation. Between 1964 and 1974 primary education, for example, had seen real expenditure increase by 54 per cent. By 1974 the economic omens were only the most threatening of many for those wedded to the new orthodoxies which had taken root in the 1960s. The Barber cuts were beginning to bite, and presaged a very different future. Local government was reorganized, the Assessment of Performance Unit was set up, Terry Ellis became head of William Tyndale primary school, Bullock recommended monitoring, pupil numbers started to fall and the permanent secretary at the Department of Education asked whether government could keep out of curriculum planning. All was soon summed up in Callaghan's 1976 Ruskin College speech.

In retrospect, circumstances in the 1960s and early 1970s had not only allowed the curriculum debate to flourish, but also to be reflected in practical school situations. The romantics, with their notion of the supremacy of the child, and experientialism, had actually been allowed to confront the educational conservatives, with their so-long-unquestioned view of education as cultural transmission. The progressives chalked up many a victory – or at least recorded them on their flannelgraphs, since in the primary schools blackboards symbolized educational prehistory. This was a revolution in government as well as education. Education had, for so long, been prescribed from above by the state, representing the élite which knew best. Child-centredness implied a very different kind of democracy. It also reflected a wider attempt at storming the cultural barricades – a clash of high culture and low culture, *King Lear* versus *Coronation Street*. It was the curricular version of the debate about knowledge itself. Developments from physics to literary criticism raised questions about whether there *was* any knowledge. At the extremes there emerged a kind of intellectual anarchy, that nothing was objectively knowable – everything was relative and constantly in flux. The manifestations in primary schools were such organizational changes as open-plan schools and integrated days, and group work, allied with such curricular changes as doing away with subjects and substituting topics.

By the mid-seventies it was all too obvious that education was not going to transform the economy or produce social equality. The debate began to swing more in favour of the Black Paperites[2] who had so vociferously complained about the lack of structure in primary-school organization reflecting a lack of structure in the curriculum – in Bantock's famous phrase, a magpie curriculum. Even before the 1979 election a reassertion of traditional state involvement in the school system and its curriculum was inevitable. That election merely influenced direction and degree. Soon, HMI pronouncements were followed, significantly, by DES pronouncements on the curriculum which foreshadowed a return to subject-based teaching. The political battle was with the local authorities, and the ideological battle with the educational establishment. The agenda had been set by the Black Papers and the Ruskin College speech – teaching according to set syllabuses and specific standards of attainment, an emphasis on literacy and numeracy. State control had been reasserted.

The state is equally concerned with the assessment of what is taught

Governments have traditionally been concerned about the nature of schooling because of education's impact on social mobility and the linked issue of economic efficiency. These have often been in conflict, and a traditional weapon in reconciling the conflict has been the examination system, inevitably yoked to the curriculum. What compelled successive governments in the nineteenth century to be circumspect in their interference was that so much of the education system was private. They had no such inhibitions regarding the elementary schools which they financed. Once the system began to run on state funds, governments assumed ultimate control. Above all, the state became involved in testing. From the first injection of state money in 1833 it was only a few years before the government began to voice those anxieties over expense which have been a constant refrain ever since. And the notion of testing as the way to ascertain whether the system was providing value for money goes back at least to the Newcastle Commission set up in 1858. By 1862 Lowe's Revised Code produced the 'payment by results' system and the most pervasive of all curricular controls had started. In the elementary schools, part of the grant for each child was paid out for attendance. In addition, the Education Department (created in 1856) approved certain subjects for grant. Teachers taught those subjects. HMI went round and tested pupils. If pupils did well then the school got its per capita grant. Here was state control of the curriculum. Subjects were taught if they were grant-earning, though the number of these was gradually widened as decades went by.

Gradually, the competitive ethic which underpinned industrial capitalism and popular Victorian values of self-help was grafted on to the education system in the search for efficiency and, ultimately, the preservation of national supremacy. Examinations became part of the British education system. The Oxford and Cambridge locals of 1858 were followed in 1862 by the Taunton Commission's advocacy of an examination for selecting free scholars – in reading, writing, arithmetic, English grammar, geography and Bible history. Again, in 1853 the Crimean War showed up the appalling consequences of incompetence resulting from nepotism. The same year saw an examination for entry to the Indian Civil Service, followed in 1870 by examinations for the Home Civil Service. Here was the beginning of a sea-change in society, the slow, and of course incomplete, transition from an occupational hierarchy based on birth and family connection to one based on merit. The educational version of the competitive ethic, the examination system, was eventually rationalized and institutionalized in 1917, with the School Certificate and Higher School Certificate replacing the myriad professional examinations which had mushroomed in the three previous decades. The scholarship examination was already in place, born of the competition to enter secondary school. So the hierarchy of examinations with which we are so familiar, grew out of the transition of a society dominated by landed élites who considered themselves as the natural governing class, to a more industrially, commercially and bureaucratically efficient competitive meritocracy, infused with the capitalist ethic. Such is the significance of education to the economics and government of the state, but equally fascinating is the way in which successive governments preserved some of the trappings and much of the substance of privilege within the changing structure.

Invaluable weapons in their armoury were examinations. Once the gap between elementary education for the working class and fee-paying secondary education for the middle class was partially bridged by the scholarship system, examinations helped to preserve the exclusivity of the secondary system. The elementary schools had to do their best to help pupils to win a scholarship and concentrated on attainment in English and arithmetic to do so. The *raison d'être* of the secondary schools became the School Certificate programme. That required a four-year course and a five-subject examination. There was a hierarchy of subjects, with some counting for matriculation. The result was that the practical subjects which the examination boards offered, for example agriculture and mechanics, were hardly ever taken up. Here was the nineteenth-century divide, in which anything which smacked of manual labour was to be avoided at all costs by respectable society, being reflected in twentieth-century examinations. Many would argue that it still is.

The system was only marginally modified after 1944. Politicians and civil servants, behind the scenes, insisted that secondary education for all should mean a modern education for most and a grammar education for the select few. The function of the primary schools now more than ever was to maximize pupil opportunities in the eleven-plus, with the result that the core curriculum of English and maths was more firmly entrenched than ever. There was no need for that core curriculum to be specified by law. O levels could not be taken below the age of sixteen, a year above the school-leaving age. The examination system was being used to combine provision of professional skills with preservation of social hierarchies. If we accept the arguments of Corelli Barnett, the purpose of safeguarding the social hierarchy took precedence over producing an economically efficient and competitive society.[3]

The history of assessment, like that of the curriculum, indicates that the change to a comprehensive system of schooling in the 1960s and 1970s was of the profoundest significance. Primary schools, apart from the occasional inspection, could get on doing what teachers wanted. This led, as simplistic analysis would soon have it, to lack of basic literacy and numeracy, associated in right-wing folklore with child-centred teaching methods and lack of accountability. The agenda for tightening up on assessment and accountability was once again set in 1976. Once the Conservatives got back in 1979 it was only the nature of assessment which was to be an issue.

Past, present, future

The school curriculum is now dominated by the legislation of 1988 and succeeding modifications. It is at this rather crucial point that the theories advanced above seem to be worryingly flawed. The facts are well known. The 1988 Education Reform Act laid down a National Curriculum for pupils aged five to sixteen, all the years of compulsory schooling. That curriculum was to consist of subjects, ten or eleven of them, common to all pupils, with the significant exception of pupils in the private sector. Various reasons were advanced for this exclusion but the fundamental one was that the state has traditionally only had responsibility for curriculum and assessment in schools which it finances. Even so, the exclusion of about 7 per cent of children in England (mainly) and Wales from the provisions of the National Curriculum is significant in terms of the foregoing arguments relating to social division. There are still separate structures, substantially class-based – preparatory schools to age thirteen, public schools from age thirteen, and an intake to Oxbridge taken from these schools which still approaches 50 per cent. This social division is reflected in the dramatic numbers of top judicial, civil service and even show business jobs still filled through the Oxbridge connection.

What of the state system? It would appear that, for the years of compulsory schooling, the curriculum is no longer an instrument of division. In all state schools there is now a common curriculum integrated with a common assessment system. The distinction between core subjects – obviously essential for coping with life in a post-industrial society – and the foundation subjects, with their attempt to provide a broad and balanced development of the individual in social, aesthetic and physical areas, is common to all. The 1988 Act laid down that the different subjects were to be specified in terms of knowledge, skills and processes. For 93 per cent of the age-range, then, it seemed as if the state for the first time ever, had sanctioned the notion of curriculum entitlement for almost all its citizens. Here were common skills, processes and knowledge which would inform and enrich the lives of its people. The age of equal opportunity, of the meritocracy, seemingly had arrived. Of course this curriculum would not of itself do anything to solve the environmental problems which have in many ways worsened in recent years. It would not counteract the effects of the widening gap between rich and poor, the breakdown of marriages, the ghettoizing of housing estates – and all those influences which, as long ago as the 1960s, Douglas highlighted as bearing on educational achievement.[4] But at least, as pupils worked their way through the common levels of attainment within the attainment targets, the impact of such environmental factors would be highlighted where before they could be blurred. And at least the principle of common entitlement was endorsed for the first time.

Since such a development is at variance with the argument that in the past the curriculum has been central to perpetuating social division, what reasons might there be for it having come about? If it had been the act of a postwar Labour government it might have made more historical sense. But to be instituted by a government more committed to the gods of the market than any since the war seems totally illogical. Indeed it was. No one in government, certainly not the secretary of state, had thought through the consequences of the proposed legislation as it affected the curriculum, and not just in terms of workload. This was why the right wing of the Tory party, and particularly the Rasputin-like figures of the Centre for Policy Studies, were so incensed. They did not want a national curriculum, they wanted a core curriculum of English, mathematics and science. The remainder of the curriculum, as Lord Skidelsky has argued, was not held to be a matter for the state.[5] That could safely be left to market forces, in which case it is certain that it would not turn out the same for everyone.

The factors at work in the fundamentalist Tory Party and government of the early 1980s were ideological – a belief in unrestrained market forces; political – an obsession with the alleged shortcomings of local authorities; economic – a concern with the inadequacy of the education system in the technological revolution through which we are living; and financial – a determination that such a major public spender as education must be quality-controlled at all levels. The immediate targets were the primary- and secondary-school systems. According to right-wing caricatures, the primary schools were full of trendy 1960s-trained primary teachers whose child-centred theories were leading to neglect of the three Rs and a contentless education, without any examination checks. The comprehensive schools were levelling down by mixed-ability teaching, a result of social theory rather than a recipe for educational effectiveness. Since wholesale privatization of the schools was not feasible, the way ahead, which would counter all these trends, was to introduce competition into the schools. They would have to be made as independent of local-authority control as possible, and this, of course, has been accomplished by Local Management of Schools and attempts to bribe reluctant clients into grant-maintained status where they could all eventually be deposited in the safe hands of a funding council. But the other prong of competition was measurement. Since value for money in the schools cannot be measured by price as in Tesco, it has to be measured in achievement, a crude version of which had existed for so long in the eleven-plus. To this end there had to be a common core to test, and a common system of testing.

In the early 1980s the activists of the Tory Party were agitating for something very simple – an elementary measurement of the core subjects in primary and secondary schools. By this means parents could choose which were the most effective schools and the traditional dividing, competitive function would be restored to both types of schools. At the same time the theorists on the right were able to argue that the core subjects, English, mathematics and science were legitimate areas for state intervention because of the state money involved and because of the practical implications for the state of its citizens mastering the basic skills. The core curriculum (not a national curriculum yet) was envisaged as limited and factual, to be tested by factual questions with, as far as possible, right and wrong answers. The last thing that right-wing market-force advocates wanted was an entitlement curriculum, a notion that all young people in the state, whatever their background, were heirs to a common heritage. Such a curriculum was at odds with 150 years of history. More, it was the ultimate endorsement of the common school, first at primary level, now at secondary level. As such, for some, at least, it was a signal of the nearest one could get to a meritocratic society, a major signal of the importance of equality of opportunity. Nothing of the core curriculum debate, except perhaps for the question of first-language Welsh, was of any relevance to distinctively Welsh issues.

The sequence of events at this point is well-known. Teacher apprehensions about this simplistic, in many ways anti-educational, proposed system did have an impact on HMI, the DES and Kenneth Baker, in retrospect a model of moderation compared with his two successors. The response was to hand the assessment problem over to Professor Black, whose task group on assessment and testing came up with a relatively enlightened model.[6] This 'ten levels of attainment' model was greeted with an enormous sense of relief by the teaching profession at the time as a great deliverance from simplistic testing of rote-learning. It was greeted with dismay by the educational right wing. Then Kenneth Baker made another momentous decision – we do not know why, but doubtless HMI and perhaps some DES officials influenced him – to go far beyond the demands of the market theorists and propose a National Curriculum which provided a common, whole educational experience rather than a crude 'teach-test' system in basic subjects. Again there was an element of relief in the teaching profession that a simplistic string of facts in core subjects had been avoided, though this was, of course, combined with anger at the undermining of professional autonomy.

The National Curriculum had elements of curricular traditions ranging from the Greeks through the nineteenth century and into the twentieth, with its variety of technologies. It was a subject-based curriculum. As such it went against the child-centred Romantic tradition; but it also avoided being a crude vehicle for assessing the worth of a school. Essentially it was a victory for the notion of education as the transmission of a nation's cultural heritage. To this extent it was enlightened. Baker instinctively put into practice the middle-class, public-school/grammar-school concept of education with which he and his officials were so familiar. The revolutionary implication of what he did in 1988 was that he made it a common syllabus for all primary and secondary pupils for the first time.

There was anger in the Centre for Policy Studies and among the Hillgate group. This was not at all what the fundamentalists required. They now had to battle on many fronts. They inveighed bitterly against the predominance of educationalists, so called, on the working groups set up to decide on the content of the various subjects, while teachers protested that there were too few teachers. There was a battle royal over history, especially, and this was no coincidence. In the light of the on-going argument, the nature of historical study at Key Stages Two, Three and Four, especially, was a microcosm of wider debate. To the right wing, if history had to be included at all it should consist of facts, testable facts, and these should reflect great episodes in the story of the British nation. This reflected, essentially, a nineteenth-century view of history, and a nineteenth-century view of teaching. There were very considerable pressures brought to bear on the History Working Group to list specific facts upon which pupils could be tested. The group parried the pressures. It specified areas of content in the programmes of study, though it had to throw in a few facts and dates to gratify the politicians. The statements of attainment were couched in terms of historical skills. This was a victory for the group.[7]

The sense of satisfaction, on this and wider counts, turned out to be premature. The seeds of defeat lay in the constraints placed on the History Working Group and on other groups. The subject structure of the curriculum is not accidental; it is based on long-established, and very different, methods of trying to understand the world around us. Individual subjects can be taught as interestingly as any topic or project work. But it was made obvious that where many in the group would like to have seen each programme of study outlined in a paragraph or so, with individual class teachers deciding how to interpret that loose specification, there would have to be more detailed listing of content. Here was a recipe for overloading. Where a few subject specialists are gathered together they will all seek to do justice to their subject. According to the terms of reference given to the group, history was to be allowed three forty-minute periods per week in the secondary schools, and an equivalent time in primary schools. This was, of course, wildly optimistic, but what were the groups to do other than accept the parameters laid down by the secretary of state? Decisions on time-tabling, out of the hands of the working groups, were, cumulatively, to help wreck the notion of a balanced national curriculum. Another, more fundamental weakness was the assessment structure. The History Working Group had no difficulty with the notion of attainment targets. It is impossible to grade or identify progress in learning facts in history. But it is perfectly possible to identify progression in mastery of elements of historical understanding. What the group was very sceptical about was the ability to do this at ten discrete levels. The group was forced into it, but at least the resulting system was better than straight regurgitation of historical knowledge as a means of assessment.

For many in Wales, there was a bonus which came with the National Curriculum. The later nineteenth and twentieth centuries steadily produced more enlightened attitudes to the teaching of the Welsh language and things Welsh. With the cultural inheritance of a nation manifesting itself in the new National Curriculum, there were basic questions to be asked about Wales. Since the curriculum was to consist of disparate subjects the Welsh experience needed to be echoed in those subjects. It turned out that elements of history, geography, music and art in Wales were to be unique to Wales. Here, at last, was a Welsh National Curriculum. With the later publication of the Curriculum Council for Wales's booklet on the *Curriculum Cymreig*[8] there was a vital move towards the integration of separate subjects into the development of a more general Welsh ethos into all the schools in Wales. Here was a real opportunity for the richness of history and culture in Wales, allied to a whole variety of senses of Welshness among the vast majority of the population, to be used to enhance the educational and civic experience of those who live in Wales.

The National Curriculum and the concomitant system of assessment, as they emerged in 1990 were not perfect. They should not have been imposed from above without consultation. They produced overloading – inevitable when there were teams of subject specialists working in isolation, wanting to maximize the impact of their favourite subject. The system of assessment through ten levels of attainment was flawed, partly because it was being used for purposes for which it was never intended. Even so, virtually by accident, we had the educational structure here for a more just, a more egalitarian and a richer society. Perhaps what happened next was inevitable, because such a society was out of kilter with Thatcherite, Majorette Britain, perhaps out of step with world developments. In a famous thesis of the 1980s Fukuyama wrote of the end of history – by which he meant the triumph of capitalism as a world economic and social system and the consigning of the alternative economic structure of state communism to the dustbin of history. Thatcherite Britain certainly institutionalized the notion of individualistic competition (there is no such thing as society) as the defining characteristic of the age. If the divisions which had always been the reflection of this in the education system were momentarily eradicated that was perhaps only a vision of what might have been, not a practical proposition.

Beware of Greeks bearing gifts. Sir Ron Dearing, avuncular, reasonable, a great listener, has taken us back to the agenda which the right-wingers of the Tory Party wanted all along.[9] Perhaps he did it inadvertently; perhaps, as the foregoing argument implies, he was the agent of forces which ultimately would have produced the same conclusion. But the thrust of the National Curriculum and its assessment have been adversely modified in such a way as to produce a situation reminiscent of the middle of the nineteenth century. Previously there was to be a measurement of progression at seven, eleven, fourteen and sixteen in all subjects, composed of a blend of teacher and national assessment. Now the all-important tests are going to be at seven, eleven and fourteen in core subjects. These tests are going to be externally set and externally marked. They will have national currency and, crucially, will be used to measure the effectiveness of schools – reminiscent of payment by results. What of the foundation subjects? Surely at the very least the inspectors will want to know about them. The inspectors do not even have to see the foundation subjects taught in primary schools – they can go on written reports. Since the production of word-processed smoke-screens is the biggest growth industry at all levels of education these days, that should not cause too many problems.

I know what my priorities would be if I were, for example, the headteacher of a primary school. I want the best for the children, and that is now going to be measured in their performance at seven and eleven, in the core subjects. Their place in a particular class in a secondary school may depend on it. Who knows, it may transpire that their place in a particular secondary school may depend on it.

I want the best for my staff. If they and I do not expend most of our energies into getting the best Standard Assessment Test results, parents will use this public knowledge to send their pupils elsewhere. I will lose capitation and, therefore, staffing. Since I do not particularly wish to be known as a failure myself I will see that the school makes a priority of the core subjects. I may find that the range of abilities in a mixed-ability class is not the most conducive to success. I will be tempted to set and stream. I may find that class teaching is more effective than group work. I may be tempted to seat the children in rows. I may find that last year's SATS are useful practice. I will be tempted to use considerable amounts of time doing practice tests. Of course the whole process is reminiscent of that which led up to that crucial eleven-plus examination. Because they are no longer to be instruments of national assessment the place of the foundation subjects in the scheme of things is marginalized. When so-called best-fit level descriptors replaced the statements of attainment in 1996 the foundation subjects became even more marginalized. Certainly in my own subject, history, the careful balance which we tried to strike between content and skills will have been undermined by ill-defined marriages of different attainment targets into vague descriptors. The emphasis will be more on the content and facts in the programmes of study.

So, there will be a curriculum of two discrete tiers – the core and the rest. The one which really matters is the one which the educational fundamentalists always wanted to matter, the core subjects which will provide a rough-hewn measure of school effectiveness. During the next five years we will see this system becoming institutionalized. Certainly practitioners want a standstill. The political parties which may be in government over the next five years both seem committed to ruthless raising of standards, however cosmetic, and weeding out the inefficient, a process in which the measuring sticks provided by SATs will be essential ammunition. Both seem committed to the competitive ethic in schools. The economic and social system within which they operate is more securely competitive now than ever. The climate in which the experiments of the 1960s flourished seems as remote as the ice ages.

The undermining of the National Curriculum, the notion of a balanced, entitlement curriculum, is bad news for the Welsh curriculum, the *Curriculum Cymreig*. For the great majority of students in Wales whose first language is not Welsh, the difference between the core curriculum in Wales and that in England is minimal. The overt essentials of the *Curriculum Cymreig* lie in the history, geography, music and art elements. Post-Dearing, all are downgraded. At Key Stage Two, I have argued that the whole assessment and inspection structure will militate against the foundation subjects. At Key Stage Four the National Curriculum has already ceased to exist. One of the benign Sir Ron's achievements has been to deliver hammer blows to the *Curriculum Cymreig* and with it, I believe, to a long-term force for communal cohesion and integration in Wales.

It is at this juncture that the argument leads us to consider the need for fundamental remodelling of responsibility and accountability for education in Wales. Since the 1880s there has been an increasingly sympathetic attitude to the Welsh language and 'Welshness' in education. Central government condescension, at its most overt in the Blue Books of 1847, has gradually been disguised and modified. Incremental educational devolution has accelerated since the end of the Second World War. By chance – legislation for a National Curriculum – and design – government by quangocracy – such increments resulted, after 1988, in the most encouraging developments in Welsh education. Sir Ron Dearing's modifications have indicated that such historical chance is an insufficiently secure base on which to build a national, Welsh, education system. However disguised, it echoes the condescensions of the last century and a half. We are led inexorably to the conclusion that the current educational deficit is a function of the wider democratic deficit in the Wales of the 1990s.

Conclusion

Wales has been transformed since the first notorious involvement of the British state in its education system. Education has played a small part in the process as a fully fledged state system replaced those voluntary efforts which the 1847 Blue Books proved to be so inadequate. That educational transformation has depended on, and interweaved with, revolutions in economics, politics, religion, language and social fabric.

One thing has not changed since 1847. The education of the people of Wales has always depended on the actions of Westminster governments. It is this essential perspective which is so well illuminated by historical example. Traditional interpretations have it that the 1847 Report was a response to individual, possibly government, anxieties about the breakdown in Welsh society brought about by economic change. The Report should therefore outline the remedies necessary to allow individuals and nation to share in the financial and cultural spoils of an English civilization at the expense of the destruction of the Welsh language.[1]

I have argued[2] that another interpretation is possible, even likely. Kay-Shuttleworth was well aware that the voluntary system was incapable of producing adequate structures of teacher training and elementary education. It is at least feasible that he hoped to shape and to use what came to be seen as the massive indictment of the Welsh nation for the purpose of exposing the folly of governmental reluctance to provide adequate schooling for its working-class citizens across England and Wales. If this interpretation is correct then, for the most enlightened of motives, Kay-Shuttleworth and his investigators used circumstances in Wales for a wider purpose. It was taken for granted in 1847 that Wales must become more like England – and not only in language – in order that its people might be admitted to some of the privileges of civilized nineteenth-century society. Wales was seen as an aberrant region, with a greater degree of social dislocation and underprivilege. Kay-Shuttleworth viewed such underprivilege from his perspective of deprivation in other regions, not for any ingredient of Welshness. In this he had much in common with eminent Welshmen of the time, as well as the English establishment.

Indeed, it was axiomatic in the mid-nineteenth century that there was no specifically Welsh perspective on the evolving state system of education other than, for example, that stemming from different denominational patterns. The state government of 'England and Wales' worked out its structures in response to political, economic and bureaucratic imperatives of the kind discussed in the previous essay. Yet occasionally a political climate developed in which Welsh needs could be accommodated if they accorded with these parameters. From the 1880s, politicians and bureaucrats were prepared to contemplate the demands of Welsh-language advocates with a little less indifference. Even structurally, there was a breakthrough when Wales was allowed its own system of secondary education in the wake of the 1889 Welsh Intermediate Education Act.

In the early years of the twentieth century the situation seemed to favour the development of a system which reflected more nearly the distinctive nature of Welsh society, as the Welsh Department of the Board of Education was set up in 1907 and O. M. Edwards took up office. There was, or so it appeared, a crucial devolution of local responsibility, too, as the new local authorities took over major educational functions in 1902. The reality was far different, as the 'Welsh Revolt' demonstrated.[3] The 1902 Education Act took no account of priorities in Wales. It was a political response to the dilemma posed by the expansionist policies of the school boards generally, and the implications which their incursions into higher elementary education had for class demarcation. There was no discussion of the suitability of the new arrangements for Wales, nor of the religious affiliations of the Welsh people which might make these modifications less acceptable. When the local authorities in Wales used their recently acquired powers to defy central government we saw the way in which central government brought them to heel. The limitations of Welsh control of its education system were similarly evident in the internal politics of the relevant government department. A. T. Davies, first permanent secretary at the Welsh Department of the Board of Education, was in constant conflict with his English counterparts in attempting to assert his authority, but he was forced to know his place. O. M. Edwards brought greater prestige to his office and a nobler vision. Yet his alternative, if Utopian, view of Welsh education had to be accommodated within the curricular and examination framework laid down by the Board of Education.

Some of those local authorities in Wales vested with an element of control of education in 1902 attempted to mitigate the worst educational effects of the economic Depression of the interwar years. As a result of economic disadvantage in industrial and urban Wales, a somewhat different pattern of education emerged in this period, particularly in secondary schooling. We have seen that, with almost all schools included in the state sector, secondary education in Wales was more egalitarian and meritocratic than its English counterpart. Local authority policies had also ensured that there were proportionately far more free places in Wales. We have also seen that local authority wishes in Wales were flouted when the government wished to economize. Means-tested special places replaced free places, notwithstanding the extent to which Welsh wishes might differ. School organization had to conform with the political priorities of central government. Any claims which Wales might have had to separate treatment counted for nought.[4]

Nothing changed when government initiatives had to be more surreptitiously exercised in the wake of the 1944 Education Act. Trends long evident in Welsh secondary education – increasing numbers of free places and selection by merit – now became part of mainstream policy. However, central government bureaucracy deemed it as important as ever that demarcation lines between different types of secondary schools were rigidly maintained. Once more Wales was not allowed to diverge. Some local authorities, notably Swansea, wished to establish common secondary schools catering for pupils of all abilities in their communities. They were not permitted to do so.[5] With very few exceptions, the shape of Welsh secondary schools was determined by the bipartite mould deemed essential to reflect wider political and class priorities. As a result, in the years following the Second World War, the most populous and influential of the Welsh counties, Glamorgan, having bid for a multilateral policy, developed one of the most entrenched bipartite secondary-school systems of any in Wales and England and eventually proved slow to adapt to the comprehensive arrangements decreed in the 1960s. Once more the theme of 'English' condescension towards Welsh priorities in matters of education was strikingly illustrated.

In the 1950s and 1960s, most of rural and all of industrial Wales was moulded into a pattern of bipartitism (there was so little by way of technical education provision that tripartism was a misnomer). From the 1960s Welsh educationists became entangled in the increasingly polarized debates surrounding primary-school teaching methods and secondary-school reorganization. The arguments coincided with an unprecedented degree of teacher and local authority autonomy. In particular, after 1974 the new counties vied with each other to fill the policy and curriculum vacuum with initiatives spawned by burgeoning advisory teams. Ironically, these developments were contemporaneous with increasing devolutionary measures in government after 1964. In the absence of the traditional degree of state control, the significance of increasing Welsh Office involvement in education was not yet apparent. It did become apparent after the change of government and direction after 1979 and, especially, from the mid-1980s. Since 1988 there has been a revolution in education and inevitably Wales has been a part of that revolution. The experience has once more made clear the constraints on educational planning for Wales.

While there has been progress in providing an education system which reflects the richness of the Welsh inheritance, developments in the last decade have also demonstrated once more the limitations of those educational institutions peculiar to Wales. Wales still has to rely on sympathetic personalities, rather than institutional independence, to safeguard its interests. The 1980s and 1990s have indicated that surprisingly little has changed in this respect since the days of O. M. Edwards. Despite Edwards's vision, his achievements ultimately amounted to damage-limitation exercises within a system patterned on Westminster priorities. In the policy revolution of the 1980s and 1990s, the Welsh Office Education Department had to react to educational Thatcherism. It will probably become increasingly apparent that it was the Welsh loyalties of Sir Wyn Roberts which helped safeguard the Welshness of the education system. It will be impossible for many years fully to assess his role in the crucial years from 1987, when the notion of a National Curriculum was being translated into reality and the machinery for implementing it being put in place, but he has claimed that it was his intervention with the prime minister personally which guaranteed the place of Welsh as a core and foundation subject. If this is the case it is indefensible that such a crucial decision about the content of education in Wales should owe as much to the chance of individual predilections now as was the case in the days of O. M. Edwards.

Just as O. M. Edwards was constrained by the traditions and codes of anglocentric civil servants and politicians, so Sir Wyn Roberts, for all the trappings of devolution, had to have regard to his political masters and, especially, to his political mistress. The people of Wales were particularly fortunate in the period around 1988 that secretaries of state Walker and Hunt adopted a *laissez-faire* attitude towards education. If John Redwood had been in office at the time it is likely that the acknowledgement and development of separate administrative and curricular arrangements for Wales would have been severely curtailed. The nature of the various educational quangos in Wales illustrates the theme. It would appear that these committees acknowledge Welsh independence and the recognition of separate needs. We have Higher and Further Education Funding Councils, but there is no evidence that they have any function other than following rigid government guidelines. As a revolution takes place in higher education in Wales, as the nature of the former constituent colleges changes dramatically with expansion and deteriorating staff-student ratios, as the federal university and some of its long-standing corporate ventures are undermined and as the former public-sector colleges redefine their role, there is no official forum in which the implications for higher education, scholarship and research can be thrashed out. There is no independence for Wales in higher and further education.

The situation would appear to be more encouraging for Welsh schools. A Welsh educational infrastructure has developed in the guise of the Curriculum Council for Wales and its successor body, Awdurdod Cwricwlwm ac Asesu Cymru. There is a differently shaped office of Her Majesty's Chief Inspector of Schools which is characterized by substantially more civilized dialogue with schools than its English counterpart. Above all, there is a different statutory curriculum, based on a distinctive cultural heritage, for pupils in all schools in Wales and this, in all but a very few schools, safeguards the role of the Welsh language. Although these achievements are spin-offs from central government policies which had nothing to do with Welsh priorities, over which the people of Wales were not consulted, this catalogue seems impressive. However, the nature of assessment policies demonstrates the extent of constraints. The transfer of assessment functions to ACAC, denied to CCW, was theoretical rather than practical, an opportunity to administer an existing system rather than mould a modified one. There is no evidence that ACAC will be allowed to make any major changes to the system of statutory testing at the ages of seven, eleven and fourteen which will increasingly modify the whole internal structure of education in Wales. Redwood's reign made it clear to education-watchers that ACAC has been ordered not to rock the boat. While all the pronouncements from teachers and their organizations indicate that a Scottish model of testing would be far more acceptable, Wales is bound tightly to England in this crucial arbiter of school priorities, all in the name of the educational market-place.

The most limited of historical perspectives indicates that the problem of standards in Welsh schools is far too complex to permit simplistic market solutions. Chapter Eight illustrates the way in which the special circumstances conditioning the development of second-ary education, in particular, allowed the flowering of Wales's reputa-tion as a nation which laid great store by education.[6] Measured by O-Level and A-Level results, as well as by 'staying-on' rates, Welsh pupils were being educated to a higher level than their counterparts in almost any of the English regions, including the south-east, dur-ing the 'golden age' of the grammar school in the 1950s and 1960s. Then came the paradox of the late 1970s and 1980s. The change to a comprehensive system which, I have argued, was more appropri-ate to the situation in Wales, was accompanied by the growing realiza-tion that pupils were, overall, less well served than their English counterparts in the reorganized system. This was revealed in research which constituted a unique initiative in the policy debate. It began with a Welsh Office conference at Mold in 1978 and came to a head with the Loosmore report of 1981.[7] Before the debate on standards had begun to take its present shape in England, investigation into school effectiveness in Wales, spearheaded by David Reynolds, was generating shock waves throughout the nation in the 1980s. Essentially, a far higher percentage of pupils were leaving schools in Wales without an O-Level pass than was the case in England – at a rate of 25 per cent in 1981.

Within a few years the Welsh debate had been subsumed into the wider rush to testing. Valuable Welsh initiatives on disaffection and underachievement ended as the work of Welsh bodies, including HMI, had to accord with new rhythms in England. Apart from Reynolds's initiative, there was no specifically Welsh dimension to the most far-reaching policy decisions on assessment in recent educational history. We now have public tables of GCSE results, vocational qualifications, truancy rates and special-needs statistics. They reveal that Welsh performance at GCSE in 1995, in terms of pupils who achieved five grade A to C passes, was lower than in England – 41 per cent in Wales to England's 43.5 per cent. Eleven per cent of school-leavers in Wales acquired no GCSE qualification at all. This is still higher than the overall figure for England (8.1 per cent), but it represents a dramatic narrowing of the gap since Reynolds highlighted a discrepancy in performance which stood at 7.5 per cent in 1988–9.[8] The publicity accorded such results may now be doing Welsh schools a familiar disservice. Reynolds's argument, in the early 1980s, that lower-ability pupils in the comprehensive schools of Wales were not being well served struck a raw nerve, and numbers of pupils leaving school without any GCE/GCSE qualifications reduced substantially. However, in England and Wales as a whole, the 1995 'league tables' indicated that the numbers of pupils leaving school without one GCSE, even at grade G, is rising – by over a percentage point in the last two years. One suggested explanation is that 'lower-achieving schools may be concentrating on improving their ranking at the expense of their weakest pupils'.[9] It occasions no surprise that the league tables in their present form will concentrate yet more schools' corporate energies on the more able, so reversing one of the healthier trends in Welsh schooling over the last fifteen years. There will be the strongest of temptations in those schools in urban Wales which find themselves substantially oversubscribed, to yield to government pressures towards limited, perhaps covert, academic selection, if only for out-of-area pupils. This, in turn, will effectively reduce the schools in less favoured catchment areas to the role of the former secondary modern schools, with the concomitant underfunding and stigmas so familiar in the post-war period. Each successive league table will weaken their relative position as the more able pupils are creamed off. That these tables are substantially, though by no means wholly, an index of economic underprivilege seems not to raise obvious issues of morality and social policy.

An underlying theme of the essays in this book is that Welsh distinctiveness in education has been allowed to express itself only when it has not conflicted with wider, all-embracing political parameters. The consequent dislocation in Wales has been most evident when state dirigisme has been most marked, particularly so since the mid-1980s, when local interests and representations, however defined, have either been ignored or destroyed in a messianic fervour of reform. It is now clear that the cumulative educational implications for Wales are so serious that its people at least have the right to be consulted as to how far they wish the system to be different from that in England, even if this conflicts with Westminster priorities. The most obvious machinery may be that of a Welsh Assembly, but in itself that is no panacea if all it allows is tinkering with centralist policies.

The catalogue of policies inappropriate to Wales, underpinned by a philosophy of the market-place in education, has now reached alarming proportions. The market-place model itself is singularly inappropriate to the whole of rural Wales, where parental choice is, practically, limited to the local primary or secondary school, but it has now generated policies involving not inappropriateness but destructiveness. The most potentially corrosive of recent market-place policies is the proposed imposition of voucher schemes for nursery education. The plan to provide a voucher to the value of £1,100 for the parents of each four-year-old as a contribution to the purchase of nursery education at any relevant private or public school has provoked universal critical comment in Wales. This stems not from political dogma but from practicalities. The imposition of the voucher scheme would result in the worsening of a situation in which over 90 per cent of four-year-olds and more than 70 per cent of three-year-olds already receive a local-authority-funded nursery education at a cost much in excess of the proposed value of the voucher. The imposition of this policy would also result in the waste of a sum estimated to exceed £600,000 to administer the scheme. That Wales is seemingly being dragged along in Westminster's wake, whatever may be the outcome of current House of Lords involvement, is the ultimate indication of the impotence of its people to plan for themselves an appropriate education system.

The voucher scheme is the worst manifestation at the time of writing, but the catalogue is extensive. The assisted places scheme for secondary education is largely irrelevant to Wales. Policy over grant-maintained schools has been rejected. There has been little support in Wales for revised teacher training arrangements which have resulted in strained relations between schools and teacher trainers, an inappropriate role for the universities and an unacceptable contraction of opportunities for considered reflection on the part of teachers in training. A far more effective system could be devised, and the imposition of a National Curriculum by the Teacher Training Agency is not it. The revolution in higher education has been brought about without any planning for the Welsh dimension of research excellence. A century-old tradition of reasonable co-operation between the colleges has been ditched without any analysis of the implications for Wales or the nature of higher education. The present disintegration of the University of Wales will in the longer term militate against the interests of its constituent colleges as well as against the academic community generally if some basis for federal co-operation cannot be found. In April 1996, twenty-two unitary authorities assumed responsibility for local government. Attempts to downgrade their role in education by relieving them of the statutory responsibility to appoint education committees failed, but there is uncertainty and concern over provision of services. The inter-relationship of school and community, particularly in rural Wales, needs rethinking in the new circumstances, both at authority and school level. An apparent political consensus, focusing on standards and league tables, demands a specifically Welsh response in the context of particular needs of schools in poor areas which require amelioration, not bludgeoning to death by market forces. The strengths of Welsh education, for example the impressive performance of Welsh-language and bilingual schools, require research and extrapolation. There should be more than bureaucratic control within Wales of in-service training, particularly since the concerns of small rural schools are disproportionate. The demands of the Welsh National Curriculum and the *Curriculum Cymreig* also make considerable training demands. The debate over the future shape of post-GCSE examinations is currently eliciting a response from Welsh educationalists. There are indications that an examination system which reflected some of the best elements of the Baccalaureate and Scottish Highers would generate enthusiasm in Wales. There is no indication that this Welsh input will have any impact on London-based policy decisions.

The Welsh educational heritage testifies to its people's laudable concern for education, for whatever motive. The transformation from reaction to Westminster policies to policy formation in the light of Welsh needs ought therefore to be a democratic right as well as being a pragmatic necessity. The Welsh should indeed go back to basics, to debate fundamentals such as the appropriateness of market philosophies to successful education, based on the premise that while competition cannot and should not be eradicated from academic or sporting life in school, it is, of itself, an inadequate blueprint for an education system. It is now common ground that education is the key to national well-being in the widest sense. It should be just as obvious that the people of Wales have the ability and the right to determine the nature of the education system which will reflect their vision of a cultured and prosperous national life.

References

Chapter 1

[1] J. Lawson and H. Silver, *A Social History of Education in England* (London, 1973).

[2] S. J. Curtis, *History of Education in Great Britain*. 7th edition (London, 1967).

[3] H. C. Barnard, *A Short History of English Education, 1760–1944* (London, 1947).

[4] James Scotland, *The History of Scottish Education*, 2 vols (London, 1969).

[5] Brian Simon, *Education and the Labour Movement, 1870–1920* (London, 1965); and *The Politics of Educational Reform 1920–1940* (London, 1974).

[6] W. M. Humes and H. M. Paterson, *Scottish Culture and Scottish Education 1800–1980* (Edinburgh, 1983).

[7] F. A. Loosmore, *Curriculum and Assessment in Wales. An Exploratory Study* (Cardiff, 1981). This study indicated that in 1977/78 27.6 per cent of pupils left Welsh secondary schools without any qualification. The comparative figure for England was 14.2 per cent; c.f. David Reynolds, 'Schooled for failure?', in *Disaffection in Secondary Schools in Wales* (Cardiff, 1983), pp. 14–27; and D. Reynolds and S. Murgatroyd in *Times Educational Supplement*, 15 February, 1985.

[8] *Times Educational Supplement*, 15 April, 1983, 31.

[9] Quoted in *Times Educational Supplement*, 21 October, 1983, 6.

[10] Gwyn Thomas, 'The First Waves', in Gwyn Jones and Michael Quinn (eds.), *Fountains of Praise* (Cardiff, 1983), pp. 123, 124.

[11] David Williams, 'Old Man of the Sea: W. J. Gruffydd', in Jones and Quinn, op. cit., p. 102.

[12] Max Morris, 'Built to last', *Times Educational Supplement*, 10 August, 1984, 4.

[13] Ibid, p. 4.

[14] E. B. Castle, *The Teacher* (London, 1970), p. 3.

[15] Gareth Elwyn Jones, *Controls and Conflicts in Welsh Secondary Education, 1889–1944* (Cardiff, 1982), pp. 26, 27.

Chapter 2

1 *Reports of the Commissioners of Inquiry into the State of Education in Wales* (London, 1847). All the quotations in this essay have been taken from the surveys of Lingen, Symons and Vaughan Johnson which precede the presentation of the statistics and individual school reports relating to their areas of responsibility. There is a mass of secondary literature on the 'Blue Books'. The most recent comprehensive study is a series of essays edited by Prys Morgan, *Brad y Llyfrau Gleision* (Llandysul, 1991).
2 D. Griffiths, 'Monmouthshire and the Blue Books of 1847', *History of Education*, XIX, 3, 261–3.
3 Ibid. p. 261–3.
4 F. Smith, *The Life and Work of Sir James Kay-Shuttleworth* (London, 1923); see also F. Smith, 'A new document bearing on the Welsh Education Commission of 1846–7', *Aberystwyth Studies*, IV, 1922, 173–8. This chapter was written before the publication of R. J. W. Selleck's biography of Kay-Shuttleworth (London, 1994).
5 These words formed part of William Williams's motion to the House of Commons, 10 March 1846, and appear on the title page of the Report.
6 There is a very substantial literature on both these subjects. The most authoritative present writings are those of Ieuan Gwynedd Jones [for example, *Mid-Victorian Wales* (Cardiff, 1992)]. E. T. Davies, *Religion and Society in Nineteenth Century Wales* (Llandybïe, 1981) provides a most useful overview.
7 S. J. Curtis, *History of Education in Great Britain*, 7th edn (London, 1967), p. 232 ff.

Chapter 3

1 T. P. Jones, 'The contribution of the Established Church to Welsh education (1811–1846)', in J. L. Williams and G. R. Hughes (eds.), *The History of Education in Wales*, I (Swansea, 1978), pp. 111–26.
2 A. L. Trott, 'The British School Movement in Wales: 1806–46', ibid., pp. 86–91.
3 T. M. Bassett, 'The Sunday School', ibid., pp. 71 ff.
4 L. W. Evans, *Education in Industrial Wales 1700–1900* (Cardiff, 1971), pp. 30–4.
5 Trott, op. cit., p. 96.
6 *Report of the Commissioners of Inquiry into the State of Education in Wales, Part I: Carmarthen, Glamorgan and Pembroke* (HMSO, 1847), pp. 55–8.
7 Ibid., p. 305.
8 Ibid., p. 13.
9 Ibid., pp. 33–44.

[10] Ibid., p. 3.

[11] Ibid., p. 32.

[12] Ibid., p. 3.

[13] Ibid., p. 8.

[14] Ibid., p. 28.

[15] Evans, *Education in Industrial Wales*, pp. 101–84.

[16] Ibid., p. 269.

[17] Ibid., p. 277.

[18] L. M. Rees, 'A critical examination of teacher training in Wales 1846–98' (University of Wales Ph.D. thesis, 1968), pp. 20–6.

[19] Quoted, ibid., p. 56.

[20] Quoted in D. R. Gwynn, 'A study of the development of elementary and primary education in south Gower 1870–1970' (University of Wales M.Ed. dissertation, 1986), 26.

[21] Ibid., p. 27.

[22] J. Fletcher, *A Technical Triumph: One Hundred Years of Public Further Education in Merthyr Tydfil, 1873–1973* (Merthyr Tydfil, 1974), p. 13.

[23] I. Davies, '*A Certaine School*' (Cowbridge, 1967), pp. 79–121.

[24] G. E. Jones, *Controls and Conflicts in Welsh Secondary Education 1889–1944* (Cardiff, 1982), pp. 3, 4.

[25] Ibid., p. 6.

[26] E. J. Davies, 'The origin and development of secondary education in the Rhondda Valleys (1878–1923)' (University of Wales MA thesis, 1965), passim.

[27] Jones, *Controls and Conflicts*, passim, but especially chs. 1–4.

[28] Fletcher, *Further Education in Merthyr Tydfil*, pp. 24–46.

[29] S. B. Chrimes (ed.), 'University College, Cardiff, a centenary history, 1883–1983' (Bound typescript, restricted publication), 16 ff.

[30] Ibid., p. 104.

[31] Ibid., p. 103.

[32] Central Advisory Council for Education (Wales), *The County College in Wales* (HMSO, 1951), p. 5.

[33] The Advisory Council for Technical Education in South Wales and Monmouthshire, *Higher Technological Education*, Publication no. 19, no imp., 1945, pp. 20–2.

[34] *County of Glamorgan, Proposals for a Scheme of the County Council . . . as submitted to the Board of Education pursuant to the Education Act 1918* (Cardiff, 1920).

[35] Ibid., p. 63.

[36] Ibid., p. 62.

[37] A. G. Geen, 'Decision making in relation to secondary education in the Cardiff Education Authority 1944–70' (University of Wales Ph.D. thesis, 1979), 79–98.

[38] *Education in Wales – Report of the Board of Education under the Welsh Intermediate Education Act*, 1938, p. 19.

[39] For details, PRO, Ed 24/588.
[40] Jones, *Controls and Conflicts*, pp. 106, 107.
[41] For a full account, ibid., pp. 142 ff.
[42] Ibid., p. 168.
[43] D. W. Dykes, 'The University College of Swansea: Its background and development' (University of Wales Ph.D. thesis, 1982), 187–9.
[44] Chrimes, op. cit., p. 104.
[45] For an account of Morgan Jones's career see D. J. Rees, 'Morgan Jones (1885–1939) and his contribution to education' (University of Wales M.Ed. dissertation, 1985).
[46] The Advisory Council for Technical Education in South Wales and Monmouthshire, *Part-Time Education*, Publication No. 8, no imp., n.d. (c. 1937), p. 12.
[47] The Advisory Council for Technical Education in South Wales and Monmouthshire, *Technical Education for Women and Girls*, Publication No. 10, no imp., n.d. (c. 1938), pp. 45, 46.
[48] For a fuller discussion see above, pp. 1–11.
[49] Cardiff County Borough Council Development Plan, WP/S 563/DP.
[50] Cardiff Development Plan, WP/S 563/DP; Merthyr Tydfil County Borough Council Development Plan, WP/S 364/DP.
[51] Glamorgan County Council Development Plan, WPS/357/DP.
[52] Swansea County Borough Council Development Plan, WP/S 566/DP.
[53] B. Simon, 'The Tory Government and education, 1951–60: background to breakout', in *History of Education*, XIV (4), (1985), 283–97.
[54] A. G. Geen, *Decision Making and Secondary Education: A Case Study* (Cardiff, 1986), passim.
[55] D. Gerwyn Lewis, *The University and the Colleges of Education in Wales 1925–78* (Cardiff, 1980), pp. 151–3.
[56] C. Williams, *Determinants of University/College Choice in Wales* (Cardiff, 1974), pp. 2–9.
[57] Advisory Council, *Higher Technological Education*, pp. 5–66.
[58] Fletcher, *Further Education in Merthyr Tydfil*, pp. 57–61.

Chapter 4

[1] N. Middleton and S. Weitzmann, *A Place for Everyone: A History of State Education from the end of the Eighteenth Century to the 1970s* (London, 1976), pp. 58ff.
[2] R. Brinkley, 'Religion and education 1660–1815', in B. Howells (ed.), *Early Modern Pembrokeshire 1536–1815* (Pembrokeshire Historical Society, 1987), p. 229; D. Howell, 'Society, 1660–1793', in ibid., p. 193.
[3] Brinkley, op. cit., p. 234.
[4] Howell, op. cit., p. 293.
[5] Ibid., p. 295.

6   Brinkley, op. cit., p. 241.

7   A. L. Trott, 'The British School Movement in Wales 1806–1846', in J. L. Williams and G. R. Hughes (eds.), *The History of Education in Wales*, Vol. I (Swansea, 1978), p. 83.

8   Ibid., pp. 83–95.

9   Tudor Powell Jones, 'The contribution of the Established Church to Welsh education (1811–1846)', in ibid., p. 108.

10   Ibid., p. 123.

11   See J. D. Griffiths, 'Monmouthshire and the "Blue Books" of 1847', in *History of Education* 19, 3, 260–63.

12   Trott, op. cit., p. 99.

13   Ibid., p. 104.

14   Jones, op. cit., p. 126.

15   The following information is based on a section of statistics in *Reports on Education in Wales*, 1847, Part 1, *Carmarthen, Glamorgan and Pembroke*, pp. 98–207.

16   Manchester Statistical Society, *The State of Education in Manchester*, 1835.

17   *Reports on Education in Wales*, 1847, p. 15.

18   Ibid., pp. 36–7.

19   Ibid., pp. 389ff.

20   Ibid., p. 390.

21   Ibid., p. 394.

22   Ibid.

23   Ibid., p. 437.

24   Ibid., p. 460.

25   Quoted in S. Bartlett, 'The Development of Elementary Education in Pembroke Borough 1814–1903' (unpublished Diploma in Educational Studies, University College of Wales, Aberystwyth, 1973–4), 46.

26   *Pembrokeshire Herald*, 25 November 1870. I am particularly indebted to David Howell for this and a number of other relevant references in the newspaper.

27   Ibid., 23 December 1870.

28   Ibid., 16 December 1870.

29   Ibid., 20 January 1871.

30   Ibid.

31   Ibid., 28 February 1879.

32   Mr Robert Smith kindly provided information about the position at St David's.

33   The section on the activities of the Pembroke Borough School Board is based substantially on Bartlett, op. cit.

34   Ibid., p. 42.

35   Ibid., pp. 50ff.

36   Ibid., pp. 64–86.

37   Ibid., pp. 71–4.

38 Ibid., p. 83.
39 Ibid., pp. 88, 93.
40 For a fuller analysis see G. E. Jones, *Controls and Conflicts in Welsh Secondary Education 1889–1944* (Cardiff, 1982), pp. 9ff.
41 G. Nicholle, 'Beyond Wales' (unpublished typescript, Pembrokeshire County Library), 130. I am most grateful to David Howell for drawing my attention to this material.
42 See, e.g. *Pembrokeshire Herald*, 23 April, 21 June, 18 July 1879 and 4 March 1880. I am grateful to David Howell for these references.
43 Ibid., 25 July 1879.
44 The events are recounted in Nicholle, op. cit. Corroborative material is available in the *Western Mail* and the *Liverpool Daily Post*.
45 *Reports on Education in Wales*, 1847, p. 13.
46 Ibid., p. 455.
47 J. R. Webster, 'The Welsh Intermediate Education Act of 1889', in O. E. Jones (ed.), *The Welsh Intermediate Education Act of 1889: A Centenary Appraisal* (Welsh Office, 1990), p. 12.
48 D. Allsobrook, 'Technical education in Wales: influences and attitudes', in Jones, op. cit., p. 31.
49 K. D. Evans, 'The Development of Secondary Education in South Pembrokeshire 1889–1939' (unpublished MA thesis, University of Wales, 1970), 3.
50 Ibid., 6. I have relied heavily on K. D. Evans's thesis for material on intermediate education in Pembrokeshire.
51 Ibid., 15.
52 Ibid., 32–8.
53 Ibid., 43–4, 137.
54 Ibid., 64.
55 Ibid., 86.
56 Ibid., 94–5, 126.
57 Jones, *Controls and Conflicts*, pp. 61–3 for an account of Advanced Courses.
58 Evans, op. cit, 150.
59 See Ron Brooks, 'Dr. J. J. Findlay, first headmaster of Cardiff Intermediate School for Boys, 1898–1903', in G. E. Jones (ed.), *Education, Culture and Society* (Cardiff, 1991).
60 Evans, op. cit., 153.
61 Ibid., 191–241.
62 Quoted in Jones, *Controls and Conflicts*, p. 141. For a full account see chapter 5 of the book.
63 For details of negotiations with the Pembrokeshire LEA and of the settlement reached see ibid., pp. 148 and 229.
64 The following section is based on papers in Welsh Office files WP/S 561 DP (Pembrokeshire Development file) and WP/S 561 DP(P)

(Pembrokeshire Development Plan Protest file). See also G. E. Jones, *Which Nation's Schools?* (Cardiff, 1990), pp. 123–5 and 154–7.

[65] W. Harrison, *Greenhill School, Tenby, 1896–1964* (Cardiff, 1979), pp. 311–39.

[66] Welsh Office, *Statistics of Education in Wales*, No. 1, 1976.

Chapter 5

[1] They often remained so after 1902. To take one example, in June 1909, Owen M. Edwards, chief inspector at the Welsh Department of the Board of Education, minuted of Brecon Boys' Church of England School: 'two rooms, head takes four standards in one small room, assistant takes two standards . . . Infants school – though not exactly a cellar it is quite unfit to be a school for small children. It is a damp, dismal, badly lighted room, and most difficult to keep warm in winter. The top is level with the street . . . and the windows are useless as they must always be thick with street dust.' Public Record Office, Ed 2/563.

[2] The most convincing interpretations of these developments, and the machinations leading up to the passing of the Education Act of 1902, are provided by B. Simon, *Education and the Labour Movement, 1870–1920* (London, 1965), pp. 176ff, and E. Eaglesham, *From School Board to Local Authority* (London, 1956), passim.

[3] R. Morant, *Special Reports on Educational Subjects*, HMSO (1898), III, 47, quoted in S. J. Curtis, *History of Education in Great Britain* (London, 7th edn., 1967), p. 314.

[4] Ieuan Gwynedd Jones (ed.). *The Religious Census of 1851: A Calendar of Returns Relating to Wales*, vols. I and II (Cardiff, 1976, 1981).

[5] T. P. Jones, 'The contribution of the Established Church to Welsh education (1811–1846)', in J. L. Williams and G. R. Hughes (eds.), *The History of Education in Wales* (Swansea, 1976), pp. 105–26. The Newcastle Commission recorded that in 1859 there were 878 Church of England schools in Wales and only 130 British Society schools, although a further 120 British schools were opened between 1863 and 1870. The differences between Wales and England are further emphasized in the multiplication of school boards. There were nearly 200 by 1874, compared with England's 641. If English numbers had grown in proportion to Welsh, there would have been over 3,000 in England. See L. M. Rees, 'A Critical Examination of Teacher Training in Wales, 1846–1898' (unpublished University of Wales Ph.D. thesis, 1968), pp. 57, 73; even in 1906 there were 650 Anglican elementary schools and 1,028 council schools in Wales. There were fifty-three Roman Catholic schools: see Kenneth O. Morgan, *Wales in British Politics, 1868–1922* (Cardiff, 3rd edn., 1980), p. 183.

[6] For a detailed summary of the provisions of the 1902 Act, see Curtis, *History of Education in Great Britain*, pp. 314–21.

[7] The fullest and best account of the Welsh Revolt is in Kenneth O. Morgan, op. cit., pp. 181–98: for Lloyd George's initial enthusiasm for the 1902 Act, see Lloyd George to Mrs Lloyd George, 24 March 1902, *idem* (ed.), *Lloyd George Family Letters, 1885–1936* (Cardiff and Oxford, 1973), pp. 131–2.

[8] Curtis, op. cit., p. 316.

[9] Schools were paid a fixed grant of 4s. for each pupil. In addition, they received '1½d, per scholar for every complete 2d. per scholar by which the amount that would be produced by a 1d. rate fell short of 10s. a scholar'. See ibid., p. 317.

[10] G. O. Pierce, 'The "Coercion of Wales" Act, 1904', in H. Hearder and H. R. Loyn (eds.), *British Government and Administration* (Cardiff, 1974), p. 220.

[11] The story of Carmarthenshire County Council's opposition to the 1902 Act and the subsequent public enquiry is told in L. W. Evans, *Studies in Welsh Education: Welsh Educational Structure and Administration, 1880–1925* (Cardiff, 1974), pp. 117–82.

[12] The figures are given in Kenneth O. Morgan, op. cit., p. 191.

[13] Ibid., pp. 194–5.

[14] Pierce, op. cit., p. 229.

[15] This claim is made for Merioneth by L. W. Evans, op. cit., in interpreting material in PRO, Ed 24/578. But this is not the policy which the county claimed to operate after the Default Act. See letter from Merioneth County Council to the Board of Education, received 9 December 1904 (PRO, Ed 92/1).

[16] The papers relating to both counties are in PRO, Ed 92/1. This voluminous file, Elementary Education, Wales: General File, appears not to have come to the notice of historians previously. However, Eric Eaglesham must presumably have consulted some of the papers, or copies of them, when they were housed in the Ministry of Education, for his article, 'Implementing the Education Act of 1902', *British Journal of Educational Studies*, X, 2 (May 1962), 152–75. His reference is to file 359 W. E. All such files were reclassified when they were transferred to the PRO. His article deals in detail with the Barry default, very briefly with Montgomeryshire's default and not at all with that of Merioneth.

[17] PRO, Ed 92/1. Letter from C. H. Wynn to the Board of Education.

[18] Ibid., memorandum of Lindsell to Morant, 11 November 1903.

[19] Ibid., memorandum of Morant to Lindsell, 13 November 1903.

[20] Ibid., letter from the managers of Llanfair National School to the Board of Education, 10 February 1903.

[21] Ibid., letter from the Board of Education to Merioneth CC, 18 February 1904.

[22] Ibid., letter from Merioneth CC to the Board of Education, received 9 December 1904.

[23] Ibid., letter from Merioneth CC to the Board of Education, 4 March 1905.

[24] Ibid., memorandum of R. P. Hills to Morant, 15 May 1905.

[25] Ibid., letter from H. Haydn Jones to the Board of Education, 6 June 1905.

[26] Ibid., letter from the Board of Education to Montgomeryshire CC

[27] Ibid. This, and extracts quoted below, are from a memorandum from R. P. Hills to Sir William Anson, 26 September 1905.

[28] *South Wales Daily News*, 20 September 1905.

[29] Ibid., 21 September 1905.

[30] PRO, Ed 92/1, memorandum written by R. P. Hills, 28 September 1905.

[31] Ibid., letter from Montgomeryshire Education Committee to the Board of Education.

[32] Ibid., memorandum of Lindsell to Kingsford, 27 October 1905.

[33] *Western Mail*, 27 October 1905.

[34] *South Wales Daily News*, 27 October 1905.

[35] PRO, Ed 92/1, memorandum from Sir William Anson to Morant, 29 October 1905.

[36] *Western Mail*, 14 November 1905.

[37] Quoted in Pierce, op. cit., p. 222.

Chapter 6

[1] John Davies, 'O. M. Edwards', *Welsh Historian*, no. 7 (Spring 1987), 26–7; A. H. Williams, 'John Edward Lloyd', *Welsh Historian*, no. 8 (Autumn 1987), 21–2.

[2] Hazel Davies, *O. M. Edwards* (Writers of Wales Series) (Cardiff, 1988).

[3] Ibid., p.3.

[4] Ibid., p. 4.

[5] Ibid., p. 21.

[6] G. E. Jones, *Controls and Conflicts in Welsh Secondary Education, 1889–1944* (Cardiff, 1982), chs. 1 and 2.

Chapter 7

[1] For discussion of this confusion, and invaluable material on both the Aberdare Committee Report (1881) and the Intermediate Education Act, see W. Gareth Evans, 'The Aberdare Report and education in Wales, 1881', *Welsh History Review*, vol. 11, no. 1 (June 1982), 150–72, and J. R. Webster, 'The Welsh Intermediate Education Act of 1889', *Welsh History Review*, vol. 4, no. 3 (June 1969), 273–91.

[2] A link between attitudes towards Poor Law legislation, administration and education is established by N. Middleton and S. Weitzman, *A Place*

for Everyone: A History of State Education from the end of the Eighteenth Century to the 1970s (London, 1976), pp. 58ff.

3 J. S. Mill, *Considerations on Representative Government* (London, 1861).

4 Schools which were popular with many of the Welsh gentry.

5 For the history of Welsh secondary education in the nineteenth century see J. R. Webster, 'The Place of Secondary Education in Welsh Society 1800–1918' (unpublished Ph.D. Thesis, University of Wales, 1959).

6 Samuel Butler to Lord Brougham (1820), quoted in Middleton and Weitzman, op. cit. p. 14.

7 This study, by Jac L. Williams, is quoted in R. M. Pill, 'Education and Social Mobility in Wales, 1938–1968' (unpublished Ph.D. Thesis, University of Wales, 1970), 35.

8 P. E. Owen, 'The Development of the Bilateral System of Secondary Education in Caernarvonshire 1903 to date' (unpublished Ph.D. Thesis, University of London, 1961), 211, 271, 272.

9 *Education in Rural Wales*, HMSO, 1930.

10 On the day during which I completed this essay, 6 February 1989, a letter appeared in the *Western Mail* from Mike Packer, in which he maintained that 'on graduation, the only option open to myself and other CDT (craft, design, technology) graduates was to accept a post outside the Principality . . . in the absence of Technology posts arising in South Wales within this academic year, I . . . will leave the profession and seek other employment.'

   A report in the *Western Mail* of 16 January 1989 was headed 'South-east holding key to "brain-drain"' and it did not refer to south-east Wales. Comparing Wales with the English regions, the report, based on the latest *Labour Force Survey*, showed that Wales had fewer graduates in employment than any of the English regions other than East Anglia. 'The figures are likely to revive demands for higher standards of employment to be provided in Wales, to prevent the region's [sic] cleverest people continuing to move to the south-east.'

11 R. Lowe, *Education in the Post-War Years: A Social History* (London, 1988), pp. 37–53, 90.

12 HMI Report on Whitland Grammar School, 1949.

13 P. Fisher, *External Examinations in Secondary Schools in England and Wales 1944–1964* (Museum of History of Education, University of Leeds, 1982), pp. 1, 2.

14 Carmarthenshire Development Plan under the 1944 Education Act. Welsh Office WP/S 554/DP.

15 Pembrokeshire Development Plan under the 1944 Education Act. Welsh Office WP/S 561/DP.

16 For detail on which the civil servants at the Board of Education decided on a pattern of segregated secondary education, see P. H. J. H. Gosden, *Education in the Second World War* (London, 1976), pp. 265–7.

17 *Statistics of Education in Wales*, no. 4, 1979, pp. 34, 96–100.

[18] Lowe, op. cit., p. 53.

[19] There is, surprisingly, no proper study of W. G. Cove. For some comments on his influence see G. E. Jones, *Controls and Conflicts in Welsh Secondary Education, 1889–1944* (Cardiff, 1982).

[20] Whitland Grammar School ceased to exist as such on 31 August 1989.

Chapter 8

[1] G. E. Jones, *Controls and Conflicts in Welsh Secondary Education, 1889–1944* (Cardiff, 1982), ch. 1, passim.

[2] Brinley Thomas (ed.), *The Welsh Economy* (Cardiff, 1962), p. 56.

[3] A. G. Geen, 'Decision Making in Relation to Secondary Education in the Cardiff Education Authority 1944–1970' (unpublished Ph.D. thesis, University of Wales, 1979), 79–98.

[4] PRO, Ed 24/2057.

[5] Ibid.

[6] Jones, op. cit., pp. 167–75.

[7] C.f. H. M. Paterson, 'Incubus and ideology: The development of secondary schooling in Scotland, 1900–1939', in W. M. Humes and H. M. Paterson (eds.), *Scottish Culture and Scottish Education 1800–1980* (Edinburgh, 1983), pp. 197–214.

[8] Jones, op. cit., passim; E. J. Davies, 'The Origin and Development of Secondary Education in the Rhondda Valleys (1878–1923)' (unpublished MA thesis, University of Wales, 1965), passim; M. Lawn, 'Syndicalist teachers: The Rhondda Strike of 1919', in *Llafur*, vol. 4, no. 1, 91–7.

[9] PRO, Ed 53/699.

[10] *Welsh Secondary Schools Review*, xxv, 2, 1939, 5.

[11] Jones, op. cit., pp. 179–81; cf. *Education in 1947*, Cmnd. 7426, HMSO, p. 77.

[12] This information and the quotation were given to me by Mr D. W. Greenaway.

[13] PRO, Ed 136/311; 136/237; 136/417.

[14] *Education in 1947*, Cmnd. 7426, HMSO, pp. 83, 84.

[15] *Report under the Welsh Intermediate Education Act*, 1938, pp. 63, 64.

[16] PRO, Ed 24/2048; 136/398; 136/594; *Education in 1947*, Cmnd. 7426, HMSO, p. 80.

[17] *Education in 1947*, Cmnd. 7426, HMSO, p. 81.

[18] Geen, op. cit., 79ff.

[19] H. M. Williams, 'A Study of Secondary Education in Breconshire since 1950' (unpublished Ph.D. thesis, University of Wales, 1975), 3, 4.

[20] Ibid., p. 12.

[21] Montgomeryshire Development Plan, WP/S 364 DP (8)/1.

[22] *Education in 1949*, Cmnd. 7957, HMSO, p. 101.

[23] *Education 1900–1950*, Cmnd. 8244, HMSO, pp. 60, 124.

24 *Education in 1961*, Cmnd. 1737, HMSO, pp. 81ff.
25 *Education in 1965*, Cmnd. 2938, HMSO, p. 91.
26 P. Fisher, *External Examinations in Secondary Schools in England and Wales 1944–1964* (Museum of History of Education, University of Leeds, 1982), p. 1.
27 Ibid., p. 2.
28 *Education in 1947*, Cmnd. 7426, HMSO, pp. 108, 109.
29 *Statistics of Education 1964*, HMSO, pp. 10–11.
30 Ibid., pp. 24, 25.
31 Ibid., pp. 24, 25.
32 Ministry of Education, *Educational Administration in Wales*, HMSO, 1948.
33 J. Vaizey and J. Sheehan, *Resources for Education* (London, 1968), p. 1.
34 *Statistics of Education in Wales*, No. 4, 1979, 34, 96–100.
35 *Education in 1948*, Cmnd. 7724, pp. 91–8; *Education in 1949*, Cmnd. 7957, p. 99; *Education in 1951*, Cmnd. 8554, p. 59.
36 *Education in 1952*, Cmnd. 8835, HMSO, p. 49.
37 *Education in 1963*, Cmnd. 2316, HMSO, p. 103.
38 *Education and Science in 1970*, HMSO, p. 59.
39 Cf. Humes and Paterson, op. cit., p. 5.
40 Cf. Timothy Williams, 'Congregations, cultures and conflicts', in *Wales 1880–1914* (Welsh History and its Sources, Open University in Wales pilot project, 1983), pp. 34, 35.
41 *Education in 1953*, Cmnd. 9155, HMSO, p. 47.
42 Ibid., p. 50.
43 *Education in 1961*, Cmnd. 1737, HMSO, p. 86; *Education in 1961*, Cmnd. 1990, HMSO, p. 85.
44 *Education and Science in 1968*, Cmnd. 3950, HMSO, p. 108.
45 *Statistics of Education in Wales*, No. 5, 1980, HMSO, pp. 53–5.
46 *Statistics of Education in Wales*, No. 4, 1979, HMSO.

Chapter 9

1 J. Bennet (ed.), *The English Works of Roger Ascham, Preceptor to Queen Elizabeth* (London, 1761).
2 Ibid., p. 191.
3 Ibid., pp. 191, 192.
4 Ibid., p. 192.
5 B. Moon (ed.), *New Curriculum – National Curriculum* (London, 1990).
6 C. MacNeil, 'The National Curriculum: A black perspective', in B. Moon, op. cit.
7 Ibid., p. 81.
8 Central Advisory Council for Education (England), *Children and their Primary Schools* (The Plowden Report), (HMSO, 1967).

⁹ C. B. Cox and A. E. Dyson, *The Black Papers on Education* (London, Davis-Poynter; originally published, London, Critical Quarterly Society, 1969).

¹⁰ N. Bennett, *Teaching Styles and Pupil Progress* (London, 1976).

¹¹ See C. Richards (ed.), *New Directions in Primary Education* (Lewes, 1982), p. 16.

¹² See above, note 8.

¹³ Central Advisory Council (Wales), *The Future of Secondary Education in Wales* (HMSO, 1949).

¹⁴ HMI (Wales), *Review of Educational Provision in Wales, 1989–90* (Welsh Office, 1991).

¹⁵ HMI (Wales), *Curriculum and Organisation of Primary Schools in Wales* (Welsh Office, 1984).

¹⁶ Ibid., pp. 7, 8.

¹⁷ Central Advisory Council for Education (Wales), *Primary Education in Wales* (The Gittins Report) (HMSO 1967).

¹⁸ R. Boyson, *The Crisis in Education* (London, 1975).

¹⁹ See C. Richards, op. cit., p. 11.

²⁰ The *Observer*, December 1987.

²¹ S. Lawlor, *The Correct Core* (London, 1988); also published under 'How clever is your child?', *Sunday Mirror*, 23 October 1988.

²² S. Maclure, *Education Reformed*, 2nd edn. (London, 1989).

²³ Ibid., p. v.

²⁴ DES/WO, *The National Curriculum 5–16: A Consultation Document* (HMSO, 1987).

²⁵ Welsh Office, *The National Curriculum in Wales* (HMSO, 1987).

²⁶ J. Rand, 'A Scottish tradition of curricular reform', in B. Moon, op. cit.

²⁷ C. Barker, 'The growth of bilingual education in the secondary schools of Wales', in W. Evans (ed.), *Perspectives on a Century of Secondary Education in Wales* (Aberystwyth, 1990).

²⁸ Ibid., p. 83.

²⁹ R. Daugherty, B. Thomas, G. E. Jones and S. Davies, *GCSE in Wales* (Welsh Office Education Department, 1991).

³⁰ Public Record Office, Ed 24/581. See also G. E. Jones, *Controls and Conflicts in Welsh Secondary Education 1889–1944* (Cardiff, 1982).

³¹ Welsh Office, *History in the National Curriculum (Wales)* (Welsh Office, 1991).

³² Quoted in B. Simon, *The Politics of Educational Reform 1920–1940* (London, 1974).

Chapter 10

¹ R. S. Thomas, 'Unity', in *Planet*, 70 (1988), p. 40.

² Ibid., pp. 39, 40.

[3] Ibid., p. 42

[4] Raymond Williams, 'Community', in *London Review of Books*, 21 January 1985, 14. See also Dai Smith, 'The Welsh identity of Raymond Williams', in *Planet*, 76, 88–98.

[5] Williams, op. cit, 14.

[6] Ibid.

[7] R. R. Davies, 'Law and national identity in thirteenth century Wales', in R. R. Davies et al. (eds.), *Welsh Society and Nationhood. Essays presented to Glanmor Williams* (Cardiff, 1984), p. 52.

[8] Neal Ascherson, The *Observer*, 1 October 1989, p. 15.

[9] Erhard Eppler, quoted ibid.

[10] Keith Robbins, 'National identity and history: Past, present and future', unpublished paper based on a talk given at the Royal Institute of International Affairs, March 1989. I am most grateful to Professor Robbins for allowing me to quote from it.

[11] Barry Jones, 'The development of Welsh territorial institutions: Modernization theory revisited', in *Contemporary Wales*, vol. 2 (1988), 47, 48.

[12] The story of the implementation of the 1944 Education Act in Wales, in which the evidence for this statement appears, is told in the author's *Which Nation's Schools? Direction and Devolution in Welsh Education in the Twentieth Century* (Cardiff, 1990).

[13] Barry Jones, op. cit., p. 54.

[14] See below, p. 162.

[15] David Newsome, *Godliness and Good Learning: Four Studies on a Victorian Ideal* (London, 1961, reissued 1988).

[16] Peter Gordon, *Purpose and Planning in the Humanities Curriculum* (London, 1984), pp. 8, 9.

[17] Denis Lawton, *The End of the Secret Garden* (London, 1979), p. 6, argues that there were still massive constraints on teachers, the examination systems in particular.

[18] David Allsobrook, '"A Benevolent Prophet of Old . . .": Reflections on the Welsh Intermediate Education Act of 1889', in *The Welsh Journal of Education*, vol. 1, no. 1 (1989), 1–9.

[19] See Chapter 6 of this volume.

[20] G. E. Jones, *Controls and Conflicts in Welsh Secondary Education, 1889–1944* (Cardiff, 1982), p. 16.

[21] See A. V. Kelly, *The Curriculum. Theory and Practice*, 3rd edn. (London, 1989), p. 29, in which he draws attention to the work of R. S. Peters, Paul Hirst and G. H. Bantock.

[22] See Chapter 6 of this volume, pp. 162–80.

[23] Quoted in O. G. Jones, 'Sylwadau Owen Morgan Edwards ar addysg' (unpublished M.Ed. thesis, University of Wales, 1976), 37.

[24] Ibid., passim.

25   *Regulations for Welsh Secondary Schools in Force from 1 April 1909 in Wales and Monmouthshire.* Cd. 4696. *British Sessional Papers House of Commons,* vol. LXVII, pp. 509ff.

26   G. E. Jones, *Controls and Conflicts,* op. cit., pp. 32, 33.

27   Central Welsh Board, *Today and Tomorrow in Welsh Education* (Cardiff, 1916).

28   *Welsh Secondary Schools Review,* vol. xiii, no. 1, 8.

29   Ibid.

30   Board of Education, *Welsh in Education and Life,* Report of the Departmental Committee, HMSO, 1927, p. 5.

31   See Gwennant Davies, *The Story of the Urdd* (Aberystwyth, 1973).

32   *The Curriculum and the Community in Wales,* Welsh Department of the Ministry of Education pamphlet no. 6 (HMSO, 1952), p. 3.

33   The most influential advocate was Lawrence Stenhouse, who entitled one of the chapters in his *An Introduction to Curriculum Research and Development* (London, 1975), 'The teacher as researcher'.

34   M. Skilbeck, quoted in Gordon, op. cit., p. 22.

35   Department of Education and Science, *Curriculum 11–16: Towards a Statement of Entitlement* (HMSO, 1984).

36   Noragh Jones, 'Blod and the Brush Salesman', in *Planet,* 76 (1989), 12.

37   Kelly, op. cit., pp. 30ff.

38   P. Fisher, *External Examinations in Secondary Schools in England and Wales 1944–1964* (Museum of History of Education, University of Leeds, 1982), p. 1.

39   The phrase is that of Ned Thomas in 'Sponsors and subversives', *Planet,* 76 (1989), 8.

Note: I am greatly indebted to Rees Davies and Richard Daugherty for their constructive criticism of an early draft of this chapter. Of course they must not be held responsible for any of the opinions expressed in it.

Chapter 11

1   *Report of the Commissioners Appointed to Inquire into the State of Education in Wales* (1847), 3 vols., c. 870, 871, 872.

2   The best-known wearer of the 'Welsh Not' was O. M. Edwards, first Chief Inspector of the Welsh Department of the Board of Education. See O. G. Jones, 'Sylwadau Owen Morgan Edwards ar addysg' (unpublished M.Ed. thesis University of Wales, 1976), 37, 39–43.

3   G. E. Jones, *Controls and Conflicts in Welsh Secondary Education, 1889–1944* (Cardiff, 1982), chap. 1, passim.

4   *Regulations in Force for Welsh Secondary Schools (1907); Regulations for Welsh Secondary Schools in Force from 1908; Regulations for Secondary Schools in Force from 1st August 1909 in Wales and Monmouthshire,* Cd 4696, British Sessional Papers, vol. LXVIII, 509ff.

[5] Board of Education, *Welsh in Education and Life*, Report of the Departmental Committee (1927), 183.

[6] *The Curriculum and the Community in Wales*, Welsh Department of the Ministry of Education (1952), pamphlet no. 6.

[7] Department of Education and Science and Welsh Office, *Task Group on Assessment and Testing: A Report* (submitted December 1987).

[8] Welsh Office, *The National Curriculum in Wales* (1987).

[9] Department of Education and Science and Welsh Office, *The National Curriculum 5–16* (1987).

[10] An unpublished research report on the first phase of this project by Illtyd Lewis, based on the work of the late Rebecca Powell, was submitted to the Curriculum Council for Wales in 1992.

[11] Research of Anthony Packer, reported in *Western Mail*, 27 July 1993.

[12] Department of Education and Science and the Welsh Office, *National Curriculum History Working Group Final Report* (April 1990); The Welsh Office, *National Curriculum History Committee for Wales Final Report* (June 1990).

[13] *Western Mail*, 12 August 1993.

[14] Curriculum Council for Wales, *Developing a Curriculum Cymreig*, Advisory Paper 18 (Cardiff, 1993), 3–5.

[15] Ibid., 9.

[16] Ibid., 11.

[17] Ibid., 13.

[18] Ibid., 15–17.

[19] Ibid., 19, 20.

[20] Ibid., 33–7.

[21] Ibid., 7.

[22] National Curriculum Council and School Examinations and Assessment Council, *The National Curriculum and its Assessment: An Interim Report* (The Dearing Report) (July 1993).

[23] Curriculum Council for Wales, *The National Curriculum and its Assessment Framework in Wales* (The Daugherty Report) (July 1993).

Note: I am much indebted to Professor Richard Daugherty and Paul Jeremy for their comments on an early draft of this chapter and to Brin Jones for a valuable reference.

Chapter 12

[1] The Curriculum Council for Wales, *Developing a Curriculum Cymreig*, Advisory Paper 18 (Cardiff, 1993).

[2] A series of 'Black Papers', condemnatory of all progressive trends in school and higher education, was published in the late 1960s and early 1970s. The first, edited by C. B. Cox and A. E. D. Dyson, appeared in 1969, entitled *The Black Papers in Education*.

[3]   Corelli Barnett, *The Audit of War* (London 1986).
[4]   J. W. B. Douglas, *The Home and the School* (London, 1964).
[5]   Lord Skidelsky, 'The future of history in the National Curriculum', *Welsh Historian* (Autumn 1993), 4–7.
[6]   Department of Education and Science and the Welsh Office, *Task Group on Assessment and Testing: A Report* (London, 1987).
[7]   The author was a member of the History Working Group and the History Committee for Wales.
[8]   *Developing a Curriculum Cymreig*, op. cit.
[9]   National Curriculum Council and Schools Examination and Assessment Council, *The National Curriculum and its Assessment, An Interim Report* (The Dearing Report), July 1993.

Conclusion

[1]   One of the most trenchant statements along these lines in recent years was that of Brinley Thomas, 'A cauldron of rebirth; population and the Welsh language in the nineteenth century', *Welsh History Review*, 13 (1987), 418–37.
[2]   See above, chapter 2, pp. 12–33.
[3]   See above, chapter 5, pp. 84–105.
[4]   See above, chapter 8, pp. 48–9.
[5]   See above, chapter 8, pp. 50–2.
[6]   See above, chapter 8, pp. 129–47.
[7]   D. Reynolds, 'Creating an educational system for Wales', *Welsh Journal of Education*, vol. 4, no. 2 (1995), 6.
[8]   'School and college performance table', *Times Educational Supplement*, 24 November 1996; Reynolds, op. cit., 8.
[9]   'School and college performance table', op. cit., 1.

Index